D1539400

In a cruel ruling in a landmark Hong Kong court case, my mother, Anna Wong Chu Yi Ching, watched helplessly as her father's hard-earned estate vanished, along with her honor. She was forced to surrender her property and life savings and stayed in detention for one week. She watched helplessly as her husband, Joseph, was held captive and tortured for four years during World War II, and eventually died of tuberculosis, making her a widow. This is the story of my mother's life. A woman with an unbreakable spirit who endured unthinkable hardship and pain, but survived it all through her unconditional love. A remarkable true story of courage, love and honor set in colonial Hong Kong.

The Bitter Battles

By Wai Yu Wong

Co-author: Nicole Dellasanta

Copyright © 2015 by Wai Yu Wong

Dedication

My mother, a widow, was one of the strongest, bravest and kindest humans on this planet. She was an elegant woman and looked particularly so when dressed in her favorite cranberry color cheung sam and pearl necklace. She was a devout Christian and a wonderful mother to her four children, two boys and two girls.

When not working as the first woman inspector in Hong Kong, she took the time to introduce us to food from different cultures and enjoyed taking us to the beaches and amusement parks and introducing us to nature. When my father passed away at the age of forty-six, she picked up the responsibility to love, teach and protect us with all her might.

Mother loved to watch dragonflies. When we lived at Tai Po Market, we walked along with the rice fields and ponds, where many dragonflies rested. We sang a Hakanese song to forbid other children from catching them. The dragonfly has been a symbol of happiness, new beginnings and change for many centuries. It also means hope, change, and love.

Table of Contents

CHAPTER 1

February 9, 2003, was a Sunday. I got up from my bed and went to check on my mother. She sensed me standing there, turned her head, and looked up at me. The corners of her mouth turned upwards. She smiled.

I smiled back. "Good morning, mother."

She blinked once and her smile got wider. "I'd like to attend church today."

Her words filled my heart with joy. My mother's faith had always been the driving force in her life, a source of comfort and hope, and the foundation of all the values and virtues in her family. My mother believed in God, but she had found Him through different paths; she had been raised in a Protestant household but had attended St. Mary's Canossian College, a Catholic school, and at the age of nineteen, she was baptized into the Catholic religion, Anna was her given name by an Italian priest named Father H. DeAngelis at the Rosary Church.

Much later in her life, at the age of fifty-three, she converted to Mormonism when she moved from Hong Kong to Canada and had remained a Mormon ever since. Throughout the immense heartache she experienced in her life, her faith always remained with her. She never blamed God for any of the unspeakable events that came her way; while others may have believed that God was absent or did not love them after such trials, mother believed that God was always there with her, through good times and worse. The tough times, she believed, were a test of her faith and love.

She had always attended church regularly until recently because her dementia had been getting worse. I didn't know what it was that had changed her mind on this particular morning; maybe it was the sun, maybe it was the lack of time she had spent at church lately, or maybe it was just a passing impulse. I'd never know. But I wasn't going to question it.

I helped her out of bed and happily began helping her with her morning rituals, arranging all the things I was supposed to do before we took taxis to church. I fixed her some breakfast, washed her face, brushed her smooth hair, and helped her select her clothes and put them on.

Mother was always neat to a tee, spotless and always matching perfectly, and today was no exception. Her clothes were made of beautiful fabrics, and she always ensured that every article of clothing matched her accessories and handbags. Because the Mormon Church she attended required all women to wear skirts, today mother selected her favorite, which was a deep cranberry color. To match, she chose her favorite shoes: a lovely brown leather pair, with cozy insoles and a leather ribbon on the top in the center of each. She had bought the shoes on sale while she was living in Canada, and they were comfortable but very pretty, matching any color skirt she had. For her shirt, she chose a dressy blouse with a high collar and a ribbon around the neck. To complete the look, I gave her a jacket to take with her, because the church was usually a bit cold.

When I stepped back and looked at her, dressed head to toe, I had to pause for a moment. This was not your typical eighty-six-year-old woman. She looked simply beautiful. Immediately when you saw her, you wanted to know her. But the clothes were only the wrapping; once you began to speak with her, you saw the gift inside. Her brightness radiated from her and filled up every corner of the room, like a rare jewel.

I finished helping mother to dress and put on her shoes, and prepared to put her in her wheelchair. I realized two things at this point. First, I knew mother disliked the discomfort the wheelchair caused her; I decided then to keep her spirits high this morning and instead allowed her to sit in the bamboo chair we had in the hallway near the front door. I wanted no distress for her today. Second, I discovered I had been so involved with her that I had forgotten to brush my own teeth. I certainly didn't want any horrified looks from fellow church-goers as they smelled my breath when I leaned in to talk to them. What an embarrassment that would be for mother's first day back at church.

I gently helped mom sit up in the bamboo chair next to the front door. I looked her over to make sure she was secured. Satisfied, I said, "Mom, I'll be right back. I just have to brush my teeth." She nodded.

Our bathroom was adjacent to the hallway. From the short distance, I could not fully see my mom, but we were very close, as the rooms were small and not far apart. I turned on the water in the sink. As I began brushing my teeth, the same thought that I had that morning came back to me. I wondered what had changed in mother this morning to make her decide to attend church. I might never know. With her dementia, it was getting harder and harder to understand her feelings. But I wasn't going to question it. It was a wonderful change after her dementia had gotten her feeling less like herself lately. I felt blessed to be accompanying her today. I thought to myself that today would be a good day.

No sooner did the thought cross my mind when suddenly I heard a tremendous thump. I froze. My toothbrush dropped from my mouth. I rushed out of the bathroom and ran to where I had left my mom.

A horrific sight met my eyes. My mother was no longer in the bamboo chair; instead, she was lying, sprawled out, on the floor in front of the chair.

My heart stopped immediately. My stomach leaped into my throat and my mind went blank. In a flash, I flew to her side. "Mom! What has happened?"

My mother has a high tolerance for pain. From looking at her, you would not know that anything was wrong. In a perfectly calm voice, she told me what had happened. Apparently, she had spotted a tiny black dot on our pearly white tiled living room floor. Being a perfectionist for appearance and cleanliness, she could not resist bending over to pick it up. In the process, she had lost her grip and fallen from the chair.

Guilt immediately began to settle on my heart. What if that spot hadn't been there on the floor? What if I had taken more time to clean it up?

7

What if I had just remembered to brush my teeth earlier like I normally did? The questions raced through my mind at light speed. If only I had been by her side…

I examined her all over. "Mom, does it hurt terribly anywhere? Where do you feel the most pain?"

She didn't answer, but I immediately found out: when I tried to lift her, she let out a short exclamation. I looked down at her. She had not screamed at all when she fell; I had only heard the thump. When she had fallen, her left side had gone down first, and from the way I was lifting her, I could now tell that that was the side that was now hurting her.

"It's okay Mom…it's okay." My words sounded feeble to me; I was trying to convince myself more than her that it really was going to be okay. Maybe it wasn't that bad; maybe she had just gotten a bruise. I tried lifting her again. She let out another short exclamation, which, with her tolerance, told me a lot. I didn't know exactly what was wrong with her, but I knew it was more severe than a bruise. Only one thought crossed my mind then: get her to a hospital.

Immediately, I called "999," the Hong Kong emergency phone number for help. Less than ten minutes later, the police were at our home. The policemen in Hong Kong were always the first to arrive at an emergency scene because they had more authority and power to control the situation; if nosy neighbors or people walking by slowed down to look or interfere in the situation, the police could swiftly hold them back. Almost immediately after the police arrived, three emergency medicinal technicians showed up from the ambulance service. I quickly explained to them what had happened, and they examined mother. They concluded that there was in fact something seriously wrong with her left side. Together, they lifted her onto a stretcher and covered her with a blanket. She was still not making any sounds, but the pained expression on her face still told us we needed to get her to the hospital quickly.

The only thing on my mind now was speed; she needed to be at the hospital, now. But the process of getting her out into the ambulance was far too lengthy because of how high up we were; since we were on the sixth floor of a high rise called Oi Chi House, the emergency medical technicians attempted to put mother on the elevator to get her down faster, but the stretcher would not fit, no matter which way they angled it. So the emergency medical technicians quickly decided to carry mother on the stretcher down six flights of stairs. A few of the policemen went ahead of us to get rid of anyone else on the stairway to give mom a clear path out.

I stayed right by mother's head the whole time, whispering to her that I would make the hurting stop very soon. She said nothing and lay very still. Her eyes were still open, but when I looked into them, all I saw was pain. Again, I felt the guilt fill up my heart. I fought back the tears that were burning behind my eyes.

Finally, when we reached the bottom floor, I was ready to get her in the ambulance and speed away. Then it occurred to me where we were: Oi Chi House was on a high rise in a square among other high rises; there were

8

no driveways or parking spaces, only a walkway between our buildings. With no room for transportation, all vehicles had to park around the back. That meant the ambulance was parked about the length of three houses away from our building. Mother, therefore, had to be carried on the stretcher that entire length to finally be placed in the ambulance.

She had not made a sound for the entire trek from our apartment, but the expression on her face was making my anxiety grow with every passing minute we spent loading her into the ambulance. I was supposed to ride with the policemen to the hospital, but I asked them immediately if I could ride with mom in the ambulance to keep her from getting scared or upset. They agreed, and as she was secured in the ambulance, I jumped in with her and stayed next to her side, holding her hand. I tried to explain to her what was happening. But because of her dementia, she would immediately forget what I had said, no matter how many times I told her. Even in the ten-minute ride to Tuen Mun Hospital, I had told her so many times that I did not know if I could tell her again.

When we arrived at the emergency entrance to Tuen Mun Hospital, I needed to register mother at the admission window before she went into the emergency room. My mother's name was Chu Yi Ching. In English, she went by the name Anna. She was born on August 28, 1917. Her address was #622 Oi Chi House, Tuen Mun.

We then went to the emergency ward. I still remember vividly to this day what it looked like on that Sunday morning: a huge rectangular room, with one side full of temporary beds, separated by white curtains, and the other side composed just of benches. Patients who were not seriously injured sat on those benches to wait for their turn. It reminded me of an army waiting room: looking around, you saw the injured, the sick, and those who may never be healed. I tried not to look at anyone, but I couldn't help it. Awful thoughts began to creep into my mind, and I began to feel panicked.

I turned to look at my mother. She was lying on the hospital bed quietly; she was all right and not in much pain, as long as she was not moving, but she still seemed confused. I held her hand tightly, trying to tell her with no words that she was going to be fine. I felt completely powerless and vulnerable. I wanted every doctor in the world to come to see her immediately. I wanted third, fourth, and fifth opinions; I wanted every nurse at her side every waking second, tending to her every need. Can you blame me? I loved mother so much that I would have sold every last penny I had to make this happen if it were possible. But it wasn't possible; and that was the hardest thing for me to accept. All I could do was wait—and that is the worst thing to tell a person who is so involved in their loved one's life.

I had been told that mother would have to wait her turn because she was not considered severely injured. But after a while, I began to wonder what the hospital considered to be "seriously injured;" we had been waiting for hours now. I glanced at the clock frequently. I paced furiously, waiting for a doctor or a nurse to at least speak to us to give us an idea of what was taking so long.

As time passed by, I realized with the growing fury that we had been waiting for over four hours in this tiny room with only a thin cloth as a partition, and no nurses or doctors had been checking on her. What if her condition had gotten worse since the time we came in? What if she had been left unsupervised? The image of her falling out of her chair earlier rushed back into my mind; it replayed behind my eyes over and over like a movie that just wouldn't turn off. I dared not walk away from her side for even a second. I shook my head to calm myself. I was fearful and impatient, but I couldn't let it show. I had to stay positive and focused for my mom.

To make matters worse, the room was freezing; for some reason, the air conditioning was on high, and it made me feel like I was in the Arctic. I couldn't stop shivering; I folded my arms tightly together across my chest, hoping to keep in what little warmth I had left in my body. With nothing in my stomach, my energy was running as low as my patience. I looked over at my mother. She was lying there with a frightened expression, covered only with a light blanket. She hadn't eaten since breakfast, and she was clearly hungry and exhausted, and still frightened and in discomfort. But she still did not make a single sound of complaint. Looking in her eyes, with no words needed, I could suddenly feel her pain. I stopped shivering and unfolded my arms. I took what little warmth I had left and wrapped my hands in my mom's hands, hoping to transfer my heat to her.

It wasn't until three o'clock when the doctor finally came to check on her. That was over four hours after we had first arrived. My impatience was nothing like it had been earlier in the day. Four hours for an elderly woman to wait! Something inside mother could have been injured even further in that time.

I tiredly repeated to the doctor the story of how her injury had happened. The doctor examined mother's left thigh and told me simply that her bone was broken. Before it could be confirmed, however, she needed to have an x-ray. That would have to wait a bit, he said, and so we waited again for another hour before we took mother downstairs to the basement where the x-ray room was located.

Her face had transformed at this point from confusion to be completely motionless. I couldn't tell if she knew what was going on. I looked at her closely, looking straight into her eyes and holding her hand, telling her that no matter what, I would be at her side every minute. But it was getting harder to read her.

The results of the x-ray came out in just half-an-hour and confirmed the doctor's diagnosis: the left thigh bone was cracked on the surface about three inches, and she would need to have an operation to heal it. I shut my eyes. Okay, I thought, an operation. That's fine; it will make her better. It's nothing too serious.

We were placed on hold for admittance to the hospital until 7pm, during which time I filled out the necessary paperwork. A hospital worker then came and brought us to the A3 Orthopedic Ward, where mother would remain until her surgery. I handed the paperwork in, and hurriedly tended to mother, helping her into what would become her bed for the next few days. Finally, mother had a place to recline and settle for a little while without being dragged and shuttled from one room to another, with unfamiliar people marching by her and poking and prodding her at every minute.

Once she was settled, I collapsed into the nearest chair and sighed. I closed my eyes for a moment. I couldn't believe what had happened after this morning. How could a day that started so brightly turn out so dark? The events began to run through my mind in a blur: the stretcher, the ambulance, the wait in the hospital, the doctor's diagnosis, and the fall that started it all...the fall. The sound of that horrid "THUD!" echoed over and over again in my ears. I shook my head and opened my eyes.

To get the sound out of my head, I looked around the room. I figured I might as well take a look at the conditions of our living quarters for the next few days. The Orthopedic Ward was very large, consisting of rows of beds, numbered from 15-24. There were two elevators, C1 and C2, which would bring us to and from the ward. It was not much different from the emergency ward: large, impersonal, and rather dull-looking. I wondered what mother would have to say about the drab-colored walls. If she were in the health to do so, she would immediately ask to speak to the decorator, I thought with a smile.

A nurse brought in mother's chart just then, and explained to me what to bring tonight and the next day to make mother more comfortable in this dreary room. The most important thing to know, she said, was that mother would have to lie on the bed without getting up to go to the toilet, so I would have to make her as comfortable as possible. Mother had already wet herself many times that day, and because we had to wait so long for the doctor, we didn't have a chance to go to the washroom. I wanted to run to the store before it closed to get her adult diapers. Before I could leave, a hospital helper finally arrived with a tray of food for her; it was the first food she had eaten since breakfast, nearly eleven hours ago. I carefully fed her the food, and when she was finished, I rushed to the nearby store and bought one dozen adult diapers.

When I got back, I asked the nurse-assistant to help her to get changed from top to bottom. It was a bit of a struggle; mother's dementia was making her fearful of her strange surroundings. Eventually, she relented, and I tried to soothe her to relax; I told her that she was okay, and that she should sleep. My heart nearly broke on my next words to her: "I will be at your side when you wake up in the morning." I had to go home, get myself something to eat, and get all of her necessary belongings that she would need to stay comfortable in the ward. I kissed her good-night on her forehead, trying not to let the tears that were welling up in my eyes drip onto her forehead.

It was 9pm by the time I got back home, almost twelve hours since the accident. I walked in the doorway and barely glanced at the bamboo chair by the doorway. It was sitting there, just as we had left it. But so much had happened in those twelve hours. I didn't want to be reminded of anything.

The day was finished, but my mind had not stopped. I ate voraciously, took a shower, and updated my sister on the accident and mother's condition. I slept on my mother's bed that night, tossing and turning restlessly.

On the morning of February 11, I arrived at her ward early, as usual, fully anticipating that her surgery would go well today. When I walked in, the nurse told me that my mother had high blood pressure, and they could not operate today. They were giving her doses of pills to lower her blood pressure.

I was a little concerned when I heard this. I had of course wanted everything to go smoothly. But I was beginning to come to agree with the reality of the situation that the nurses and doctor were aware of—that at mother's age, there could be no room for error. So I stood by as mother was given pill after pill to push her along to her eventual operation. I couldn't help but let those bad thoughts creep back into my head; with every pill, mother took into her once-smiling mouth, my anxiety rose a little more.

That afternoon, two nurse assistants came in and took off all of mother's clothes, put her on a stretcher with a light blanket to cover her, and pushed her to the bathroom to wash her fully from head to toe. I followed close behind. A bath was a good thing, I thought; I was glad that mother would be able to feel clean again, and I was hoping that this would be as refreshing for her mind as it would be for her body. Hopefully, some of my own worries would wash away down the drain as well.

The scene that unfolded, however, did little to wash any of my fears away. As I watched the way the hospital workers handled my mother, my blood and anger began to boil as hot as the water she was washed with. Like a farm animal being herded off and hosed down, mother was placed under the water head and bathed quickly and roughly: one assistant held the shower's head to spray water on her whole body, getting it everywhere, in her eyes, ears, and mouth—and the other used a cloth with soap to scrub her, hard, fast, and with no care. The soap looked dried and old, and they rubbed it on her with an ungentle force, scraping it on her skin, up and down, back and forth. They did not seem to notice they were handling a human being, let alone a confused, elderly woman. They splashed and scoured mother everywhere, forcefully and hastily; I had no idea what the temperature of the water even was.

My mouth dropped open. Was this how they treated patients here? It was too painful for me to watch. Mother remained silent and motionless throughout the ordeal. I couldn't tell if she was really in pain and was holding it in, or if she didn't know what was happening. Either way, her silence was the greatest pain of all.

With the way I had seen them treat her today in the shower, I wanted her in the hands of more skilled professionals. The next day, she was moved to another ward, D1-D4, which was on the same floor but on the opposite

12

side, closer to the operation area. This was a special ward for patients who were scheduled to be operated on within the week. Mother's age and her condition were not the only reasons that her surgery was to take place so quickly; Tuen Mun Hospital did not have empty beds very often, so the doctors liked to treat patients and send them home as quickly as possible.

After seeing the way mother had been treated by the assistants yesterday, I began to have serious doubts about this hurry; since she was in her eighties, could the doctors really rush this procedure without any side effects or harm to her? Were they really analyzing her objectively as a patient—or did they just want the bed? It was a disturbing thought that I couldn't shake. Mother was still taking heavy doses of pills to lower her blood pressure; I began to wonder if that was really the best course of action for her.

But her health began to improve slightly, so I put my doubts aside for the time being. The next day, the 12th, she had her first bowel movement since she had been admitted to the hospital. My mother used to have bowel movements regularly, and never once had constipation, until now. Then on the afternoon of the 13th, although it was not her turn, the nurse had sent an order for her to bathe. But after what had happened last time, there was no way in hell anybody but me was getting near my mother.

I told the head nurse that I would take care of giving mom her bath on my own. She explained impatiently to me that it was hospital policy for the nurse-assistants to give the baths. I looked her in the face; she looked into mine. I repeated my story, with gritted teeth. She said nothing to me, but told the waiting nurse-assistants to leave. She then agreed to let me wash mom on my own.

I took mother into the shower room and helped her under the shower head and gently began to rinse her. I took the old, aging, crusty soap and did my best to get it soaked with enough water so that it had a softer texture. I rubbed the soap over my mom gently, taking care to wash every part of her body. This was exactly how it should be, I thought to myself as I washed her. This was what mother had taught me: this was unconditional love. I was carrying out the most important virtue that the beautiful woman in my arms had taught me.

With all of my frustrations with the hospital, I was hoping that they would not disappoint with mother's scheduled surgery. On the morning of February 14th, the doctor told me that mother's blood pressure had successfully lowered significantly, and they were ready to operate that very day at 1:30pm.

I had mixed emotions as I signed the necessary papers. I was still fuming over the incompetence the workers had shown towards mother, and I just wanted her to be in the hands of excellent, skilled surgeons. As she underwent the two-hour operation, I waited anxiously outside with the other patients for the entire time. I was a nervous wreck. All the worries I had been trying to hide rushed back up in me like a blast of wind. I kept thinking to myself everything that could possibly go wrong. What if her blood pressure rose too high again and they had to stop the surgery? What if she reacted badly to the medicine they gave her? What if the surgeons made an error? I couldn't sit; I was on pins and needles. I paced back and forth in front of the waiting area like a caged tiger. Every time a doctor passed by, I looked up eagerly; every time a nurse walked through, I wanted to ask her to go into the operating room to check on my mother. It was all I could do to keep my mouth closed and my mind as positive as possible.

Finally, the two-hour mark passed, and suddenly, the doors to the waiting room opened. I looked up in eager anticipation. The procession of doctors and nurses seemed endless. But then suddenly, there she was: sleeping, safe and sound, on her hospital bed, with bandages around her left thigh, and healed!

I breathed a huge sigh of relief. I wanted to cry with joy. She was in a deep sleep from the exhaustion of the surgery and from the medicine they had given her, but the doctors assured me she would be fine when she woke up later. The operation had been a complete success, and now, mother was being pushed up to a brand new ward, B9—the recovery ward. The words sounded wonderful to my ears.

As I watched the nurse help her settle into her new ward, I thought to myself what a long few days it had been. It was hard to believe that I had originally only come to Hong Kong for a visit a little while ago, just to see how mother was doing. It seemed like a lifetime ago. Now there was no way that I was leaving her anytime soon.

Her recovery progressed as equally successfully as her surgery. Aside from some constipation, mother overall was progressing fine. She showed no clues of any complications or signs of alarm. I began to believe I could forgive our time here at the hospital if she was going to continually improve. This, I believed, was the light at the end of our tunnel; if all went well, we would have a clear path to good health from here on out.

I visited her every day around 8am to give her company while she was eating her breakfast. She was the only thing on my mind when I woke up in the morning, and she was the last thing on my mind when I went to bed.

But on the morning of February 17th, her progression stopped dead in its tracks. After breakfast, we talked for a while, having our usual conversation, about nothing in general, just enjoying each other's company. Suddenly, mother stopped speaking. She raised both her hands straight up; she went completely silent, but her eyes bulged wide open.

I panicked; was she choking? I examined her; that wasn't it. Was she having a reaction to her medicine? I tried to find a nurse or a doctor, but none of them were around. What was happening? What was wrong with her? Memories of her fall came rushing back into my mind. I didn't dare to walk away from her as I had then.

14

I did not know how long it was, but my mother calmed down. The nurse finally came, followed by the doctor; he used a light to check her eyes and told me that mother just had a stroke.

Oh my God. I couldn't believe it. I tried to listen as the doctor explained to me what this meant. A stroke is a cerebral-vascular disease that affects the arteries leading to and within the brain. It is similar to a heart attack: in a heart attack, the blood flow is interrupted in the heart, and it doesn't get enough oxygen; in a stroke, the blood flow is interrupted to the brain, causing a lack of oxygen.

My mother had a right brain stroke. The right side of the brain controls the left side of the body, which controls thinking and cognition; a stroke to the left side can cause changes in communication, movement, vision and touch, and behavior. A right-brain stroke can cause symptoms ranging from a loss of movement on the left side of the body to a heightened sense of confusion about simple facts like dates and times to an aggressive, irritable, and temperamental personality.

I could barely process all the information the doctor was telling me. I buried my face in my hands. Mother was already suffering enough with her dementia; I knew the stroke was only going to make her worse. How badly was her mind damaged now? How was she going to be able to function?

I asked the doctor how this could have happened, and he told me that it was sometimes a side effect for an elderly person after surgery, especially for someone in mother's condition. It could happen to anybody, though, he told me; there was nothing anyone could do to prevent it.

I held back the tears that stung the back of my eyes. That still didn't make me feel any better. I had so many questions and concerns. What was going to happen now? How do you heal a stroke? How long until she was back to normal again?

I could barely think with the anxiety that was starting to settle over my chest, but I could think clearly enough to ask about one thing: immediate treatment. I was at least thankful that we were in a hospital surrounded by doctors and nurses, who could immediately start her on the appropriate medication. I expected the doctors and nurses might give her some kind of injection or medicine.

The doctors simply checked her over, confirmed that she had a stroke, then left. They didn't tell me anything—never gave her a prescription, never treated her. I just assumed that they were coming back. Mother wasn't in any pain; she was just exhausted and confused. I felt her hands; they were cold from only wearing her thin hospital gown. Her face was weary, and her eyes were watery.

I stayed there by her side for a long time, holding her hand, talking to her gently. As we waited, I counted every moment that passed. Lunchtime came and went; still no doctors, no nurses—not even a meal. Mother's stroke had happened right after breakfast; surely that was more than enough time to wait. I walked out into the hall. No doctors or nurses were in sight.

I went back into the room and began to pace back and forth in front of my mother's bed. With every pace, I got more and more anxious. Soon, that anxiety grew into fury. Where were they? Weren't they going to do something for her? Give her medication, give me some instruction—give her some food at least?

The afternoon came and went—still nothing. No doctors, nurses—not even any meals. Finally, my temper reached its breaking point. I had had enough. I was not going to stand idly by while mother was not given the care she deserved.

I left mother for a moment and went to the front desk to ask when someone was coming to see her. The nurse at the desk looked at me strangely and told me the doctors had all left the hospital for the day and had returned to their offices until tomorrow.

I felt like I had been hit with a bucket of cold water. Was she kidding me? I thought it might be some kind of cruel joke. What kind of place was this? A patient suffers a stroke and was not treated? Why did no one come, not a single soul, doctor or nurse, to help my mother? After their diagnosis, they had simply left as quickly as they had come, leaving mother and me there.

I wanted to bang my hands on the desk and scream like a child until a doctor came. Mother was uncomfortable, and I wanted so badly to help her, but I dared not move her, even to change her diaper, even though in the time since her stroke, now several hours ago, she had wet herself many times. I didn't want anything else to happen to her and have no one there to help her. So I gritted my teeth and went back to my mother's room.

It wasn't until 4pm when a nurse finally came to inject a saline solution of sucrose intravenously into mother's left hand. She felt the pain then. At 6pm, a CAT scan simulator confirmed mother had a stroke. I sighed with impatience. We already knew that; I wanted the treatment!

I was later informed that in America, there is a medicine administered within twenty-four hours of having a stroke, in which a patient is usually injected on both sides of the abdomen to help revive them. In Hong Kong, nothing like this injection was given, nor were there any pills or even food administered. I spent the remainder of the day with my mother; she was not given anything else to eat for fear that she would choke. We didn't hear from the doctors at all that night; we had to wait until they came back the next morning. I wondered if the nurse had come in to give mother the IV only because I asked. If I hadn't said something to her, mother might still just be lying there.

The next morning, we still didn't get to see a doctor. Doctors usually checked on patients between 9am to 10:30am, but on the morning following mother's stroke, the speech therapist came to evaluate mother. This was no replacement for the actual doctor; I was annoyed that we still were not getting any concrete treatment for mother. The speech therapist concluded that mother could not eat at all. Mother had to starve another day again. It was bizarre; after a patient had a stroke, the doctor was supposed to look after his

16

patient in this ward, but ours had not even shown up or prescribed any medicine.

I was still infuriated. But what could I do? I didn't have the authority to go running to the nurses, screaming at the injustice of the situation. I couldn't protest or write an angry letter to the hospital administrators. None of that would make my mom better. All I wanted, I thought to myself with exasperation, was for a professional to examine her and take care of her—not see her once, after something bad occurs, and then disappear. That to me was common sense—when someone was injured, you take care of them until they get better. Apparently, I was speaking a different language than everyone else.

On the 19th, I arrived at the hospital at my usual time, early in the morning. Today, mother was scared and had forgotten why she was staying in the hospital. I told her many times, but she kept forgetting because of her dementia. Then she suddenly began asking me who was next to her on her left side. At first, I had no idea what she was referring to, but it dawned on me that when mother felt someone next to her, what she actually felt was her left limb. She still could not remember that she had been paralyzed from her left side that started from her left lip down to her toes. It depressed me to know that mother did not recognize the full side of her body. I began to wonder if she was going to ask me every morning who was on her left side. I didn't know if I could take that every day.

After a short visit from the doctor at 11am, who simply examined her over and did not give her any medicine for her stroke, I was about to reach my breaking point. But then, at 4pm, we finally started to get some answers. We had our first visit from mother's case worker, Cybie Mok. She worked at the Ming Sum Lau clinic, a psychiatry clinic, as a dementia senior co-coordinator. She would make home visits once a month to us to help us all adjust and manage mother's dementia. Ms. Mok kindly and patiently walked me through all aspects of mother's health and personality that would now be affected by her stroke – especially her dementia.

Mother had first shown signs of dementia in 1999. I had received a phone call at my home in Worcester, Massachusetts saying that mother had gone out and had forgotten how to get home. She had waited by herself, panicked and frightened, in the middle of the street for twenty minutes. When she finally remembered how to get home, she never wanted to go out again by herself.

This concerned me greatly when it happened. I recalled that about a year before that, mother was helping a staff member from the gas company check on the meter in her kitchen by standing on a stool. Suddenly she fell; when she fell, she hit her head and developed a large dark patch on the left side of her face. After going to the doctor, she said she felt fine, and as the patch gradually went away, she showed no other signs of illness. I wondered if this was a delayed result of that fall.

After I had a discussion with my husband, we decided to have mother and my sister Agnes come and live permanently with us in

Worcester. On May 23, mother, Agnes and I took United Airlines flight 896, a little over fifteen hours, directly to O'Hare Airport in Chicago. We passed through the Immigration Counter, checked our luggage, and transferred to a domestic flight to Boston in the evening. By the time we arrived home in Worcester, we had spent over twenty-four hours during our long journey. All of us had jet lag, but at eighty-four years old, mother was already very tired. She woke up many times during that night. The weather also affected her. That year in May, it was a bit chilly in Worcester, and with the weather so humid and hot in Hong Kong, in a matter of two days, we were already separated into two different worlds.

After we were settled, I took them sightseeing both in Worcester and Boston to enjoy some of the highlights for tourists. I also took her to visit Worcester Polytechnic Institute where her granddaughter Stella graduated. On Sundays, I accompanied mother and Agnes to attend the Mormon Church nearby our neighborhood. Once I returned to work, mother was not comfortable in this new place. She was always panicked and questioning our conversation or intentions. Mother also never slept well during the nights; she had anxiety and the tendency to become frightened.

I had no knowledge of the causes behind mother's behavior. Finally, she decided she wanted to return to Hong Kong. On June 16, we flew to Chicago for a connecting flight. Stella took her daughter Stephanie to meet us at the O'Hare Airport, and mother was very pleased to hold her great-granddaughter in her arms. We then caught our flight back to Hong Kong and arrived there the next day.

Over the next several months, I phoned Hong Kong as often as possible. The distance between mother and I unnerved me. Everything seemed to be fine until November 2001 when I received a call from Ho Yuk Wah, mother's church friend. She told me that mother could not sleep during the night. To figure out what was wrong, she took mother to see Dr. Chan, and he diagnosed her symptoms as depression.

I was shocked. I flew to Hong Kong to see her on November 16, 2001. Once I arrived, I discovered that she was taking 20 milligrams of Prozac Isatuein/Deprexin and 25 milligrams of Cinnarizine. This was not appropriate medicine for depression; this was an overdose of treatment for a mental illness. It was now causing mother to sleep excessively. I removed the pill of Prozac gradually, little by little, day by day.

I was then scheduled to return home to the States on November 30. It was painful to leave mother. Yuk Wah had been cooking for mother part-time since last year; now, I hired her to work full time to attend to mother's needs. But I still worried constantly. Over the next year, I phoned Hong Kong as often as possible for updates. Yuk Wah continually assured me everything was fine, but the distance between mother and I still made me anxious.

In the early morning of May 16, 2002, I arrived again in Hong Kong. I took mother to see a doctor in the afternoon at the Ming Sum Lau Clinic. It was here that the doctor officially diagnosed her with vascular dementia. Vascular dementia occurs when the blood supply carrying oxygen and nutrients to the brain is interrupted by a blocked or diseased vascular system. Unlike a stroke or heart attack, however, dementia's effects are much more progressive; if blood supply is blocked for longer than a few seconds, brain cells can die, causing damage to the cortex of the brain—the area associated with learning, memory, and language. People with dementia experience impairments in all of these areas, and can also demonstrate significant changes in mood and personality. Dementia isn't always obvious, as was the case with mother; this explained all the changes in her behavior over the past couple of years.

On June 20, I left Hong Kong. By the time I returned home, I constantly worried about mother and called her several times daily, so I decided to take early retirement. On September 24, 2002, I decided that my next trip to Hong Kong would be to monitor mother as closely as possible to see how much her dementia was affecting her and decide the best course of action to take. Larry would accompany me but would stay only for a little while and then fly back to America alone. I planned to stay with mother until March 2003, around which time my elder daughter was due to give birth to her second son in America, and I would fly back to be by her side.

I had been learning about dementia since mother's diagnoses, and Ms. Mok had offered very good information and advice. I was pleased that Ms. Mok would now help me understand how to handle mother's dementia and stroke together. We went over some of the things that mother, as a dementia patient, would now be experiencing as a right-brain stroke patient as well. With both her dementia and the stroke, we now needed to keep both illnesses stable and under control in order for her to gradually improve. Otherwise, she explained to me, her mind and memory would steadily decline, like a roller coaster going down a hill.

We first went over the most obvious skill mother had lost: her movement. A stroke patient may lose coordination in any part of the body, and become tired and fatigued very easily. With her left-side paralysis, mother of course had lost all movement on the entire left side of her body, from her face down to her toes. I told Ms. Mok that mother kept asking me who was seated to her left; she explained that was a normal effect of her stroke, since mother now had no perception of her left side. She advised me that in the next few days not to place any significant items to her left, and that if mother had visitors, I needed to tell them to approach her either directly in front of her or to her right. Mother could become more disoriented if people constantly stood or spoke to her from her left. However, she also said that once the immediate effects of the stroke began to gradually wear off and mother began to show a little less confusion and disorientation, it was important for us to approach her from her left side, so she could become aware of it again.

I thanked Ms. Mok for her time when we finished speaking; she had been the only one so far to really take time and explain things to me. I felt like part of the burden had been lifted from me. Before I left around 8:30pm, I

19

gave mother a big hug. She looked at me, depressed and still confused. I wiped back the tears in my eyes; I kept my brave face for her.

On the following day, the 20th, when the doctor came to check on mother at 9:30am, he told me that my mom needed a speech therapist, Ms. Wong, who would come soon. She arrived at noon, at which time she fed some rice congee to mother. Rice congee is a type of porridge that is eaten in many Asian countries, made by the extended boiling of rice in water. Some congee had flavor, adding meat or fish; some was just plain, however, which would clean our internal systems when we were sick.

Now, mother had not eaten for several days. So when the congee gently touched mother's lips, she took it all into her mouth at once and gulped it down as quickly as she could. Naturally, the food came right back out; in eating too fast, she began to choke. Ms. Wong stepped back, startled; I moved in to help as mother coughed up the last of the food and swallowed what she could.

She was okay after a moment. I looked over at Ms. Wong, expecting her to begin feeding mother again, a bit more slowly this time. Instead, Ms. Wong swooped in and removed the bowl of food immediately, and began furiously scribbling on her chart.

"I'm not going to feed your mother solid foods again," she replied, not looking up from her chart.

"Excuse me?" I said. "You know, she hasn't had solid food for days. She's obviously more than a little hungry."

"This patient clearly is not able to eat solid foods, so I'm putting her on a feeding tube for now," she said, her eyes never looking up at me.

I froze in shock. "A feeding tube?"

"Yes," she replied, "from the nose."

"A feeding tube from the nose? Is this really necessary?"

"Yes," she said. "It's the easiest way to get your mother to eat." She clicked her pen, turned on her heels, and left, taking mother's chart and dignity with her.

I was still standing in place. I couldn't move. Had I heard right? Did she not just witness what had just occurred? Had she not heard my explanation? How could she come to this conclusion? My goodness, mother had not eaten for five days, of course she would be starving!

I had hoped I could trust her not to be like the doctors. I wanted her to actually sit with mother, spend some time with her, and understand her needs. But she was just like the rest of the doctors—harsh, abrupt, and not able to see what was right in front of her.

The culmination of my anger and frustration came at 4:50pm that day: the time when the feeding tube was first administered to mother. As four nurses entered our room, I wondered to myself, with a harsh, ironic laugh, where all these nurses were while mother was having her stroke. The corridors were empty when a patient was in a fatal situation, but more than enough employees appeared out of nowhere for a completely unnecessary procedure.

20

Was it really going to take four nurses to insert a simple feeding tube into an elderly patient?

As I watched the horrific process begin to unfold before my eyes, I wished with every fiber of my being that everyone would suddenly disappear like they had when mom had her stroke. Mother's nose suddenly became the excavation site of four miners who would stop at nothing to get inside, using every cruel and inhumane strategy to reach their goal. As I watched, I felt like I was bleeding through my own nose; I couldn't imagine what mother was going through. It took all four of them first to hold mother down, like an animal being subjected to torture. One nurse held her legs, two others held her hands on each side, and the last nurse had the unlucky job of pushing the tube through her nose down to her stomach. I stood by helplessly as mother struggled with all her strength against the pain. It was a very delicate process; if the tube went too low and touched the wall of mother's stomach, then she gagged, the tube had to be taken out, and the process had to start all over again. The nurse had to try one more time until the feeding tube was placed accordingly. I thought back to the way mother had been handled in the bath. That was nothing compared to this. This was the cruelest thing I had ever witnessed.

This was a dreadful process in the first place, but the nurses did not handle her properly. They treated her like a science experiment to be jabbed with cold instruments, not like a human being in pain who needed to be handled with tenderness and care. The most visible evidence was mother's blood splashed all over her apron; that blood to them was like water, just another everyday liquid, not the lifeline of a human being. There was the proof, the proof for all the doctors and nurses and anyone who walked by to see—that it was not just my eyes that were seeing how mother was being mistreated.

And yet I still couldn't do anything to help. When they finished and left quickly without a word, I rushed to mother's side and grabbed her hand. She looked at me, lying still now after the ordeal, but with an expression of sheer pity on her face. I wanted then and there to break down and cry at her bedside, to let me tears fall and splash onto her face, and tell her that I know it was not fair, that I was doing everything in my power to keep her comfortable. But I couldn't. I simply comforted her with my words that she would soon be all right. My heart suffered so bitterly; words could not express how much pain I had. To my mother, I hoped my words and tone sounded soothing. To my own ears, my words were shaking and quivering with my doubts and fears.

The burden of mother's pain lay heavy on my heart. It was not even a bright spot for me when mother was transferred out of Tuen Mun Hospital and moved to Pok Oi Hospital on Friday, the 21st of February. The night before she was transferred, they didn't even allow her the dignity of her own room: the staff had simply left her lying in her bed in the hallway all night.

These horrible memories of what had happened to us at Tuen Mun would follow us to every other hospital, doctor, and nurse that we would

21

encounter. It had planted in my mind and heart a strong distrust of those who were supposed to be taking care of mother. But it had also taught me something: I knew now, after all of our experiences there, that I was still the one who had mother's best interests at heart. There was no one else; it was me and me alone.

CHAPTER 2

When we arrived at Pok Oi on our first day, and had gotten mother settled into her new room, C5 ward, bed B10, she suddenly grabbed my arm. I looked down at her. She was looking at me intensely.

"Take me home," she begged.

I was wordless. Every ounce of me wanted to take her right back home with me. I wanted to be home right then at that moment, curled up on the couch with my arms around her, holding her tight, back safe in the place that we both knew so well. It took all of my energy and every last bit of strength not to cry in her arms and tell her how much I wanted to go home with her, too.

But I knew I couldn't take her home if I wanted her to get better. So I chose to say nothing to her. When I looked in her eyes, I couldn't tell anymore if she felt anything but pain. I wondered if she still believed that I still had her best interests at heart, and that I was doing the right thing for her. I stayed with her that night until very late, watching her with unease.

If I was a coward, I would have brought mother back home with me, shielded her from the awful doctors and nurses, and took care of her myself. But something somewhere inside me kept telling me that I was doing the right thing. These people at that hospitals might treat her improperly— but this was the best shot mother was going to have at a fully recovery. They had the proper resources to take care of her; I didn't.

As we began our first week in the new hospital, I would need my courage more than to stand up for mother. After our experiences in Tuen Mun, I knew that I had to prepare myself for more mistreatment and lack of care. I was ready to take on the challenge.

But I had another challenge in simply getting to the hospital to be by mother's side every day. Pok Oi Hospital was located in Yuen Long, but far away from Yuen Long's central city; I needed to take a special mini-bus from Yuen Long to reach this hospital, the green 609 mini-bus that ran from 7:30am-8:30pm. If I stayed out past 8:30, I would miss the mini-bus and have to walk down the steep hill. From Tuen Mun I took a light-train, 614, back to Yuen Long downtown. I walked a short distance to this mini-bus station and followed a queue line. It took around another five miles to reach Pok Oi Hospital. This was how I traveled every day to visit my mother from early morning at 6am until very late at night at 9pm; usually I took the last ride down to the city. It was a very steep area, and it was hard to walk up and down the hill. At night, walking back, it was very dangerous; the cars' headlights would blind me, and I wouldn't be able to see the road. You could never tell who or what would be out there at night. There was the ever-present danger of a car not seeing me and hitting me, or me tripping over something I couldn't see in the road, or falling into a hole or ditch.

Luckily, I had the good fortune of having a kind neighbor show me an easier way to get to the hospital. Instead of my usual route, my neighbor told me to take the number 720 light train to Hung Shui Kui, transfer to the number 614 at the Yuen Long light train station, then walk across the street and wait for the mini bus to climb up the hill to the top of the hospital parking area. It was half an hour faster, and this allowed me more time to spend with mother. I was very grateful to my neighbor for this handy piece of advice.

After I began taking this new route on February 22, a sunny Saturday, arriving at the hospital at my usual 8am, I found yet another horrific site. Arriving at mother's bed, I found her tied up like a mentally ill patient. She wore a sleeveless jacket that covered her body, and both of her wrists had been tied with thick straps to each of the railings of her bed; the feeding tube was still hanging from her nose.

I was astounded and outraged. What could my elderly mother have possibly done to be tied up and strapped down? What was she even capable of, at her old age?

I wondered if one of the nurses was going to tell me some ridiculous story. They explained to me that mother had removed the feeding tube out of her nose; because of her dementia, she was confused about the tube that she found in her nose when she awoke, so naturally, she simply pulled it out. The nurses had tied her wrist down so that she would not pull the tube out again.

I shut my eyes tight. It took all of my willpower not to cry in front of mother. I opened my eyes and looked down at her. She looked back at me with tearful eyes. I shut my eyes again, trying to keep my breathing even. My heart was bitter with tears at the injustice of what they had done, but I knew if I cried in front of mother, she would only become more miserable. So I tried to take mother's mind off of her pain; I told her jokes, asking her silly questions about the other patients, anything to draw her attention away and bring her out of her sadness, anything to make her forget she was being held like a prisoner.

I tried to draw her attention out of the window she had next to her. Mother's bed was the last in a row on the right side of her ward; in total, there were thirty beds, fifteen on each side along the wall. Each bed had a small end table placed next to it on which you could leave personal belongings, and mother was lucky to have a window on her other side, so she could at least look at the sun and sky instead of the other sickly patients.

As I sat and talked with her, I noticed that she was coughing and choking from time to time. I checked her tube and discovered that the milk that was feeding her was going at a very rapid pace. No one had adjusted it.

That was it. That was the last straw. At that moment, I decided that enough was enough. These people were not taking care of her properly; I didn't care about doctor's order or hospital policy anymore. Instead of going to find a nurse, I would take care of it myself. On the top of her IV milk bag was a knob that controlled how much milk she received. I turned it one way slowly; the milk came out too slow, only one drip at a time. I kept turning up slowly until mother was receiving her milk at a reasonable speed, and she would not choke or cough on it. She looked at me; she was more comfortable.

I sat back. I felt more powerful, and I felt some of my stress faded away. I realized that what I had been worried about for so long was not just

24

mother, but myself—that I had not done all that I could to help her. That was going to change.

On Monday, February 24, I arrived at my usual early time to the hospital, and mother had already woken up. She was having her so-called breakfast – milk through the nose tube. I greeted her with a warm hug and kiss on her forehead. When I pulled back and looked at her expression, I knew she was not comfortable with the jacket tied up around her. So I loosened both of the cotton straps. I wasn't going to wait any more for orders or instructions. Neither the nurses nor her doctor showed up to check up on her. It wasn't until later in the day when a nurse discovered that mother was out of the straps. But I was prepared for her. I told her firmly, "I am going to be at my mother's side at every moment. I personally will make sure that she doesn't take the tube out of her nose."

As I stood there, not moving, the nurse fell silent; any protests they were about to give were stopped short. They could see my fierceness; they complied, and decided to let me stay with mom and leave the straps off of her.

As they left the room, I turned to mother. She was still confused about her tube; to keep her from taking it out again, I lied a little, and told her that the tube was a special tube for her, and she could not remove it or else she would suffer a lot of pain. She agreed, and remained calm, and she did not have to wear the restraints again.

My next battle came with the nurse-assistants who were scheduled to give mother a bath. I had not soon forgotten what the previous hospital workers had done to mother in the same situation, and I was cautious to see if this would be any different.

It wasn't. Two servants arrived soon to help mother prepare. These servants were two strangers, and taking a bath is clearly something very personal. But instead of comforting mother, treating her like a person, speaking kindly to her, and assuring her that they would take good care of her, they removed all her clothes wordlessly, like mother was just another nameless patient off the street. They then put her into a plastic stretcher, covered her with a thin cloth and pushed her to the bathroom where she would have her bath. There was no conversation; I guessed that these two workers saw mother as just another old lady that needed to be cleaned up and shipped back to her room. They probably had dozens of other patients just like her.

When mother was helped into the bath, they used a long handled shower head to water mother down from her hair down to her toes. It was clear to me that they couldn't tell the difference between giving an elderly woman a bath and hosing down a farm animal, just like the first two assistants back at Tuen Mun Hospital. One thing these servants did not care less about was whether the water was too hot or the right temperature for this old lady. They didn't speak to her, or let her feel the water first to see if it was the right temperature for her. They simply turned on the water and started spraying her down.

At Tuen Mun, I had stayed silent as I had watched this same scenario unfold before my eyes. Not this time. I yelled loudly at them. I went and tested the water myself until I got the right temperature. I stopped them from doing the quick, rough strokes up and down mother's body that they had been doing. At that point, the whole process was finished for them, and they left quickly without a word, leaving behind a dripping wet sick woman.

Good riddance to them, I thought. For them, she was just one more patient, one more bath to give before they could leave for the day and go home. They had no idea that this was someone's mother. I wiped and dried mother's body carefully with a towel and dressed her properly.

Over the course of our first few days at Pok Oi Hospital, I began to feel increasingly triumphant, like I had just won a series of very small but very important battles. To anyone else, I was probably just another daughter trying to look out for her ill mother; to me, every conversation was a battle, and every battle won was a victory, no matter how small. I had not been doing enough; I was not going to stand by anymore and let things happen to her. I was going to do my best to nurse her and protect her in every way possible. At least while I was at her side, mother was free.

Mother's daily exercise regime was my next task to take on. Because of her stroke, it was essential to her health that mother begin to exercise to start to improve. I expected that for an old woman, these exercises would begin slowly, maybe for an hour or so each day. Although she had a stroke, she was still fragile, and she was not young; you couldn't push her to do something she wasn't capable of. But I was wrong. In the afternoon of the same day of her bath, mother began the first of many weeks of a strict exercise regimen. She was placed on a very tight daily schedule; she exercised on the fourth floor from 8:30 am to 11:45am, then was pushed back upstairs to her ward to rest for 15 minutes, then ate lunch for a half hour, and was then pushed downstairs again for her other exercises until 4pm. That's an entire day of physical exercises. I didn't know any healthy people that subject themselves to exercises for that amount of time each day. But because she was paralyzed on her whole left side from her lip, arm, and hand to her leg, the doctor wanted to ensure that her joints and muscles could still mobilize properly in order for her to fully recover.

To get down to the fourth floor, two assistants would come up to mother's room and put her in an upright sitting position in her bed. One person would get on either side of her and lift her up from underneath her arms, and lift her into her wheelchair. Once she arrived down at the fourth floor, she would begin her hand exercises. Her left hand would be placed onto a small board that had four wheels attached to it, similar to a very small skateboard. Her upper arm would be immobilized; she would use her right hand to hold on her left arm with the board, and would push the board back and forth on the table to ensure that her joints would not tighten up. In the afternoon, she had to grab onto two bamboo pulleys that would extend her arms up and down to stretch her muscles. She was usually very frustrated, and would not move herself; I had to help her move.

26

For a sick patient like mother, I thought this was cruel. I knew that the exercises were of course nothing too harsh, but it was quite a lot for mother to do. Mother gave me that sad look as she was being pushed off every day, begging me with her eyes not to let her go. What was I supposed to do? I just embraced her, and accompanied her to the exercise room.

The worst part about these exercises was that mother was still required to wear her feeding tube, so she had to exercise with it in. That feeding tube was awkward, dangling, and swinging here and there. But the doctors had told me, "If you want your mother to improve, she has to exercise even with the feeding tube." Watching as it dangled from her nose as she feebly attempted to do the exercises, I wondered if this was the breaking point. She looked so pathetic, and I felt so awful for her; I wanted to just give up and bring her home.

There was one incident that almost did make me bring mother home for good. One day, I noticed a bruise on mother's left leg, which was her paralyzed leg; I pointed it out to the nurses and asked them what had happened. They looked at me with surprise, and immediately accused me of being hasty and sloppy with mother, and that had what had caused the bruise. Oh no, I said to them, there was no way that was the case. The bruise was at the same height as the footholds on mother's wheelchair; I deduced that one of the footholds had hit her when someone had not been gentle with mother when helping her in or out of the wheelchair. The only time that mother was moved into the wheelchair was when she had to go do her exercises, and it was the hospital assistants who moved her then. The wheelchair was also not ours to keep in our room; it belonged to the hospital, and I did not operate it without the presence of a hospital assistant.

I asked the head nurse to investigate further, and come to find out, just as I had suspected, two of the hospital assistants, while they were helping mother into her wheelchair, had carelessly hit her leg and not told anyone. Mother of course did not feel the pain because it was her paralyzed side, so she was not even aware of it. Well, the evidence was there now, right there in black and blue. The head nurse admitted it was their fault and apologized, but that really didn't make up for their carelessness. I had a feeling it was just going to happen again.

I was right. A few days later, while she was being moved again into the chair, all of a sudden, I noticed her left fingers were clustered in the metal part of the wheelchair, looking as if they were about to be crushed. She couldn't feel a thing, of course; the sight horrified me. I yelled at the assistants; I ran over to take her fingers out as gently as I could. The assistants didn't apologize; they just looked at me and wheeled mother out, just another number on their list of patients that day.

I had no patience left to deal with the inhumanity and carelessness of these workers. The nurses and assistants obviously had many other patients that they needed to care for, and I wanted someone with my mom at all times, not just to aid her if something happened, but to be there with her to prevent anything from happening. So I hired an outside assistant with experience in

27

caring for paralyzed, elderly people. The person I hired had taken care of her paralyzed father for many years until he passed away. She was the complete opposite of the hospital workers: careful, attentive, and patient. She was exactly what I had been looking for, the answer to my prayers.

After I hired our new assistant, something began to change in mother. She had always been the strongest woman that I, and most other people who knew her, had ever known. As she had been getting battered down, humiliated, and mistreated, something inside her had taken the dark and turned it into light. Before my very eyes, mother began to improve, both in health and in spirit, little by little, day by day. As careless as these hospital workers were, my mother worked twice as hard to overcome her obstacles. They would never know how well she was improving, with or without their so-called help. Everything they were doing just made her tougher.

As I began to realize this, a series of small but bright lights began to shine for us when several special events began to happen, all right in a row. The first happened on Tuesday the 25th. Dr. Ng came to see mother at 9:45am that day and gave two weeks to review her case. These two weeks meant that mother would be monitored as she improved, and she might have a chance to eat or to practice eating again without her feeding tube. My spirits lifted at hearing this news.

Then, that afternoon, mother's spirits were lifted too in ways that I had not witnessed in a long time. Mother's cousin Wong Yee Chun, or Rosie, and her daughter Karen came to visit from Wattle Grove, Australia. Mother recognized Rosie immediately; the sight of her had made a light switch flip on in mother's brain. She suddenly seemed almost like her old self again, full of as much energy as she used to have, laughing and chatting, thoroughly enjoying talking about the old days. I remembered that Ms. Mok had said that visitors were an excellent way of energizing mother's spirits and creating a joyful environment around her. It had not occurred to me how important this was, but if mother's almost instant change in personality when she saw Rosie was any indication, I knew that I was going to be asking for a great many more visitors for her. As Karen and I watched the two of them converse animatedly, I marveled silently at how happy mother truly looked. Their two-hour stay seemed far too short, and after they left, mother remained in good spirits for the rest of the night.

Our second instance of good luck came with mother's progression in her physical health. On February 26 from 3:00pm to 6:45pm, mother sat up in a chair for the first time since her stroke. She had a little help, but this was very good progress for her. She did, however, sit up for a little too long, and her back and feet began to hurt; the nurse who had helped us had disappeared, and I couldn't find any other worker to help move her back to bed until 6:45pm.

At 9:30 on Thursday, the 27th, a kind and patient speech specialist came to feed my mother. Let me tell you what a difference kindness makes. Both this specialist and I supportively encouraged mom to swallow the soft food that was given to her. Lo and behold, she did eat it, one mouthful at one time! I was so happy; this meant no more feeding tube in her nose and no more suffering! Halleluiah! This was our most important accomplishment yet.

Then, on that very same day, my grandson Ryan was born to my daughter Stella. Ryan was a big baby, over ten pounds! I told my mother and congratulated her on being a great-grandmother; she smiled back at me and congratulated me on being a grandmother. It was a lovely and joyous break for my mother and I, a beautiful little light in spite of all this dark sadness.

Our successes continued from there. On February 28, mother could take a bath again; I was ecstatic she could feel clean and fresh. I fed her breakfast and lunch, which was always congee. Since mother could not swallow the congee alone, it would be much better to add "Thick and Easy," recommended by the doctor; otherwise some of the liquid from the congee would run straight to her stomach and her throat could not stop instantly, end up she would choke. When mother swallowed the bowl of congee with Thick and Easy, it would help the food go down to her esophagus easily without choking, and she could not suffocate or develop pneumonia. This was a long process to feed her to ensure that this did not happen; it usually took an hour to feed her one bowl of congee. But she always enjoyed eating the entire bowl.

Our housekeeper would bring over the congee at 11:00am every day, with enough for mother to have lunch and dinner. Even though half of the congee would be saved for dinner nearly five hours later, and even though it took mother an hour to eat, her congee would never grow cold in the bowl while she ate, or in between meals. The special container that the congee was kept in was designed to keep the congee hot for up to five to seven hours. The container was small, but was insulated with aluminum on the inside with an additional compartment as well, in which the congee was kept, and was therefore surrounded by two walls of heated insulation. The container also conveniently had another small bowl in which you could store other foods without touching the congee. I usually kept my mother's fish in there if she desired it. It was easy for our housekeeper to carry it to and from the hospital, and because the container kept the congee steaming hot for several hours, she did not have to make the long haul back and forth from mother's home to the hospital twice a day.

By March 2, mother was eating congee for most of her meals with little chunks of meat. I hired a housekeeper to cook some fresh fish to put on her congee. Mother loved fish because it was easy to digest; she used to eat fish every day at home. She was pleased to see it again in the hospital. Later that day, her son Stephen also came to visit her from Canada, bringing with him two bags of diapers for her to get more comfortable. Seeing her son and having fish that day were big highlights for mother. I could see she was slowly getting better, both physically and mentally. I wanted to invite that therapist Ms. Wong over to mother's room for dinner sometime, just so she could watch mother eat and swallow the congee all on her own.

It was a strange feeling for me these past few weeks, seeing mother progress so well. I almost didn't know how to handle it; I was so used to having everything fall apart and fighting for her in ways I didn't think I had the strength to. I wondered if God was giving me a break; now that I realized the reasons behind all of this pain for mother, I wondered if He was letting me rest for a while.

I decided to take the rare opportunity to put my worries aside for just a single morning. My entire focus had been on my mother for the past month—every waking and sleeping moment had been dedicated solely to her and her improvement. On March 3, I had an appointment for myself, so I could not go to see mother as I usually did early in the morning. I went about my business, and went back to see mother later that morning.

I should have known better. A constant caretaker can never rest—ever. That morning, the hospital took my absence as a window to do things their way.

By the time I arrived to see mother at 10am, the milk tube had been placed up her nose again. Somebody had fed my mom breakfast that morning, and she had choked; then they put the tube back in her nose. When I arrived, her apron was splattered with her own blood, just as it had been on the day the tube was first put in.

I couldn't begin to describe how horrible that day was. Mother had no idea what was going on; I was frustrated and mad as hell. She had been progressing perfectly fine up until this morning; I stepped away from a few hours in the morning and everything was back to where we started. I didn't believe the nurses' stories; how could I? My mother had been fine every day, and now, all of a sudden, she's back on the tube. It had been placed so forcefully up her nose that she was clearly in a lot of pain. I felt almost the same pain as my mother; as she looked up at me with those same tearful eyes she had on the day the tube was first inserted, I could only look back at her with as much love as I could show her.

On the 4th, because of what had happened the previous day, I arrived extra early. I discovered that my mom had pulled out her tube. I didn't tell anyone. At 7:15am, I fed my mother congee with no problem. I knew the tube was useless.

At noon, our housekeeper brought in the congee with the fish for lunch, and I prepared to feed her. The head nurse caught me suddenly. She demanded that mother's tube be put back in. I thought she was overreacting; everything with mom had been fine when I left this morning. I really didn't care what she said to me at this point; she could have called the police on me and I would have chained myself to mother's bed. I was not budging. The nurse knew me by now, especially how stubborn I was. She saw the anger and the fierceness in my eyes, and I guess this morning she decided not to challenge me herself. She told me to wait until 12:30pm, when the speech specialist arrived, and I could feed mother in front of her to prove that I was not lying. I agreed.

The specialist didn't show up until almost 1:30pm. My mother furrowed her brow when she saw her; who could blame mother for being scared of her? But she had not eaten since 8am, and she was starving. I began feeding her the congee just like I had that morning. She ate ravenously; as she ate, I enjoyed seeing the expression on the speech specialist's face turn from skepticism to disbelief. When mother had finished every last bite, the specialist looked at me, then quickly shifted her eyes down to her paperwork and wrote a report that allowed my mother to eat solids again.

Finally! Some justice for mother! My persistence had paid off. What a mistake the therapist had made! I felt so triumphant that mother was finally getting the proper treatment that I asked for a written apology from the therapist. She had almost damaged my mother's life after all, if she had authorized the tube to be reinserted. But just like with everything else from this hospital, I never got an apology. Their unwillingness to budge infuriated me; they would not listen to reason at all. I couldn't believe how my mother was being treated by these irrational people. I was the only one who could see the truth in her situation; I was the only one who held my dear mother's best interests at heart. Not even her doctors could see what she really needed. If I had left her alone with the doctors and nurses, she would only become a victim.

After witnessing my mother eating, at least the head nurse knew I was right; I had stood up for my mother. From 3pm-5pm, mother sat up on the chair that day; she was very tired. I fed her dinner, and I watched as she fell asleep. It had been a long day; both of us were tired and we needed some well-deserved rest.

I was exhausted. I felt like I had run a marathon and that I wanted to sleep for a hundred years. I wanted everything to be perfect again, over and done, so mother and I wouldn't have to worry about anything anymore. That was wistful thinking on my part; my brain knew better. I think my heart did, too. Even as I was resting, my mind kept whirring like a machine with thoughts of mother's health.

The next day, with my faith in the improvement that had come mother's way recently, I wanted to ensure that the effects of her stroke would continue to improve as time passed. I hired Mrs. Tsang, whom I had been introduced to by Ms. Mok. Mrs. Tsang was a special advanced physical therapist, and I hoped that she would be a good fit for my mother, after our awful recent experiences with therapists. She was a bit expensive on our budget ($700 per one-hour session, with the first session costing $1000), but as I soon discovered, it was all worth it.

Her first visit was on March 6, and after she had reviewed mother completely for the first time, her report was better than what I was expecting: she concluded that mother one day would be able to walk again, with the assistance of a helper!

I was ecstatic at hearing this from a professional. This was simply the most fantastic news we had received yet; it was the news I had been waiting to hear for such a long time. Imagine—an elderly stroke patient, gradually growing stronger until one day, she would stand and walk on her own! It was extraordinary news to my ears.

I asked her how she had come up with that conclusion. None of the doctors thus far had given us anything except a bleak outlook for the future. She explained to me that when she examined mother, her left side had actually responded; if time proceeded, with daily exercises, massage, and acupuncture, her left side would eventually be brought back to life, and she would then be able to exert full control over herself again.

This was such wonderful news. Why hadn't any of the doctors told me this before? Then I remembered—to diagnose a patient, you have to properly assess them. Thinking back to how doctors had ignored mother immediately after her stroke, I wondered how they would feel now if I walked back to them and told them that I knew that mother would one day recover. I would love to see the looks on their faces. Mrs. Tsang was the first professional in a long time that I began to trust, beside Ms. Mok. As she spoke, I listened to her intently; I could tell this woman was an excellent therapist, and I was planning to follow all of her advice.

There was no time to waste anymore. Now that I had found someone who had assessed mother properly and cared about her as a human being, I didn't have the time or the patience to deal with any more of the hospital's incompetency. The victory with the speech specialist and the optimistic news from the physical therapist had given me a new breath of life. Now that I knew there was a real, solid chance that mother could improve, I was ready to get started on the right path. With all of these worries suspended for now, I had time to think, not only about how to continue to improve mother's health with nutrition and food, and exercises, but also how I was going to be able to care for mother once she got out of the hospital. There were two things I now needed to do: find us a new place to live, and find us an excellent caretaker who would help me to watch over mother night and day.

On March 8, two days after Mrs. Tsang's first session, through word of mouth, I quickly hired a woman named Ah Ding. She was quite a smart woman; when I met her, I knew immediately that she was well-equipped for the job. Her responsibility was looking after mother in the hospital from morning till night, and even overnight if needed. Because I hired her to be on call round the clock, she stayed with us at our home at night. After I hired her, we sorted out how things were going to work with mother, and then I put her right to work. She began her first day with us on March 8, only two days after Mrs. Tsang's initial session. From the first day, she proved herself to be worthy of the job.

Mother's body and mind soon began making steady but remarkable improvements. She started to notice things around this ward, and people started to speak with her; sometimes, she joined a conversation or just offered a friendly hello. It lifted my heart a little every time I watched as she spoke with others; it reminded me of how wonderful and friendly she used to be when she was younger. Even with an aged face, she still had the same spark of energy in her eyes and her voice that could light up any conversation.

Ecstatic with the change Ah Ding had helped bring out in mother, I quickly decided to have mother receive calls and visitors again to ensure this show of personality kept up. On March 18, the phone in our room rang, I picked it up and handed it to mother. "It's for you," I said with a grin. As she listened to the receiver, her eyes widened. Her face lit up, and her mouth spread into a huge grin. Suddenly, she was chatting away, barely able to contain her excitement.

On the other end of the phone call was my mother's best friend since childhood, Kwok Wing Shui, or Mrs. Man. Mrs. Man and my mother had kept their friendship going strong for over six decades; that was an extraordinary friendship between two wonderful women. Their strong friendship came from the many traits they had in common that had discovered during their childhood. Mrs. Man told me in her later years that she had always admired my mother's beauty and intelligence; she told me that my mother looked like an angel. As the two of them kept their friendship over the years, Mrs. Man further admired mother's constant diligence, hard work ethic, and unwavering perseverance. Now, listening to mother talk over the phone to her, I could tell that nothing had changed between them. Mother was lucky to have a friend like her, someone who had remained in touch all throughout her life. They had a good fifteen-minute conversation over the phone, and when mother hung up the phone, her smile did not leave her face for the rest of the night.

I would see this same expression on mother's face again when a few days later my mother received a visit from someone else from that same time in her past: Chan Bo Chun, or Mrs. Ho. There were few other people who meant as much to my family as Mrs. Ho; she was one of those rare jewels who showed more than enough generosity to people whom she cared about.

We had first been blessed with Mrs. Ho's presence when she had been a student of my mother's sister Lily at St. Rose of Lima's School, at 4 Embankment Road, in Kowloon. At that time, Mrs. Ho had my mother as her godmother when she was baptized. Lily knew that mother was the best person suited to be Mrs. Ho's godmother because of her strong character; Mrs. Ho realized this too, and she formed a bond with my mother that was stronger than friendship. She looked up to my mother like an elder; she respected her opinions, her advice, and the way that mother treated others. They were two like souls that had found each other. Even now, while mother was in the hospital, she had been calling me asking if there was anything she could do for us. I knew that she really cared; she was not simply asking out of politeness.

It pleased me greatly to see these people that meant so much to mother come back into her life. If mother was just another patient to the hospital staff members, she was the world to these few dear friends. Privately, I also remained glad that their visits were clearly helping stimulate mother's mind.

33

On March 19, Dr. Ng came early at 8:30am, just for a routine checkup. Everything was looking good; in fact, he seemed a bit surprised at how well she was improving. On the morning of the 25th, however, I discovered that mother was experiencing a bit of pain. Since mother had learned to sit, her back started reacting to the new position painfully. That day, the physical therapist found out that her shoulder had actually been dislocated; this had most likely happened at one instance when she was pulled out of her wheelchair and transferred to another sitting area. I wasn't aware of how painful this must have been for mother; she had not shown any signs, except for today. We made her comfortable as best we could until the doctor could fix her.

On Wednesday, the 26th, I noticed something far more serious; mother started to speak funny and unclearly, slurring her words. This was odd, since she had only been getting better each day. Dr. Ng came in to analyze her, and told me mother had another stroke—a small one, but a stroke nonetheless. It had most likely been caused by a small seizure she had earlier that day, he said.

I was confused. She had been progressing so well; what had gone wrong? Dr. Ng explained that sometimes, these things just happen; there's no reason for them, and sometimes it's impossible to do anything to prevent them. He then prescribed her a small dose of Aspirin 81; that was the only counter medicine for my mother after her stroke.

I sighed to myself as mother took her medicine. Only a week earlier, she had been vibrant, alive, animated when she was talking to Mrs. Man. Now her speech was broken, slurred; if Mrs. Man called again, I wondered if she would recognize mother's voice. What if it happened again tomorrow, or the next day and the day after that? I couldn't watch mother be full of life one day only to see her become helpless. I only wanted an uphill progression from here on out—I wanted nothing but improvement. Every stone in the road, no matter how big or small, was a roadblock for us. I wanted all of them gone to have a clear path to recovery.

As mother continued her uphill battle every day, I would usually stay by her side, keeping her company. Sometimes I would walk along the corridors, either on my out for errands or to speak with a nurse or doctor. It was while walking along the corridors of the hospital on the day of March 28 that I first heard the rumor about a man who had died of SARS in the male ward next door.

This news didn't ring any alarm bells for me then. SARS was a new disease back then in early 2003, and it was only just beginning to spread. I did not even know exactly what type of disease SARS was or what effects it had on someone. To me, the man who had died from it was just another patient with a sickness. I felt bad for the man's family, but I put it out of my mind for now. I had more essential things to be concerned with.

But within a matter of days, SARS wouldn't be just another rumor in the ward next door. I would know all too well what SARS was.

CHAPTER 3

Two days later, on March 30, a woman who was just three beds away from my mother died in the late morning. I had already noticed that for the past two days this woman was not feeling well; the nurses had been using a thin curtain to separate the woman from the rest of us. I had seen people going in and out many times from that area, crying bitterly. I felt bad for the woman's family, just as I had felt bad for the family of the man who had died two days earlier. But this was a hospital; people died every day here. I could not concern myself with it.

But this time, the same rumor began again that this woman had died of SARS. Suddenly, the name shot through me like a bolt of lightning. Now I was paying attention. This deadly sickness suddenly frightened me to a great degree. I had no idea what it was, but it had just killed two patients, both in close proximity to my mom. Mother was sharing a big room with more than twenty beds; the disease was bound to spread.

Our ward was not the only one infected. As I listened to more conversations, I became aware of the alarm this disease was causing outside all over Hong Kong. Over the next week, SARS spread like wildfire across Hong Kong. The most alarming thing about it was not the sickness itself; it was how quickly the patients were dying from it after diagnosis. Usually, the infected patients died within only days. There was no known source of it, so there was no way to treat it in time. Suddenly, it had become the single worst epidemic that Hong Kong had seen in over half a century.

News of it grew to epic proportions; there was no news program or paper that was not covering it. Every Hong Kong newspaper ran giant banners that loudly announced that the "Invisible Killer" was here. One newspaper wrote: "Fears Grow in Hong Kong as Disease Spreads;" fifty-eight new cases of the deadly flu-like disease were reported in just one day. The disease itself, and news of it, began to spread to other areas of the world, but global health officials called Hong Kong the most severely affected area.

Within a week, there was quiet hysteria around Hong Kong. Banks and other offices closed, and much activity ground to a halt. One of the only places that stayed open was of course Pok Oi Hospital. The fear was palpable there; I was right there along with them. Since mother was living in this crowded environment with thirty people jammed in this ward, with one man having died three days ago in the other ward and one woman dying three beds across from hers, mother was very susceptible to contracting SARS. There was no question that mother, like anyone else, would be gone in an instant if that happened.

I sure as hell was not going to take that chance. Mother was not scheduled to leave the hospital yet, but I made the executive decision to take her out. It was not worth risking her life.

Immediately, I set out in search of a new apartment for mother and me. I needed a place that could accommodate mother in every way. I wanted some place sunny, cozy, and with easy access to transportation. Most

35

importantly, I wanted someplace far away from the congested rooms of public hospitals and other buildings where SARS was running rampant.

Finding a nice apartment was not that easy; all the bathrooms in the apartments I looked at were very small, and didn't have enough room for even one wheelchair to get in. I looked at over twenty-five apartments during that week and all of them were almost the same with a single small bathroom; some couldn't even close the door from behind if the wheelchair was there. I didn't know what to do. And every day, I had to hear the horrible news about the deadly weapon that was killing many people over the whole of Asia. I went to bed every night with a heavy heart and a worried mind.

Something happened during the night of April 1, however; somehow, God gave me a blessing just when I needed it. The next morning, when I woke up, a light bulb went off in my head. I thought to myself, if the bathroom was too small for the wheelchair, mother might be able to shower in the kitchen. Many kitchens in Hong Kong have drains in their floors for water to go down. I remembered the apartment I visited recently in a place called Tai Hing Garden with such a kitchen; it would be the perfect fit for my mother.

It was an apartment in a series of twelve blocks of high rises that were thirty-five stories high, and were situated high atop a steep hill. On each floor, there were only six apartments, which you could access by a quiet elevator. The apartment I wanted was facing both east and south, with plenty of sunshine coming right to the living room, as well as into one of the big bedrooms. We had a far-reaching view of the city below; when the night came, we could see the sparkling lights twinkling like stars beneath our eyes. We could even see the swimming pool by looking down from up above from our living room.

I immediately called the owner, Mrs. Chan, to look at the apartment again. I told her my intention, and asked if the kitchen's drain was good for the water to go down. She told me that if the water overflowed, then all her hardwood floors would be destroyed. That didn't deter me; I went to a nearby shop and hired a plumber to come and work with the drainage. Mrs. Chan agreed to give me the apartment, and the plumber fixed the drainage in less than twenty minutes. On April 2, I paid the deposit—it was a steal at only $4,500 Hong Kong dollars—and just like that, mother now had a new place to live.

Our new official residence was Tai Hing Garden, Block 11, Flat A, 13th floor (which in Asia is actually a lucky number), Tuen Mun. One of the best things about this place was the beautiful fauna, flora, and trees which surrounded the bottom of the apartments. If you followed the path of red pebble stones, with rows of exotic flowers planted along both sides of the path, you would eventually come to a swimming pool and athletic courtyards. The rows were also lined with stone and wooden benches everywhere for the tenants to enjoy.

The only problem now was that we had no furniture with which to fill our new space. The first and most important thing was to buy all of the special equipment that mother would need. The first thing she needed was a special hospital bed that moved both ends upward and downward, and hand rails on both sides for protection to prevent her from falling, as well as a metal triangle pulley to hang above her bed. I also had to get her a shower chair with wheels. Along with that, I had to order a five-gallon electric shower heater for the kitchen which was eighteen-and-a-half inches by thirteen inches, to make sure mother had enough hot water when she took a shower. I also had to include a washing machine and air-conditioning.

With all of these essentials needing to be ordered, paid for, and delivered, I was running around like a mad dog! I had to divide my time between the apartments to be there when the furniture arrived, as well as at the hospital for my mother. Between our old home and the new apartment, it was only three stops by light train, but I was usually too exhausted to move by the time I got back home at night. But I remained extremely relieved that I had found this place; not only would mother escape the SARS threat, but the beauty of this place, in contrast to her dreary hospital room, would hopefully lift her spirits.

As I was busy preparing our new home, I still had to worry about mother's well-being at the hospital. The threat of SARS's exposure to the community had only intensified, and the panic had grown to epic proportions. Extreme precautions were being taken everywhere, including at Pok Oi Hospital. No one was allowed to go in to visit the patients at all, except for the doctors and nurses; there was only one designated hour in the evening when family members and relatives could come and visit. When they did come in, everyone had to wear a mask and wash their hands before walking in.

I really had no choice but to obey the procedures. That meant that I couldn't be with mother as often as I wanted to be. But I did request one special favor: since my mother ate her meal very slowly, I asked to feed her in the waiting room, away from the other sick patients in her ward. The nurses allowed me to do so. It became clear to me that they said yes because of the commitment to my mom they saw that I had. Soon, some of the other patients' families saw me with mother in the waiting room, and they bugged the nurses for the same treatment. I listened to them with one ear, and kept my mouth shut. The nurse always snapped back at them: "Would you be able to do the same thing as her? Would you be willing to come here early in the morning and stay until after dinner, waiting for your loved one? Do you know at exactly what time your loved ones eat lunch or dinner? Do you know every single detail about every moment of your loved one's day?" There was always silence. I smiled to myself, and kept feeding mother silently. The other people did not ask the nurse again.

When I couldn't be with mom, I surrendered most of my duties in taking care of her over to Ah Ding, who had proved herself a very good, full-time caretaker. I still needed to focus on finishing everything for the apartment. My mother's furniture would not be delivered until Saturday, April 12. But SARS was spreading like wildfire around the hospital. The masks and the hand-washing were not helping much. It had gotten so bad that you could sense the panic in some of the doctors and nurses. With mother's condition, I had a decision to make. Even though our apartment was not ready, I finally decided to discharge her on April 7.

That will be a day I will never forget. It was a day that went down in the history books in our family. I still tell the story to my children, and I hope they will tell it to theirs. For all the serious issues that were occurring around us, somehow, we managed to turn the day into a hilarious adventure.

Mother was all packed up with her few belongings and ready to go in the morning. I had already figured out how to go back home, which had taken some time and consideration. Since she could not even stand up with helpers on both sides, taxis were too small for her to fit in. I tried to find a van to transport her in her wheelchair, but I was not successful. So with no van, no taxi, it was up to me and our assistants to take my mother back home by light train.

Let me tell you – what an experience that was! First, we had together all of mother's belongings and odds and ends that she had accumulated while she was in the hospital – every pen, every cup, every bowl that was left on the table. Ah Ding and our housekeeper, Ah King each had their hands full with all of mother's belongings. That left me to push my mother in her wheelchair. I had no idea how to work all the different levers on it.

To make matters worse, when we went outside, it was raining. Ah King, with her hands full of mother's things, had to make room to hold an umbrella over my mother, so she would not get wet. As the four of us ventured outside in the pouring rain, we did not have a straight path to walk to the light train station. The road was hilly, and we needed to go down it. The rain was so bad that all we wanted to do was get dry. So we picked up speed as we walked. As we went faster down the hill, the wheelchair went a lot more quickly than I thought. Every time I pushed it, it would go in a direction I did not want it to go—and mother of course would go right along with it! She was holding on for dear life! The rain on my glasses also prevented me from seeing clearly, and I hit several bumps and potholes as we travelled. And every time I hit a bump or hole, my mother would shoot up out of her chair!

"Sorry Mom!" I would yell to her. She did not say a word to me as we whizzed along, just patted me on the hand. I felt like we were in a comedy show!

But even despite our hilarious trek to the light train station, we got back to our old apartment at Oi Chi House safe and sound. I couldn't wait for mother's new apartment at Tai Hing Garden to be finished. I had never realized how tiny our 350-square foot apartment was, especially now that four people were going to be living in it—myself, mother, my sister, and Ah Ding; Ah King only came to work with us during the daytime. The living area was like an open studio, and the bathroom was off the living area, and had only a toilet and shower with a floor drain; the sink was hanging in between the bathroom and kitchen's wall. The only good thing about the apartment was the price; this low-cost housing complex charged only around $845 Hong Kong dollars, as opposed to the $5,000 that most people had to pay in other areas. Since this was considered lucky, no matter how small the apartment was, I couldn't complain.

My mother had always kept this apartment very neat and welcoming. There were two beds in an L-shaped in the farther corner of the living area, separated with two end tables. The Chinese beds usually were only twenty-eight inches wide, which was considered a standard size of Hong Kong, but mother ordered the beds thirty inches wide. Two big wardrobes were placed against the other side of the wall; a round folding table covered with laced table cloth, with four folding chairs, was placed near the center of the room. A Chinese wooden bench with its cushions was in front of big windows, and a TV set was on a low bookcase. Mother was very artistic; she always decorated her windows with nice flora curtains with hanging rods; very often she matched with their bedspreads too.

Because of mother's paralysis, once she was in bed, she could not turn over by herself. Ah Ding then devised a clever way to help mother move; she placed a large blanket underneath mother in the bed, so when mother needed to sit up or be turned, Ah Ding could simply stand over her and tug the blanket to help her move.

Little accommodations and new tricks like that were helpful for the time being, but I was relieved when the building manager confirmed that the new furniture I had ordered would arrive at the new apartment at Tai Hing Garden on Monday the 14th. That meant that we could move in on the 15th. So on the morning of the 14th, Ah King and I waited at the new apartment to make sure all parts would not be missing. We also cleaned all the furniture and dusted the whole house again, including climbing up and down to the tall windows. There were still a few key pieces of furniture that had not been delivered—beds for Ah Ding and me—but the house was ready for mother, and that was what mattered most. We brought mother to the new home, got her settled with all of her belongings, and soon, there we were—in a new, beautiful apartment with gorgeous surroundings that would hopefully lift her spirits and her health.

While I was quite happy—happier than I had been in a long time—I was mostly relieved that we were finally free and far away from the dark disease of SARS down in the hospital. I felt like I had made the right decision; there were still questions in my mind—how was I going to care for mother out of the hospital, for one—but for now, I was content with my decision.

Ah Ding and I did not have a bed to sleep in for several days. Our beds, along with some other necessary amenities, like our phone, didn't arrive until the 21st, almost a week later. It didn't really matter to us; on the first night, we just rolled out some old comforters on the floor and slept. We were too exhausted to think, but we still got up to check on mother periodically; after all, this was a new environment to all of us.

On our first morning, we awoke happy and excited to start our first full day in our new home. It was time for new, good thoughts and energy to flow throughout the rooms. Things got off to a great start. Mother began the day with a nice warm, long bath with Ah King and Ah Ding. She also showed a good appetite and good sleeping habits, and she was excited when my brother Stephen came to visit the same day the rest of our furniture arrived. Stephen had two homes, one in Vancouver and an apartment at Sheung Ping in China. He was in China at this time, so he came to visit mother. He brought his favorite saxophone, and as he played for mom, she grinned, moving around as best she could to the music. I danced along as Stephen played. Mother looked between the two of us and her grin grew wider. She was content to see her grown-up children.

Although Tai Hing Garden was not a home for senior citizens or physically incapacitated patients, I wanted to use mom's new apartment as a kind of beautified care-taking home for her. I knew she needed the best care possible, and I wanted to make her new apartment just the right place to keep her healthy as well as happy. Unfortunately, one of the key elements to making mother happy and healthy was about to leave our life. Ah Ding announced with sadness and regret that she had found a different job and that she would be leaving us.

I was devastated at this news. I was genuinely happy to see her get a good job, but I was extremely sorry to see her leave us. She had been such a big help, not only to mother, but to me too. She had made all of our lives much easier with the care and kindness she had shown us; she helped mother through some of the most difficult transitions in her life, and for that and so much more, I would remain forever grateful to her. As Ah Ding and I said our goodbyes on her last day, April 28, I wished nothing but the best for her. I owed much of my mother's health and well-being during that time in our lives to Ah Ding's care and patience.

But as sad it was to see Ah Ding leave, our lives had to move on; so two weeks before Ah Ding officially left, I had urgently called my friend Ms. Tao, who knew a lot of good people through her connections; she recommended a nice young woman named Chu Shui Lin, or Ah Lin, to take Ah Ding's place. I agreed immediately. I trusted Ms. Tao, but more importantly, I couldn't afford to go a day without having mother look after. When I said that, I meant it; on the same day that Ah Ding left, Ah Lin arrived at our door.

I was very pleased with Ah Lin when she arrived. She was exactly how Ms. Tao had described her: pleasant, smart, willing to learn, and very energetic. I could tell she would be perfect to take up the big responsibility that Ah Ding had previously had. I introduced her to mother, and right from that moment, I could tell that she and mother were going to get along just fine. Mother liked her immensely as they began to spend time together, and it made my heart soar to see mother so happy. It was wonderful to have someone working with us full-time that mother liked so much.

As my mother's personal caretaker, Ah Lin did everything that Ah Ding had done for mother that was essential to keeping her healthy. With both her stroke and her dementia, we had to maintain a stable condition between both of these sicknesses; otherwise, her memory would steadily decline like a roller coaster down a hill. When she was first diagnosed with her dementia, the doctor told me that the most important thing I could be to build and maintain a stable environment that wouldn't upset or frighten mother easily, but rather make her feel secure and safe, and that was exactly what Ah Lin and I would do for her.

But there was one additional responsibility that Ah Lin had that Ah Ding hadn't: keeping a logbook of mother's health. I had the idea one day to start a log of mother's health movements to keep track of her daily occurrences. This wasn't something that I had to do or that was recommended by the hospital, but I felt satisfied knowing that we were doing everything we could to keep mother's health where it was.

I started the logbook on April 21, and Ah Lin kept it very tidy, and each day she kept track of everything that my mother did—and I mean everything. The notes I recorded were much detailed than the ones from the nurses in the hospitals. On April 30, for example, we recorded that mother held the railing with her right hand for the first time, but she told us her hands and feet were very painful. The next day, we recorded that the swelling in her hands and feet had gone down, and she was able to do it more comfortably. Every day, we noted what mother ate for all of her meals and in between her meals—in the logbook, I separated each food group and had Ah Lin make a check under every type of food mother ate, and also had her write exactly what she ate—for example, a banana, some milk, or a bowl of cornflakes. In addition to her food intake, we also recorded every one of her liquid outputs and her bowel movements and what time they occurred, to make sure her digestive system was working properly. We recorded the results of mother's occupational therapy with David Lau, whom she began seeing twice a week starting on June 26, and her physical therapy with Ms. Wong, whom she began seeing once a week beginning on July 2. Everything mother did relating to her health was recorded in this logbook; it became like a Bible to me.

I also had Ah King shop every day to get mother the freshest food possible. I preferred that mother ate fresh food, including fish, meat and vegetables, because there was more nutrition in fresh products. That was why mother had improved well, without swollen hands and feet, in such a short period of time.

We also kept track of mother's daily exercises. As she had at the hospital, she followed a daily routine at home five times a day. Ah Lin and I helped her to do these exercises, which ranged from her shoulder all the way down to her toes, all of which worked out the left side of her body. Ah Lin used her ten fingers to press gently from mom's head first, down to her neck, and to every section of the joint; then she would move down to her left side shoulder, upper arm, lower arm, wrist, and every section of her five fingers in the same fashion. She would then continue down to her body down to her five toes. After that, she did the same thing to the right side. After she finished with all the joints in mother's body, she then went back to

41

mom's left arm, and put her left hand on the triangle rack, so that mother could stretch her arm for a short while, depending on how she felt.

The five times per day was a lot of exercise for an elderly woman. But mother was very cooperative, and would do everything Ah Lin said without a word. If she felt pain, she would make a noise to let us know, and then Ah Lin would work more gently. Sometimes I joined in to help, so that Ah Lin could eat earlier or run her personal errands.

Mother also had the wonderful benefit of a massage twice a day, starting on May 15, which helped her blood circulation and flows remain intact. Ah Lin worked on the top and I worked on her leg and toes. These massages always put mother in a great mood; we always joked around during these massages, and mother liked to tease Ah Lin.

Usually, helping mother with her exercises and taking note of all of her vital signs would take up a good part of our day together, since she needed to be checked so often. But we had time in the mornings, after all the business was finished, to get out of the house and go for a short walk around the building. Mother, Ah Lin and myself would stroll around the beautiful lanes with flowers on both sides, warmly greeting the neighbors we saw out and about. This was nothing like the hospital; we were not speaking with rows and rows of ill patients lined up in a dreary ward. Many of the tenants in our new building were married couples and had young children or babies; mother often liked to point out which baby she liked most, and sometimes she just watched the toddlers play. It was at those times when I saw my mom in the light I had always seen her in: as a mother. When she looked and smiled at the babies playing, I imagined that was how she used to look at my siblings and I when we were younger. The thought warmed my heart; it made me realize that no matter her age, she was still my mother.

In addition to maintaining our daily activities and exercises, I also had the task of keeping up with mother's expenses. When mother's dementia had gotten worse in 2002, the government assigned a social worker, Ms. Wong, to be my mother's caretaker, since all of mother's children were living outside of Hong Kong at that time. Mother's Hong Kong pension and her disability income now needed to be reported to the social office once a month. May 9 was the first appointment I had to report to the social worker how I, as her new caretaker, had been using her money.

As I sorted out the expenses I had been using for mother, I was pleased with what I saw – I, like my mother, had been working diligently to remain as frugal as possible and spend only what I needed to. I knew that mother had worked hard all her life; she used every penny wisely and never wasted anything on an unnecessary item. When I visited mother in Hong Kong back in the days when she travelled frequently between Hong Kong and Canada, I observed my mother's frugal spending. She told me that was her duty as a mother: to love and to serve her loved ones, and to always sacrifice.

I still remember seeing how frugal she was when I visited her in the summer of 1979, while she was living in Vancouver. When we went out shopping for food, she would only buy the heads of grouper fish instead of the entire fish, which was an unusual thing to do. I was curious why she decided to do that. She explained to me that it was for a couple of reasons: first, it was much cheaper to buy just the head than the whole fish. Second, nutrition wise, this was far better than the whole fish, because the bone added flavor and calcium. It turned out to be tastier too: she cooked the head with carrots, celery, and ginger, and it was very delicious indeed.

The same situation occurred again in 1998 when I visited her in Hong Kong. Usually mother shopped twice a week, not in nearby shops, but instead travelling forty-five minutes by light train to Yuen Long, where most of the food was much cheaper than Tuen Mun. On that day, three of us – mother, myself and my sister Agnes—were pushing a food-cart went to Yuen Long market to shop. Mother was eighty-one years old then, still healthy enough to go up and down the light train, and walked speedily like the young people when she walked across the street. Instead of shopping for fresh chicken, mother brought frozen chicken thighs and legs. Mother told me it had the same nutrition and the price was almost fifty percent cheaper. She learned this from a local college in Canada, and had followed this advice ever since.

All of these memories bubbled in the back of my brain as I sat in the social worker's office as she tallied up mother's expenses. Yes, everything seemed very expensive now, but as far as I was concerned, mother should spend every dollar she earned comfortably. Now, because of her low income, another $2,400 Hong Kong dollars was added to her spending (which was substituted for all old aged and disabled seniors). This was good, because all our funds were already stretched to their limits. But mother was of course worth every single penny. The social worker was satisfied with our expenses and spending, and I left her office feeling equally satisfied.

Life at our new apartment was comfortable and secure. Some days I couldn't believe I had lucked out and found us such a wonderful place; some days I was just grateful to be out of the hospital and away from SARS. The disease did not concern me that much anymore; mother had shown no signs of contracting it, and we were far away from the congested, dirty air of the hospital. I had been so concerned about the big picture for the last few months that I almost didn't know what to do with myself when everything had finally settled. It was around this time that I forgot almost completely about the fears I had had about caring for mother; now that I had provided her with a home and a caretaker, and successfully got us away from the threats of the hospital (the cruel and inept workers, the lack of proper diagnosis and treatment), my mind began to settle on the day-to-day things we had lined up. This involved, first and foremost, improving mother's health, little by little, day by day.

Most of the things that were recommended for stroke victims were things that we did. We tried to approach mother from the left side, which made her more aware of the left side to help with left-side neglect. The repetition of our day-to-day routine would help her memory. We wanted most of all to get mom's strength and confidence back. With rehabilitation exercises five times per day and lots of hard work, mother could improve. It is very time-consuming, but you have to be very patient and success will come the more you work and never give up hope. The person may not be perfect, but eventually the person may be able to function to a point of needing less and less help.

In addition to our daily exercises, I also wanted to start mother on a vitamin B-complex injection once a week. May 14 was Mrs. Cheung's first visit; Mrs. Cheung would be administering the injection, as well as checking mother's blood pressure. During her check-up, we noticed mother's blood pressure was too high at 162/90. (An ideal number would be 140/70.) She told us not to worry, and to continue what we were doing daily, and mother's blood pressure would gradually go down. I desired to go towards the best possible number she was capable of. We kept up her daily routines, and as we continued to record mother's progress in the logbook Ah Lin and I had started back in April, we now included her heartbeats, her high blood pressure number, as well as how swollen her hands and feet were. This way, we could notice any major changes in mom's health, and prevent anything else serious from happening.

I also wanted to learn more about how to help mother improve physically. I hired Mrs. Tsang, the physical therapist who had checked on mother while she was at Pok Oi Hospital, to make house calls to us. On May 29, Mrs. Tsang came and taught us how to extend mother's exercises. Ah Lin and I stood and watched intently, taking note of her every move. Mother also listened and cooperated patiently as Mrs. Tsang directed her movements, even despite the pain and uneasiness we could tell it sometimes caused her.

The new work that Mrs. Cheung and Mrs. Tsang had encouraged us to pursue paid off; after her first two weeks of extended exercises, on June 13, mother turned herself over completely on the other side of the bed for the first time since her stroke. Now, this may seem like a small occurrence, but remember: less than three months ago, she had asked me in the hospital who was standing next to her when she felt brief sensations in her left arm. Now, mother was able to take control over her body and turn herself over by herself.

To us, this seemingly small bit of good news was like a giant hole had been opened in a dark tunnel. All we could see now was the light. Ah Lin and I helped mother to continue her exercises five times per day, and kept up massages two times daily. Mother's small signs of progress slowly evolved into a steady, continuous improvement, as we helped her in every way that we could. Our uphill climb began to subside; we began to head into an easy coast.

As her physical health improved, her spirit began to lighten with it, mostly thanks to the old friends and family members who suddenly reappeared out of the woodwork to see mother. On June 19, mother's good friend, Tony Wong, brought his family to visit mother. My sister Agnes had stayed with his family in Sheung Shui, Tai Tau Ning Chuen from 1980-81, after mother had become friends with Mr. Wong through the Mormon

Church while she was living in Canada. The whole group of Tony Wong's family, including his mother, wife, children and his sister Sally all gathered in our apartment to see her. It was clear that mother was very pleased to see all of them. We had a lovely time, chatting and laughing. Mother was her old self again, bright, beautiful, the center of attention. After they left, she smiled happily. She slept well that night.

As mother improved every day, we had to make sure she was remaining comfortable. Hong Kong weather begins to get hot in June, and since mother's mattress was made from foam material, it would be too warm when mother was lying down, without air circulation below. So on June 17, my brother Paul accompanied me to buy a gel pad. Paul was my mother's second child and first son; and he lived in Vancouver. He was a businessman, and he would come to Southeast Asia once or twice a year on business. He loved and cared for mother very much, and he wanted to make sure that she was okay for now.

The gel pad cost $5,500 per piece, two inches thick, to put on top of the mattress. It was very heavy, and needed two people to handle it. I laid on it to feel it before we brought it home; it was cool, so my mother's back would feel cooler. After we brought it home, mother seemed much more comfortable.

I didn't know if it was the gel pad, the visitors that kept dropping in, or just the change in weather, but mother's progress suddenly began to skyrocket. On June 24, while we were holding mother up from her bed, our intention was to move her to her nearly custom-made long bench chair. To my surprise, I noticed mother's left foot and toes were standing flatly on the floor. The doctor had told me that my mother would not ever stand again, even with helpers on both sides. Simply amazing!

The next day, I received a call from Father Ho Siu Keung, who was the priest in the local Tuen Mun Catholic Church. I had heard of him through a friend at church; he was well-known for his gift for healing people after he offered prayers for them. He had been praying for mother all this time.

It was then that I began to realize that outside help existed; it was not just up to me to carry this burden of getting mother healthy. God had been listening and had answered our prayers. With all of mother's progress lately, I had automatically credited it to the hard work that mother, Ah Lin, and I were doing. But it occurred to me that something else had to be at work. My belief in God had never ceased; but lately, with all of my busy work, it seemed like I had forgotten about Him—not on purpose, but just sort of pushed to the back of my mind. It's funny how He seems to pop up at times when I need Him most and when I least expect Him.

I thanked Fr. Ho for his prayers, and as I spoke with him about our activities, he was very pleased with mother's improvement.

Later, that day, Sister Wut, from Holy Redeemer Church, Tuen Mun, came to visit mother. Sr. Wut did not know my mother personally— she was simply the nun from the local Catholic Church whose duty was to visit sick parishioners. Since she was a stranger to mother, I thought this

45

would be a great opportunity to try and revive some of mother's memory by telling Sr. Wut a bit about mother's life.

We introduced her to mother by bringing out mother's old photo album of her past, and gave her a bit of a background story. Opening the book was like opening a part of mother's heart that had been closed or forgotten about for a very long time. When we opened the book, Mother's eyes lit up; I saw an expression of recognition cross her face. She smiled brightly, and she pointed to the various pictures as we told Sr. Wut the stories of my mother's past.

The first page we turned to was from May 8, 1969. On that date, mother was elected as Hong Kong's first Model Mother of the Year by The Chung Sing Benevolent Society, a famous non-profit organization. This was a brand-new award, honoring strong mothers who were devoted to their children and had raised them properly and successfully as an asset to our society. There was no one more deserving than mother, and she secured her place in Hong Kong history by becoming the first person to receive it.

Mother had been nominated for the award by her brother-in-law, Mr. Law, a Protestant minister in Tai Po Market, who had submitted an essay detailing mother's extraordinary life. Out of five hundred nominees, mother was then chosen as the final recipient of the award. At a ceremony held in City Hall in Hong Kin, she received a plaque that had her name engraved in bronze, hinged on a wood stand. It was handed down to me in the year 2000, included among all her personal memorable items when I went to visit her in Hong Kong.

The next event we looked at in mother's photo book was from June 27, 1969. On that date, mother retired from her work, ending her sixteen years of service in the Preventive Service as the first female Revenue Inspector. She had first joined the Preventive Service as a Revenue Officer, Class II, in 1953. She was promoted to Class I in 1957, and Revenue Sub-Inspector in 1958. Mother was the first woman to be appointed a Revenue Inspector in 1967.

To mark mother's retirement, the Assistant Commissioner of the Preventive Service, Mr. A. L. Tokley, presented her with a gold medallion at a ceremony held in the Preventive Service Senior Officers' Hall. During her duty of work, she was also awarded many appreciations from Colonial Secretary Mr. M.D. Irving Gass, Commerce and Industry Department, Mr. E. I. Lee and Director of Commerce and Industry, Mr. H.A. Angus, to praise mother's work and outstanding performances. Her retirement party was not a typical celebration; she was honored as one of the most respected and distinguished employees that ever worked for the Preventive Service. As the first woman revenue inspector ever in Hong Kong, she had commanded a sense of utmost esteem and honor with all of her colleagues. She had overseen a staff of twenty-two people, all of whom had admired and appreciated mother as their boss.

As we looked through the pages of the photo album, mother pointed here and there to the photos to show Sr. Wut. There were letters of recommendation from various government officials who had known or worked with mother, all stating their satisfaction of her work performance. Page after page was filled with glowing letters, awards, and certificates displaying mother's splendid attributes. These fragments of her past began to come back to mother as if she was reliving the events over again. I began to notice elements of mother had returned that had not been there while she had been in the hospital; she was more animated, more awake, and more alive. She seemed like her soul had been buried somewhere deep in a black hole for the past few months; suddenly, it was like it had returned.

As we continued to look through the book, one photo stood out to mother: a picture of her sitting among her staff taken during her retirement party. Mother pointed excitedly to the woman standing to the left in the front row. "Do you remember her?" I asked her. "Of course!" she replied immediately. It was Lan Je, or Mrs. Fan, the mother of her son Stephen's wife. Mrs. Fan was similar in age to my mother, and the two of them enjoyed each other's company, and they had often conversed together after work. She is shorter than my mom, very slender, and fashionable. We never saw her in anything but beautiful, modern clothing, usually custom-made Chinese garments from a tailor. Her daughter, my sister-in-law, is very smart and very persuasive. She could argue and debate passionately and logically, whether in writing or in conversation, both in English and Chinese.

Mrs. Fan had worked on mother's staff for a long time, and she had watched mother's children grow from their teenage years to their adult lives. As Stephen grew to be a successful young man, Mrs. Fan introduced her daughter to him one day over tea. After they met, Mrs. Fan began to tease my mother about how nice it would be if her daughter would one day marry the handsome Stephen. After Stephen and her daughter had their first date, Mrs. Fan's dream came true—they soon fell in love and were married! As we sat there, laughing and joking about the beautiful romance that had blossomed between them, mother's eyes glazed over the picture, her eyes twinkling with bliss. I smiled. Sr. Wut's visit to us was more of a blessing than I had expected.

On July 7, Sr. Ho Chi Ching, my Auntie Lily's best friend, came to visit mother. She was a retired kindergarten headmistress from St. Rose of Lima's School. As she walked in the door, you couldn't miss her: her tiny height (under five feet) made her instantly recognizable. But once you got past her height, you then recognized the same firm, strict, and stern walk that she had back when she was headmistress. She had always held the belief that good character needed to be taught to children from a very early age, and so she taught her kindergarten students the rules of obedience and discipline, which she carried out in her own life. But after years of knowing her personally as a friend of the family, I knew what was underneath that stern gaze. Sure enough, as soon as she saw mother, her face melted into a pool of warmth and joy. Even now, in her eighties, it was clear that her firmness was her school persona; outside of work, she was a friendly, personable, and pleasant woman.

Seeing Sr. Ho always reminded me of my auntie Lily. Lily was a vital part of my mother's life. Her given name was Mo Ching; Lily was her baptized name. When she became a nun, her name became Wing Cho Philomena Chu. That name was too long for me to pronounce when I was younger, so I affectionately called her auntie Lily. My mother's elder sister by four years, she was five foot one, which, like my mother, was considered well-built for her generation of Chinese women. Auntie Lily was just like my mother: affectionate, kindhearted, and intelligent. She was a kind and pure woman, always happy, polite, calm, and ladylike. Although she was rather timid, she was still very sociable, and had many friends.

She had graduated from St. Mary's Canossian College in Hong Kong, the same school that my mom would later graduate from. It was a rare feat for a woman to graduate high school in Hong Kong in the 1930s. She did not stop there; she continued on and eventually graduated from Hong Kong University in 1937. From there, she received her first position teaching at Sacred Heart Catholic School in Macau.

After World War II ended in 1945, she left Sacred Heart and then professed to become a nun at the Franciscan Missionaries of Mary. It had been an honor for my grandfather to see his daughter Lily graduate from Hong Kong University; he was hoping she would then use her education to take over the family business. What a surprise to him when she announced she was becoming a nun!

She then moved on to teach at St. Rose of Lima's, a school for girls founded in February 1948 by the same missionaries. The school's curriculum fit perfectly with the values my grandparents had taught auntie Lily; it focuses on strong morals and ethics, and allowed teachers to work closely with parents to provide a firm education for its young women. When auntie Lily taught there in the 1950s, the school only provided a six-year primary course (Primary 1 to Primary 6) and two secondary level classes (Form 1 and Form 2). More secondary classes were added as time went by and eventually, students began taking the Hong Kong Certificate of Education Examination was a standardized examination. The first Arts A-level class sat their examinations in 1986 followed by the first Science A-level class in 1991. As the curriculum expanded, and more girls were attending the school, the secondary school moved to 29 Ngan Shing Street in Shatin in September 1999, and given the term "college," while the original school on Embankment Road remained the "primary school."

Auntie Lily loved St. Rose of Lima's, and she worked there as a primary headmistress until 1958. From there, she taught Form 4 and 5 classes in English (which is the equivalent of the American grades 11 and 12), as well as translating Chinese to English. She remained there for the rest of her life. She was well-known for her excellent teaching abilities and for helping Chinese students prepare for and pass the difficult standardized tests. Despite the difficulties that come with teaching new students every year, auntie Lily remained virtuous and kind; she joked and laughed a lot, and this was why every student remembered and loved her. She remains famous as one of the most influential teachers there to date.

Sr. Ho had been best friends with Lily all throughout their lives. When Lily died of cancer on April 24, 1972, at the age of 59, Sr. Ho was right there next to her bedside, praying on the rosary. Suddenly, as she was praying, part of the rosary broke. At that very moment, Sr. Ho looked up and saw Lily take her last breath, before she passed away. At Auntie Lily's funeral, she had many important people from her school and university days attend. Even forty years later, her students remembered her very well, giving wonderful anecdotes, recalling that they were never bored in her English classes.

Walking up to mother's bedside, Sr. Ho greeted mother warmly, but mother did not recognize her. One of the reasons I knew was because Sr. Ho's nun's habit had changed. She used to wear a white veil with black trim, a long, white robe, and a cross always hung down on her chest. Now, since their Franciscan organization had changed dramatically because of our society, they did not wear the habit anymore, just a casual long-sleeve shirt and a short black skirt. To my mother, this was not really a nun in her image, and it was certainly not how she remembered Sr. Ho; she had never seen her out of uniform.

As Sr. Ho chatted and spoke at length with mother, very often mother would look over at me and ask me who she was, and after I told her, then mother would still have no idea whatsoever. Still, although she did not recognize her, mother enjoyed her company. After Sr. Ho left, mother settled back with a smile. She had received lovely visits from wonderful people lately, and she seemed to be content from them for the most part. They had all brought back lovely recollections from her past, something that mother remembered surprisingly well. All of their visits were of equal importance to mother: every interaction, every phone call, every smile from a loved one gave mother another ounce of energy, another incentive to work harder, another reason to keep improving. The advancements that she had made over the past months were astounding; even her doctors and therapists, some who had diagnosed her with a much different, darker outcome, agreed. This was extraordinary progress for an extraordinary woman.

CHAPTER 4

Three months had now passed since mother was discharged from Poi Oi Hospital. It was now July 25, and mother had her first appointment back at the Tuen Mun Daily Clinic since she had been discharged. I was not looking forward to it. Ah Lin and I had spent so much time on our logbook, and I clearly knew what I was doing in hiring outside therapists and specialists to help mother. I didn't really see the point of exposing mother to SARS again, which had still not been contained. But my grumblings aside, I did know that it was still important for mother's health that she see a real doctor.

It was my first experience with a new doctor for mother's appointments. The Tuen Mun Daily Clinic specialized in out-patients who had a stroke. I figured this at least wouldn't be as bad as the regular hospital, where we would have to wait with patients of all diseases, illnesses, and medicinal needs. Hopefully, we would be able to get mother in and out of there as quickly as possible.

But I had a problem. To transport her there, I had to hire a special van that could support her wheelchair. I had no experience using such vans, and no connections to someone who might know how to even find one. So I figured, what place is more likely to have such a van than a nursing home? I picked up the phone and began randomly calling each of the local nursing home's offices to see if they could provide us with the van I needed. Most of the answers I heard, rather rudely, from the other end were that use of their own vans was restricted to their own office.

After many failed attempts and many rather abrupt "goodbyes" from the offices, one nurse was finally kind enough to direct me to a local businessman who was connected with a number of different kinds of businesses in the area; a van service might be one of them. I thanked the nurse, searched for his phone number, and called to tell him about my situation. I was prepared for the usual "Can't help you, sorry," that I was accustomed to, but instead, to my surprise, he was impressed. He told me that he might have someone for me, one of his former employees, Mr. Mok Man Kin, or Man Kin, who had such a van.

Hope fluttered in my heart. To my good fortune, once Man Kin found out about our situation, he was very interested in working for us. I didn't expect much from him, maybe just a one-time thing, and then I might have to find another way to transport mom; but he expressed interest in remaining with us and helping mother with any transportation she needed. And so he quickly became mother's private chauffeur. He would drive her back and forth to the clinic on the days of her appointments, to the restaurants we went to, or other places mother liked to visit. I was quite taken aback at his generosity; he quickly became a significant part of our family unit, and not just for his van use. He was, quite simply, a wonderful man. I felt blessed at my luck and at the generosity of everyone down the line who had heard my story and passed me along to this gold at the end of a rainbow.

On the day of mother's first appointment, with mother safely secured in her van, we set off for the clinic. We were scheduled for 9:45am. When we arrived, exactly on time, the doors to the elevator opened, and we were met with the sight of a long queue that snaked around the corridor. I didn't know if all of these people were lined up to see one doctor, or if there was a problem. We joined the queue; by the time we reached the desk, we discovered it was the line for registration. We had already booked our appointment; why did we need to register? I handed the white appointment paper to the staff at the desk; she then asked me to wait in the big hall to wait for our announcement.

I groaned to myself. This was exactly what I had been afraid of. Memories of waiting for hours after mother had first fallen came flooding back to me. It was a nightmare all over again. And now, we had the added threat of SARS. Every one of these patients near us was coughing, sneezing, and breathing all of their germs into the open air.

There was no way I had taken my mom out of one hospital to save her from SARS only to have her contract it while waiting to see a specialized doctor. So I compromised; instead of taking her out completely (which wouldn't have done her any good), I had Ah Lin push mother outside the clinic hall to wait while I kept our spot and waited inside the hall with all of that dirty air for my mother's name to be called.

I waited for a half an hour; then, finally, the loudspeaker announced "Chu Yi Ching!" I immediately jumped up and went over to one of the nurses' tables. Now were we about to see the doctor? Oh, no; now they gave me a tag with a number on it. My fury grew. I went back to sit down and wait again.

By this time, the three of us were all hungry. I had not anticipated being here for this long, so I had not brought any lunch with me. I had to send Ah Lin off to get some junk food, because I could not leave the hall—not even to go to the bathroom. Mother herself already had a wet diaper, but I couldn't even leave to change her. If they called mother's number while I was gone, even for a minute, I would lose my place and have to start the whole procedure all over again. I just prayed that both of us could hold on a little longer.

Finally, after waiting for what seemed like an eternity, the nurse announced our tag's number. I felt like I was waiting for a lottery and my lucky number had just been called. I leapt up, and Ah Lin, mother, and I went to another room adjacent to the hall. The room, like the hall we were just in, was not a private area, like you might see in most American doctors' offices. These were simply open stations, with just a thin wooden wall on either side, or a curtain to shield the patient from the waiting hall. There were six stations all together; the nurses would have six patients lined up in their office, and when the floor supervisor called out a room number, the nurse would usher the patient to the desk. It almost had the feel of cattle lined up to be herded into stalls.

As we entered one of these little stations, one of the nurses followed us in, and took down some general information, asking us general questions about mother's illness. Then we shuffled off to line up at the doctor's station for the full check-up. When our doctor came to meet us, I couldn't believe my eyes; his face showed so much youth that he couldn't be any older or more experienced than an intern or university student. I frowned. I did not like the idea of having an inexperienced doctor examining my mother. Sure enough, as he asked us questions about mother's health, scribbling his notes down in his notebook, he never once looked up at our faces or even at my mother to examine her. He was writing and asking questions at the same time, without looking at my mother or us.

My temperature boiled. Clearly, this doctor was just fulfilling a duty; he had no intention of getting to know mother any further than her name and her ailment. How could he possibly prescribe the best treatment for her if he wouldn't even look up at her? His "examination," if you could call it that, was brief, and his prescription for her was the same thing she had been taking, Aspirin 81. And that was that; chart closed, pen clicked, and the young doctor was out the door, my mother already only a distant memory to him.

It was now 1pm. It had taken us three hours to sit in a room full of threats of disease and deadly germs, only to be examined by an inexperienced physician and be given the same prescription we were already using. I was completely silent on the way home. I just wanted to get back home and away from everything having to do with government hospitals as fast as possible.

Luckily, mother's next appointment was at a smaller clinic, this time in Ming Sum Lau. I was hoping that with the specialization of this particular clinic, mother would get the individualized treatment she actually needed. This clinic was nothing like the free-for-all, impersonal hospital; it was reserved only for seniors on particular Wednesdays, and the doctor that she would be seeing specialized in brain illnesses. Her appointment was on Wednesday, July 30, at 2pm, and since the clinic was smaller, I figured that 2pm actually meant 2pm—not waiting in line for three hours.

On the day of mother's appointment, Man Kin helped her in and locked everything secure at the back of the van, while Ah Lin and I sat behind the driver's seat. I was still expecting our appointment to be right on time, at 2pm; when he gave me the tip that we still needed to go at least half an hour early to register in order to be on time to check out. I groaned to myself— still the same old hospital routine—but I was grateful that he had at least warned me ahead of time, unlike the nurses at the hospital.

Mother's appointment at Ming Sum Lau was more intensive than her former basic appointments at the hospital. Since this clinic was specialized, I learned much more information about mother's disease. From that first day at Ming Sum Lau, I remembered almost every word that doctor told me about dementia. If I wanted to maintain the basic level of my mother's memory of what she had left now, I needed to learn more professional techniques to reach the goal, from both physical and mentally. Otherwise, like ordinary dementia, it would decline like a sharp, downward arrow. In other words, mother was still declining, but gradually stepping forward, in slower, every other step.

In order to improve and maintain my mother's memory at this time, I learned several further tips and suggestions. When we talked to mother, we kept our voices at a reasonable tone, and did not make a lot of noise to upset or surprise her. We never asked her questions if we knew she could not answer them; she would then get frustrated and angry. This was the worst thing we could possibly do to her. If you wanted to talk to her, you would sit next to her and pat her on the arm gently. Once she gave you her full attention, you would look her in the face to speak with her in a quiet voice. Before mother started to eat, we would let her say a prayer before each meal. When she was eating, we would ask her to look at the plate of food at everything on the dish; the color, the texture, smell and taste before she started to have her meal. We made sure her food was cut into small pieces, and watched her while she ate small bites at a time to see if she enjoyed the food, and we would ask her if she needed any salt on it. This way, mother could enjoy her food thoroughly. It was also an activity for us, the other adults, as well as mother; we were learning how to speak more respectfully to her.

The feeling of having every detail of mother's illness explained to us by kind professionals was very reliving. I still recognized good care when I saw it. I was going to take advantage of every piece of advice she gave me, and that started with an excellent outlet that would really let us try out these new sensory techniques: mother's birthday. I decided to throw a party for her birthday, which was fast approaching on August 28, and I was hoping at this party we would all be able to use different activities to help trigger more of that step-by-step improvement.

I immediately began planning. Everything was running smoothly so far, and I was hoping things would go well. At 9am two days before mother's birthday, I was sitting next to mother's bed, talking with her like we usually did. I don't even remember what we were talking about; probably something not important.

Suddenly, without warning, mother's eyes rolled up in her head. I could only see the whites of her eyeballs. Her teeth suddenly began biting down hard on each other, making a loud grinding noise. Her entire body began to shake uncontrollably from head to toe.

What the hell was happening?! I panicked. I screamed for Ah Lin. When she raced to mother's side, her expression turned to one of complete horror. We had no idea what was happening to her. We immediately called for an ambulance. Before the police and emergency medical technicians arrived, mother's attack had already calmed down, and she was regaining consciousness. When the police and emergency medical technicians arrived, she was fully awake, with no recollection of what had just happened.

I had timed it; the entire attack, whatever it was, had all happened in exactly one minute. With the terror that Ah Lin and I saw, it had felt like an eternity. I would never get rid of that image of my mother's eyes rolling back in her head like we were in a horror movie.

Mother was perfectly fine now; but because we had called for help, even though her attack had passed, and she showed no symptoms of it, she still had to go to the hospital and check in to the Emergency Ward.

When we arrived, we waited for the usual several hours that had been accustomed to, and after she was finally examined, the doctor there confirmed mother had a convulsion. This was typical, he said, for patients recovering from a stroke. He suggested that mother be admitted to the hospital for observation overnight.

I would not be having that—not after the poor care she had received here. I thought this overnight observation was useless—they were spending more unnecessary time focusing on a one-minute convulsion than they had when she had her stroke. I refused to let her be admitted. The doctors could not legally keep her there; I had every right to take her home.

I was relieved for a moment, but then I realized I had a very big problem getting her home. When we went to the hospital, the ambulance had a stretcher to carry mother; now we didn't have her wheelchair to bring her back. Suddenly, I realized we had no way to transport her back home. My panic began to rise. It was already 10:30pm. Ah Lin looked at me, worried, and I tried to focus so I could think.

At that very moment, an idea popped into my head. I quickly made a phone call to Man Kin and told him about our day; immediately, without hesitation, he came to the hospital with his van to bring us home. I breathed a huge sigh of relief. An angel from heaven, sent down to rescue us! It had been a thirty-five-minute drive for him from his house, and it was late at night, but he had still come for us. When he arrived, he borrowed a wheelchair from the hospital; these wheelchairs had two long poles on each side that prevented the chair from fitting into the van. As fast as lightning, he went into his van and emerged with a set of tools, and immediately unscrewed the poles from the chair and finally, successfully, got mother into the van. We sped off into the night, leaving the hospital in the dust.

I felt like cheering at the top of my lungs into the night air. I couldn't even begin to tell this man how grateful I was to have him in our lives now. If he had not generously shown up, mother might have been forced to spend a dreadful, uncomfortable night in the hospital. I would have felt like a failure, having promised both mother and myself that I would never again subject her to that kind of mistreatment. Man Kin later told us that on his way to the hospital, he flew his van without stopping for red lights; I told him that it was because he was our angel.

I needed another angel to watch over us the following morning, which was mother's first day after her convulsion. I was worried about how mother would feel and act, but when she awoke, she seemed fine, just a bit tired. I wanted to keep monitoring her closely over the next day, because I still planned for her birthday party to go on, since I had already invited friends and decorated the living room.

54

Her health remained on the rebound. On the morning of August 28, her eighty-sixth birthday, the best gift of all was that she showed absolutely no signs of having pain, discomfort, or any remembrance of what had occurred two days earlier. We all breathed collective sighs of relief; I had made the right decision to take mother home from the hospital. I tried to put the incident out of my head for now, but I'd continue to watch her closely throughout the day to make sure nothing excited or upset her too much to cause another convulsion.

Soon, the guests arrived, the games were laid out, and the party began. As we began celebrating this wonderful gathering for mother, we hoped to collectively raise her spirits.

I invited my sister Agnes, my brother Stephen, Ah King, Ah Lin, and two friends to come join us. I had decorated the living room with colorful ribbons, since that was the area of the house where mother lived. Mother would not be lonely like most people hiding in the bedroom; in the living room, mother could see everyone whether they were going into the bedrooms, bathroom, watching TV, in the kitchen or even going out. She was stationed at the center of the living room like a security guard. She would be busy just watching people come in or go out from this direction to other parts of the apartment, never feeling lonely or deserted.

Besides the colorful décors on the walls, we also had custom-made party hats with colored tissue paper. I had even carefully selected her favorite music. Everything was bright and lively, all intended to give mom a burst of happiness and joy. It seemed to be working; as the guests all filed in and began talking animatedly to mother, she looked like a child at her first birthday party, surrounding by all those who loved her. There was a beautiful smile on her face and humor in her eyes; we could all tell that she felt alive and spirited, like she was young again.

Aside from the ecstatic look that did not leave mother's face for the entire day, the best thing about today I knew was going to be the series of games we would play. My intention was to use the games not only to play with mother, but also to help stimulate her memory. Ms. Mok had told me that one of the effects of dementia is difficulty completing normal tasks, and one of the best ways to combat this is by practicing following and remembering step-by-step directions. These games would greatly help mother's thinking and perception skills.

In total, we had seven people to play, divided into two groups: my mother, Ah Lin and her sister in one group, and my sister and the rest in the other group. I was the judge. Mother was the center of the games, while the rest of us were there to help her along.

The first game involved playing with colorful cards; there were four sets of color cards, which I had mixed on the table, divided into two piles. The players would have to match them. No sooner had I finished announcing the rules, mother immediately picked and correctly matched all the color cards. I grinned. My plan was working! I took mental notes about mother's movements and her brain function as she played. Her motion of picking with only her right hand was quick, and her speed at matching the correct cards showed me that her mind was still improving. We applauded mother's victory, and her smile beamed back at us like sunlight.

For the next game, we used the same pack of cards, but this time, the rule was to match up the numbers on the cards, both even and odd numbers for all of us. Before we started the game, I removed one card and hid it; we called this game "chasing ghost." None of us knew which card was singled out until the end. Everyone's heart was beating to chase around that unknown card. When we revealed the card, mother's face lit up in recognition. I smiled again. Another victory!

The third game was speaking without words but with action; in America, it is called charades. One person picked out one card, looked at the word and acted it out without speaking; the other partners would guess what the word was. Our crazy and hilarious motions filled the living room with loud noise and laughter. Mother picked up most of the words that we acted out.

Next, we played a game that involved clapping hands and changing actions by touching some parts of our body, similar to the American game "Simon Says." The leader would suddenly change action by touching their nose and see who would be the last to follow, and then that person would be punished by doing some silly action. Mother was having a grand time; she showed her happiness by clapping not with two hands, but instead clapping her good hand on her thigh.

We all cracked up at the following game, where we each thought of a flower's name and tried to eliminate people who could not come up with one. We played the game for quite some time, and since many flowers had already been named, when it was my mother's turn, she said "senior flower." We all laughed at my mother's clever creation. I took mental notes again; I was very glad our games seemed to be working to keep her mind intact.

After the games, it was time for the guest of honor to open her gifts. All the guests filed up next to the presents that were stacked on the table, and I took each gift one by one and handed it to mother. The way that mother opened these presents was something we all enjoyed watching tremendously. This was no impatient five-year-old tearing up the wrapping on her Christmas presents; mother took care to unwrap each part of the gift individually, as if every piece of tissue paper held a diamond inside. With Ah Lin's help, she would open each gift, carefully taking away layer after layer of wrapping paper, her eyes lighting up with delight after each piece was stripped away. When she got to the bottom with the real gift inside, her face could not contain the smile she had. I took lots of pictures of her curious expressions.

The process of opening the gifts became pleasantly overwhelming to mother. By the time she got to Ah King's present, she was barely paying attention to what it was as she opened the small box. It was a small, brown bear that made a noise when you squeezed it; when mother took it out of the box, she didn't glance to look at what it was. I could see that her mind was questioning it; she shook it—no response. Then she squeezed it—ah, it had a noise! Mother finally recognized it and smiled at its cuteness.

Last was my present; it was a white box, stuffed with loose papers and cotton materials. Mother searched through the papers carefully, gently lifting one piece at a time, until at the bottom of the box, she found out it was a bottle. Ah Lin helped out and let mother blow on the round lop, which carried bubbles; mother played with it continuously with fun, and Ah King tried to catch and chase bubbles. Mother's face was positively glowing with happiness and laughter as she watched her.

As I laughed along with everyone else, I watched mother closely. The light that was emanating from her told me something that I had been worrying about for a long time: that deep down, beneath the disease that was changing her brain, beneath the paralyzed nerves on her left side, the same, warm heart still beat strongly. She was still the same person: charming, keen, and full of personality. The physical problems she had would never overcome her spirit.

Mother's eighty-sixth birthday party was a beautifully bright spot for all of us in the middle of a year that had been plagued with dark times. On the roller coaster of emotions, we had hit a high point. I kept up this positivity now by helping mother settle into a steady routine of exercise, both intellectually and physically.

Although mother's entire left side, from her lip down to her toes, was paralyzed, she could still exercise and maintain her right side, which she did regularly. Ah Lin and I did several exercises with her every day, and our physical therapist came to help her exercise twice a week. These exercises helped mother maintain her physical fitness and would improve her motor skills. During the day while she was awake, mother always sat in a straight-back chair that dipped down the back of the seat that resembled the kind of chairs you find in movie theaters. I had the chair made especially for her in order to keep her posture straight. The chair also had a straight board that went across the front, much like a child's highchair; this was to prevent her from falling over on to the floor. When the physical therapist came, mother would be sitting in the chair, and we would do exercises together. The therapist would have her lean over every day with her right arm, a little further each time, so mother could extend her arm.

We also passed a ball around several times; if mother could not pass it a certain way, we began back at the easiest exercise. The point of these exercises was not to heal mother completely, or to make her frustrated or angry; we wanted to do the best we could for her with the strength that she had. That was why the therapist did not push her too hard; if he gave her an exercise she couldn't do, she would simply refuse to do it. So he started off easy, and gradually, day by day, worked in more difficult exercises and activities.

Ah Lin and I helped mom emotionally too; the therapist would help her with her exercises, and we would offer mom encouragement. Even if she had done a very simple exercise, we would still praise her and tell her she had done very well. We kept up with all the good exercises several times a week.

Besides keeping mother physically fit, we kept up at maintaining mother's intelligence. I spoke English with her frequently. Neither Ah King nor Ah Lin could understand English, so every time we spoke together, Ah Lin would ask mom if she could learn. My mother would tell her, "sure, absolutely—how much will you pay me?" and hold out her hand. Ah Lin would say that she had no money, and mother would joke with her and slap her hand to tell her she better pay her soon if she was going to teach her. Mother had not lost her good humor, and would frequently joke around with Ah Lin especially: if she pronounced an English word incorrectly, mother would yell to me to get the scissors to cut off part of Ah Lin's tongue!

Mother's memory was also aided by the frequent visitors she had. Many of our relatives continued to stop by during this time. We kept her chats about her happy memories, and often times, her visitors would still ask her for advice. Even despite her condition, they still valued everything that mother had learned, and believed they could still learn from her. I would try to stimulate mother's memory by asking questions about the old photos and documents we saw in mother's photo book, and she would usually remember quite a bit of detail about it.

One of the most frequent questions her visitors had for her were tips on travelling, since they all knew what a world traveler mother was. I would tell my mom to look through the photo albums and try to jog her memory of all the places she had gone when she had been a world traveler.

My mother of course had not been wealthy enough to jet off to different places whenever she felt like it. Her travel experiences came as gifts. Throughout her life, my mother had been generous to many people, all of whom now lived all over the South Pacific and some across the globe. Her generosity had been felt so deeply by these people that some of them, never forgetting the kindness she had once bestowed on them, now wanted to pay her back—by offering to pay for her to travel to different places around the world to visit them, completely free of charge. They believed it was the least they could do for mother's compassion towards them. My mother therefore became a world traveler, flying all over the southeast corner of the world, including Singapore, Malaysia, the Philippines, and Japan, and as far as London. Every trip gave her lovely sights to see and new opportunities to experience, and she was grateful for every trip that she took.

One of my mother's favorite trips came in 1985, when she was living in Vancouver. My auntie Theresa (Chu Fook Ching) and her husband Ming Leung Sun were living in Brisbane, Australia at the time, and invited mother down to visit them and their family. Theresa, a bright, open-hearted, and hard-working woman, like my mother, had also graduated from St. Mary's College, studied in England and graduated with a degree in nursing. Her husband was also an extremely intelligent man; he was the youngest man ever at that time to have graduated with a Ph.D. from Cambridge University, at the age of only twenty-seven. My mother had shown incredible generosity towards Theresa throughout the difficult times in both their lives, and Theresa wanted to repay mother. She and her husband paid for my mother to travel with them all over Australia, up and down the coasts, and to the larger cities like Sydney. They also went to visit one of my mother's bridesmaids, Claire, and her bridegroom, Joseph; it had been over forty-five years since the wedding, and it was a joy for my mother to see them. The entire trip was wonderful for mother to experience, and she was grateful for Theresa's kindness.

Now, looking back at the photos from all of these fantastic trips with her frequent visitors, I would try to stimulate mother's memory by asking questions about the old photos and documents we saw, and she would usually remember quite a bit of detail about it. It was not simply something to talk about or a way to pass the time; talking about the past was an exercise to keep mother's sharp mind intact.

With mother improving every day, I decided to consult a private doctor, who specialized specifically in gerontology, named Dr. Ng Hing Wai. A good private specialist like him was very expensive; just the consultation fee alone was over $1,500, not including the medication. Regardless of the pricy consultation, I still wanted to make mother's situation even better.

Since his office was in Kowloon, we transported mother by Man Kin's handicapped van from our home in Tuen Mun, which took 45 minutes without traffic. It was a long trip for all of us, but mother trusted me; she knew I would do anything for her benefit. When we arrived, Dr. Ng examined mother and asked me many questions regarding her first stroke and convulsion. He then told us frankly about my mother's case; it was not wise to bring mother from a long distance to see a doctor. She had a stroke, she had dementia, and she was getting old; he gently instructed us to just let her be comfortable as much as she could be.

For a moment, I did not quite understand what he was saying. Then suddenly, it hit me. My stomach sank. My head began to cloud, and my chest began to tighten. Dr. Ng did not tell us directly, but I knew from his words that mother's time with us would be over soon.

As we walked out of the office, I immediately pushed all bad thoughts out of my head. I could not accept anything except positivity and improvement right now. I would continue to dedicate every moment to helping mother be as comfortable, healthy, and happy as possible.

After the appointment, mother, Ah Lin and I went to have tea at the oldest restaurant in the area, the Nathan Tea House. Chinese tea is an ancient tradition, and holds many significant meanings. It was a pleasure for us to be able to take mother out to have tea.

In Cantonese, tea time is called "yum cha," which involves both drinking tea and eating "dim sum" dishes. Dim sum is a Cantonese style of bite-sized or individual portions of food served in small steamer baskets or on small plates. We would enjoy yum cha and dim sum at local tea houses, similar to American coffee houses, where people young and old meet to talk, catch up, or go on dates. Unlike what you would see in American coffee houses, however, there is much etiquette and practices involved in yum cha, and during other Chinese meals as well. First, it is customary to pour tea for others before yourself; when pouring tea for people on one's left side, the right hand should be used to hold the teapot and vice versa. To thank the person pouring the tea, a single person taps their bent index finger, and a married person taps both their index and middle finger, symbolizing bowing to someone in appreciation. If you do not need a refill when it is offered, the fingers are used to "wave off" or politely decline more tea. Leaving the lid balanced on the side of the tea pot is also a common way of attracting a server's attention, and indicates a silent request that the tea pot be refilled. Since tea is often poured many times in a meal, these gestures prevent any disruptions to the conversations.

As we sat and enjoyed our tea time, I remember how mother once told me she used to come here once in a while with Amy Yuen, her former sister-in-law. Amy, the wife of my father's brother Ambrose (Wong Chi Yan), was one of the most beautiful people many of us had ever seen. My mother always remained very close to her. Amy lived in Heung Bun Mansion, across from this restaurant. She was two years older than my mother, and she was lucky to have a faithful Philippine helper named Tina. Recently, she had many sicknesses from her diabetes; doctors had removed half of her foot and a few toes from the other, and she was also blind and deaf. She was in and out of the hospital frequently. Her son Thomas and his family lived in Singapore, and very often, he came over to Hong Kong to visit his mother.

Mother missed her a great deal. As we sat now, I looked at her and saw all of that same emotion she had back then reflected now in her eyes. I wondered, as I always did, what she was thinking. I wanted to unlock the mystery of what was behind her beautiful eyes.

Seeing mother in great spirits had made my day-to-day tasks a lot easier. One of the things I now wanted to do for her was to get her a new wheelchair. I wanted one that would allow her to lean her head back and lift her legs up in a reclining position. The chair that I found was only available, however, in Kowloon, inside of Hong Kong Polytechnic University, in the physical therapy department. You should know by now that a small matter such as location was not going to stop me.

On September 4, mother and I traveled to the university to meet with the man in charge of the department, Mr. Lo. We were scheduled to meet him at 2pm; mother had a light lunch, and we arrived there fifteen minutes early. As we waited, I glanced around the room we were waiting in; I was surprised and impressed to see that there were all kinds of equipment and tools, and fancy computers.

Mr. Lo walked in then and introduced himself and his products. His demeanor and his intelligence impressed me as much as his products. He informed us that he customized all his products from scratch according to the patient's need. Analyzing mother's situation, he showed us the reports on how the current way mother sat would cause her pressure on her back, bottom, and legs. The new wheelchair that he could customize for her would solve all those problems spots.

I was ready to jump at his offer, but then he told us his price: $55,000 Hong Kong dollars. I cringed. That was way out of my price range. I didn't want to push him about lowering the price; he had been very kind to us. I'd have to leave that offer sitting there on the table, and as we left, the idea of mother's customized wheelchair taunted me and made me turn back, just for a moment. But I couldn't argue with reality; I simply did not have the money. I turned back around and headed out the door with mother. I really wasn't even that dismayed; at least I had tried. My newfound hope told me to let it go. It was out of my hands. Besides, at least I had gained some useful knowledge; now I knew what areas of mother's body to exercise a bit more now with Ah Lin.

Ah Lin truly had become a blessing to us. In Hong Kong, most servants stayed with their employer for twenty-four hours a day, seven days a week, even on Sundays and holidays; they almost never went home. Ah Lin worked hard, especially in my household with mother, and she deserved every bit of money I could give her. We paid her monthly, plus tips on special holidays. My personal favorite was paying her for these holidays, but I also paid for all of her personal necessities (toothpaste, toiletries, etc.), in addition to her food and all of their seasonal clothes. At every meal, I always sat down and waited for her to come to join me for dinner or lunch. After all the work Ah Lin had done for mother, I wanted to show her my gratitude in every way possible.

Ah King, our cook, had been with us for quite some time, but on September 5, she was sadly leaving us. In the late afternoon on that very same day, our new cook, Ah Fan, arrived from mainland China. Ah King still came to teach her to do the cleaning around the house, as well to cook, until Ah Fan was capable enough to do the job on her own. Ah Fan learned quickly, and was a hard, diligent worker; however, she was a very shy young woman. Mother would tease her good-naturedly, mostly about her accent and the fact that she did not speak correct Chinese. Ah Fan took no offense to this, and as she got more comfortable around us, she began to open up, and we saw how good of a sport she was, going along with mother's jokes. She and Ah Lin made life much easier around our house; I was blessed to have two wonderful, capable, and easygoing assistants to help us, and I tried to keep the friendliness abundant.

I kept right on going with our daily routines at home; my mother kept right on progressing in her health, little by little, day by day, right through September. With Ah Lin and Ah Fan's assistance—as well as visits from her physical and occupational therapists, and visits once a week from Mrs. Cheung, who checked on mother's high blood pressure and injected her with vitamins B & B6—mother kept right on plugging away. It really was quite remarkable how well she had improved.

It was around this time that I had a quiet moment to myself one day, and as I sat back in one of our comfortable chairs, I felt another good feeling

61

stir in my heart, but the sun was still beaming brightly through our windows. I was suddenly reminded of that Sunday back in February, over eight months ago. I closed my eyes. I could still picture the morning exactly—the beams of sunlight on mother's face when she woke up; the soft, pressed linen of her best skirt pressed up against my hands as I helped her dress; the look of content that she had as I had placed her in the chair by the door, like an angel waiting patiently for God. I remembered then the thump I heard from the bathroom; the sight of mother lying there on the floor; her yelp of pain when I tried to lift her; the frantic call I had made to the emergency personnel, and the anxiety I had in trying to get her out to the ambulance as quickly as possible.

I squeezed my eyes shut as tightly as possible. Suddenly, the picture turned; I began to see mother being visited in the hospital by her family and friends; I saw the youth return to her face as she recalled her past; I saw our new apartment, beautifully furnished and waiting for us to move in; I saw her birthday party, mother in her chair surrounded by those who loved her, eyes lit up like birthday candles.

I opened my eyes and looked across from me. There she was, sitting there as she had every day. At that moment, at full force, it struck me what a courageous woman she was. Tears began to well up in my eyes. After everything she had been through—she was still sitting here. There she was, right in front of me. She had come so far—and I was proud of her.

I had a decision to make. I had been in Hong Kong for exactly one year. I was missing my husband Larry and my own home deeply—my own bed, my own kitchen, my own comfortable chairs. Larry knew my mother was the most important person in my life, and he never complained, not even to my being away from Massachusetts for a full year. My stay with mother had only been intended as a visit; I had to decide if I would make it longer.

In the end, with mother in her current condition of steady improvement, and with so many people in place to care for her, I decided to go back home. I had done what I could for now; the situation was right for me to step back and let mother continue on with her new daily life. Looking at her beautiful face, I felt content that I could leave her now in good hands, and she would be all right.

On the morning of Saturday, September 20, I left Hong Kong and headed home to Worcester by way of Logan Airport in Boston. I would have a stopover in Chicago, but that was fine with me; in those days, United Airlines had just started to offer direct flights from Hong Kong to Chicago without refueling, which I was glad for, because it shortened the length of the flight from twenty to seventeen hours. After I landed in Chicago, I had to wait another four hours in the airport for my connecting flight. Another three-hour flight followed before I finally landed in Boston at Logan Airport. From there, I reserved a door-to-door service Worcester Limo van to take me back to Worcester. All through the drive, I kept looking out the window and marveling at what I saw. I couldn't believe I was backing home. I was so eager to sleep on my forty-eight-inch wide bed.

As soon as the van arrived at my doorstep, I wanted to get out and kiss the ground. I leaped out of the van, got my luggage, and went inside. I inhaled deeply. There it was; the smell of my own home. It was like no other. Larry greeted me warmly, and I greeted him in kind. As we hugged, I began to feel my jet lag settling in; I suddenly wanted nothing but to crawl into my own bed and fall into a deep and dreamless sleep. I went into my bedroom and found it just the way I had left it; and there was my bed, beckoning to me to pull down the covers and let all of my stress fall away.

As I rested my travel-weary eyes and let my head fall back on the soft pillows, I allowed all the thoughts that had been piling up in my head and my heart to flow freely. It was hard to believe what I had witnessed in the past year; it had seemed like everything happened so suddenly. My mother had hit rock bottom and I had hit it too along with her; there were low points where I felt saddened and angered that mother's health had not been taken care of properly. But along with those low points were high ones; the image of mom's birthday party ran through my head like a filmstrip. I saw her beautiful face, her brow furrowed with curiosity as she opened my birthday gift to her. I remember the look on her face as she joked with Ah Lin sitting next to her, and her grin as she looked around at all the colorful decorations I had put up. I remembered the day we had brought her home from the hospital, and the laughter we shared when I took her speeding through the rain in her wheelchair. I could almost feel her hand gripping mine again, with her soft fingers touching mine and telling me that she didn't mind what I was doing, and that she trusted that I would take care of her.

But now, lying alone, in my own bed, twelve hours away from her, I reached out my hand to try and touch hers. But all I felt was darkness.

The transition back to Worcester and away from mother was more difficult than I had anticipated. An ocean and two continents couldn't separate my heart and my mind from mother, and, as I soon realized, it couldn't cure my anxiety. Although I had left because she was quite stable and in good and capable hands, I couldn't help but worry about her constantly. I wondered if Ah Lin was still keeping the records; it was silly, because I knew she was. I worried that mother was still doing her exercises; that was silly also, because I knew she was doing that too. My anxiety got the best of me; I called her home in the morning, or evening, just to make sure everything was all right. Each time, they assured me things were fine, and I would have to hang up, thousands of miles away, and let my worries overtake my sleep for another night.

It finally became too much for me. I devised a new plan: I would stay at home in Worcester for just one month, then fly back to Hong Kong to see mother, this time again with Larry. Since Larry was living alone, and our winter in the States was very cold with freezing temperatures, I didn't want him to be alone in the cold for health reasons. He would stay with us for half a year until the late spring, when I would bring him back to the States. This way, I figured, I could have all of those I loved and cared for around me in one place.

63

A month later, on October 24, we caught our early morning flight from Boston to Chicago, where we stopped to visit my daughters, Stella and Iris, and their families. We were ecstatic to see our grandchildren Stephanie and Ryan, and we all stayed at Stella's house that night. The next morning, we went to have tea in Chicago's Chinatown, and we had a lovely time together as a family. Seeing my children and grandchildren together was the only thing that could truly warm my heart to the core and lift my worries a little.

On Sunday, the 26th, we left my daughters and grandchildren in Chicago and finally headed back to Hong Kong. It was odd; every time I went back to Hong Kong, I never had jetlag. Something was wired in my brain to tell me to forget my own tiredness and stay awake. I had an important goal to take care of that required my full, undivided attention. As we landed, instead of the usual tiredness I felt, my brain snapped away from the wonderful time I had with my children and grandchildren, and automatically shifted back into the work mode I had whenever I was here.

Even though it had only been a month since I had left, I felt incredibly relieved to see everyone again, and to see that everything and everyone was still in good shape. Mother especially was very happy to see us, and it warmed my heart to see her in such good spirits when she saw us. As I hugged her, I looked around; everything looked exactly the same. I breathed a little sigh of relief. I had been worrying over nothing. Maybe I just needed to see mother in front of me again to believe it.

With my anxiety somewhat settled, our trip began to take on a very different feel than my previous visit only a month ago. Now, we were all a bit more at ease; with the addition of Larry, it made things quite interesting. Since Larry does not speak Chinese, he, mother, and I spoke English very often instead of Chinese. Ah Lin, however, still did not speak English at all, and because of this, I gave her an English name, Linda, which she still continues to use to this very day. Very quickly, Linda learned English from mother, and picked up on what she heard from our conversations so that she could communicate with Larry in a simple way. So, every morning, when Larry got up, Linda asked him what he wanted to eat for breakfast. Although Linda had already learned one word at a time from mother, she was still learning, and her conversation was not always clear; sometimes, mother would have to correct her a few times before she spoke proper English. Because of the language gap, jokes came along with laughter. And poor Ah Fan never even got an English name, because she could not even pronounce Cantonese well; the difficulty of the English language would be almost impossible for her to learn.

With the ease that we were creating in our home, it was no surprise to me how quickly I settled back into the routine I had left only month ago—taking mother to her appointments, checking and maintaining the logbook, and allowing friends and relatives in to see mother. Her next appointment that I'd get to take her to was on November 14 to get a refill of her Aspirin 81 pills, at the place I knew all too well, the Tuen Mun Daily Clinic. This was where we had waited for three hours to see the young, inexperienced, and rather impersonal doctor. Her appointment was at 9:45am, but I knew the drill already. I went first to hold our place in line, I let mother arrive around 11am, which, lucky for us, was almost around the time the nurse called her name. I had successfully learned my way around these obnoxious policies, and mother benefited from it. Everything was normal with her, and she received the same dose of pills, and just like that, we were done.

Five days later, on November 19, Mr. Alphonsus "Nelson" Chan, a member of the Community of Ministries, came to our home. I had previously requested someone from the Catholic Church to deliver the Holy Eucharist to my mother, and today would be the day. Although mother had been a member of the Mormon Church since 1970, her Catholic upbringing still ran so strong in her blood that she still wished to receive the Holy Communion from the Catholic Church. Even with her fading memory, she remembered her prayer "Our Father" by heart. She had never renounced her faith; she had switched churches, but she had never abandoned her faith in God. After all He had put her through, she had not pushed her faith away. I believed that many people who had been through half of the things she had might lose hope, and become angry or hurtful. But not her. Even now, when she could not remember our names or recognize our faces, she could remember her prayer without blinking an eye. As she spoke and recited the holy words, I felt tears sting my eyes. I knew that God would always hold a special spot in heaven for her.

Mother continued on with her physical exercises as well. On November 26, mother learned a new exercise called the "trunk movement," where she moved the core of her body. She liked it; for her, it was a new challenge. But one of her favorite exercises involved nose punching: the therapist would taunt and tease my mother and try to persuade her to punch him in the nose. He would have mother stretch her arm out as far as she could, and lean in and out to get her to move her arm back and forth. Since mother had a quick wit, this was one of her favorite exercises to do. The servants and I would do the exercise with her as well – but we would tease her more than the therapist did! It was the therapist's job to keep mother's body healthy, but it was our job to keep mother's spirits up. The more exercises we did, the crazier we got. It was an entertaining way to get mother to do something she otherwise might not want to do.

As the year began to wind down, our normal routines were interrupted by two important events, one good and one bad. In late November, I received a surprising phone called from my younger daughter Iris. "Iris" means "colorful rainbow," a beautiful image that symbolizes someone who is full of life and personality. This was indeed my daughter! Calling us now, Iris had landed in Hong Kong on the 24th and was staying with her friend. So the next day, I told mother that Iris would come to visit her on that Friday. Mother was ecstatic; Iris used to visit mother very often when she used to work in Hong Kong for some years, and mother cared for her a great deal. Mother was more eager than I had seen her in quite some time, and when Friday afternoon came, and Iris arrived; I thought mother's smile was going to crack her face in two! Iris hugged mother tightly, and told her how glad she was to see her. She sat and talked with mother for a while, and showed her recent photos and explained every one; mother listened, nodding her head with a smile at each photo. I took a few pictures, and in the photos, you can see the pure happiness on the faces of both grandmother and granddaughter. What a blessing to have three generations of women there together! That night, mother's excitement from seeing Iris was contagious; we shared a good, long chat and laughed over the joys of having our own children.

But then, at 8pm on Tuesday, December 2, mother's heartbeat reached 120, which was far too high. Looking back at our logbook, we knew that she had high blood pressure a few times per day, but usually her heartbeat was below 70. Her heartbeat started at 119, but when we checked again two hours later, it had climbed higher to 120, and immediately, we got her an appointment to see a private doctor for the following day. (We had already learned this clever shortcut; seeing a private doctor was much faster than going to see the government's doctors, and we could bypass all the ridiculous waiting.) So the following afternoon, we pushed mother to Tuen Mun Daily Clinic again at 3:30pm. When the doctor checked her with the EKG, her heart beat still read 120. The doctor prescribed her 10 mg of a special medication called "Isosorbide Dinitrate," which she started taking on Thursday. To our relief, three days later, mother's heartbeat came down to 53, and her blood pressure stabilized at 134/85.

The day that we got home from the clinic, I sat back down on the same comfortable chair that I had sat on before I had left for America. As I looked around our apartment, with everything reminding me about what had transpired over the past year, the exhaustion that I had been pushing away for so long finally settled on me. I felt so many emotions at once, I could barely take it. I rubbed my hands over my eyes. I only had a single phrase to describe the year: a tormented whirlwind.

2003 was a milestone year for my mother and her illness. While she would never fully regain her health or strength, she had made tremendous improvements in areas where weaker people might never progress. She had gone from having a feeding tube inserted in her nose to someone feed her blended soft food to eating normally by herself. Mother had made good progress in her occupational and physical therapy and her massages. She had only had a convulsion twice: two days before her birthday on August 26, and again on September 21. Our hard work with her and the prayers that many people had sent her way had certainly worked.

Remembering back to mother's birthday in August, watching her open her presents with delight, I felt something deep in my heart that I thought was the beginning of sincere hope. I had never stopped believing that mother could recover; now, after seeing her improve so much over the past year, after everything she had been through, the light at the end of this long, dark tunnel now seemed to be growing even closer and closer every day. With this genuine sense of hope, my daily tasks seemed much less of a hassle. All the problems we had encountered last year—the arguments with the hospitals, finding a new place to live, getting mother new facilities, signing for this and that, taking care of all the day-to-day things—were only minor roadblocks in our pathway to success.

No matter how many obstacles there were, they would never overshadow my pure, single goal of making sure mother was always properly cared for. No action that I would take, no thought that would cross my mind, for the rest of my life, would be free from the events that had happened. There was no one else in the world who had watched mother's every move as I had—from her fall in early February, to her steady physical and spiritual progress up through her birthday in late August, to our conversations about the past only a month earlier. Her well-being would always be my lifelong dedication; every part of me, body and soul, was now, and forever, hers.

CHAPTER 5

At the start of 2004, I was cautiously optimistic. Only a year after mother's accident, we had come a long way from uncaring doctors and nurses, long lines at the clinic, cruel feeding tubes, and inhumane hospital procedures. Now, we were happily settled far away from chaos and confusion in our humble new home at Tai Hing Garden. Linda and I worked like clockwork to make sure mother's days were guided by order and routine. Five times a day, mother exercised every part of her body she could move. Weekly, she had her occupational and physical therapy appointments. We played games, talked and laughed together. Our apartment remained a bustling center of energy.

With everything in our household running smoothly, I thought it might be time for a short vacation for me. With everything that had happened over the past year, I needed some time away to clear my head. The more well-rested and clear-minded I was, the more helpful I could be to our household.

I decided that my husband Larry and I would take a vacation together. Larry was still living with us here in Hong Kong; we were having a particularly cold winter in Massachusetts that year, and it was too dangerous for him to suffer the frigid temperatures alone in our house. I was happy to have him with us in Hong Kong – and so was mother. Every day, as Linda and I would go about our work, Larry's naturally humorous personality would lift all of our spirits—especially mother's. The two of them, who were so alike in their cleverness and quick wit, could have formed their own comedy team together. I was glad he had stayed with us and made our positive energy even brighter.

I allowed myself to become a little excited as I thought about where Larry and I should go. Larry had been to Hong Kong many times with me before, and he had seen most of the traditional sights. Suddenly, I realized that there was only one place Larry and I needed to go—my childhood city of Macau. I had not been there in a long time, and Larry had never been there at all. It was settled; Macau was our destination.

I arranged all the necessary travel plans, and on January 12, Larry and I boarded a hydrofoil ferry for the hour-long boat ride that would take us across the sea to our destination. Macau is located on the western side of the Pearl River Delta, across from Hong Kong to the east; it is connected only to mainland China to the north. Thus, the ferry is the only means of transportation to get there. I had not taken one of these ferry rides in quite a while; the sea air felt wonderful, fresh and crisp, as small pellets of water splashed up around us on the deck of the ferry, lightly hitting our faces.

As the land rose into view from the ferry, I was met with sights I had pushed back into the deepest parts of my memories. Everything around me—the smells, the sounds, the taste of the air on my tongue—suddenly rushed back to me in a storm of familiarity. I inhaled deeply to take it all in. I already felt energized; I couldn't wait to explore the places of our past.

After our ferry docked at the wharf, Larry and I got a taxi and I asked the driver to find my desired first destination: a very specific European cemetery. It was not the cemetery itself I wanted to visit; it was the building that, hopefully, still stood next to it. There were many residential buildings in Macau that matched the description of the one I was looking for, so I figured we'd have a better chance of finding the building if I instead described the European cemetery to the taxi driver.

As we drove around, I closed my eyes and began to dig deep into my memory for every detail I remembered about this building. It was very tall, like all the others around it, and each outside window was covered in old, wooden shutters, and had a narrow, green balcony attached to it. The memory of the image began to assemble in front of my eyes like a photo.

When I opened my eyes, the taxi driver had stopped. We were at the cemetery. All around us were sharp, sleek, modern high rises that had been constructed after the other older buildings had been torn down. But in the middle of all of them was this old building, still standing like a tall, firm beacon of hope. It had certainly been worn over time, but one side was still rooted firmly on the land. I looked up and saw that the green balconies I remembered so vividly were still there, hanging overhead. Even the windows looked the same, with their original wooden shutters still attached.

Inside this building was the former home of my second auntie on my father's side, Wong Shui Kwan, her husband, Mr. Cheung Fai, and their seven children, the youngest of whom, Rosie, was the same age as me. Their home was one of my most vivid childhood memories; aside from our own home, this was where mother and I used to spend most of our time. I remember that inside, the stairs were long and straight, with no handle. I remember when I was younger, when mother would drop me off here to play with Rosie while she needed to do errands, we used to climb these long and straight stairs. I remembered mom holding my hand carefully, step-by-step, as we ascended up the stairs. Her skin was soft and warm, and she gripped my tiny hand tightly, reassuring me that she would not let me fall.

As I stood there in front of the building I had known so well as a child, I felt as though mother was standing right beside me in spirit – beautiful and strong, gripping my hand tightly as if she would never let go. As Larry and I traveled throughout Macau over the next few days, at every location we saw, every building we visited, I felt mother there with me.

On our third day in Macau, Larry and I went to visit my old nanny, Ah Mg. She was eighty-three years old now, and lived in a Catholic nursing home on Lou Wan, a lovely island that was connected to Macau by a long, tall bridge that the government had built to allow easier travel to and from the mainland. We took a taxi across this bridge, arriving there in less than an hour. Larry and I took her out to have Chinese tea at the local store in Lou Wan, where we sat and drank tea together, laughing over old times.

Ah Mg had first come to work for mother back in 1952, when my family lived in a first-floor apartment at 20 Wuhu Street in Hung Hum. At that time, mother was working eight hours a day at the Hong Kong and

Whampoa Dock Company Limited, very close to our apartment, to support her family. Our old nanny, Ah Yee, who had already been working for us for a short time, had received a different job opportunity elsewhere. She introduced us to Ah Mg; though her full name was Tsai Lai Wah, she was called "Mg Tsai," which in Cantonese means "number five," being named so because she was the fifth girl in her family. She came from a wealthy family from Canton. After Mg Tsai's parents died in World War II, she went to Hong Kong to rely on a relative and her relative's family. They lived in a small apartment that was 1200 square feet in total and separated into five rooms, with one family living in each room, and everyone sharing the same bathroom and kitchen. The living situation was not ideal for Mg Tsai; what was worse, however, was that this relative treated her like a slave, slapping and beating her. Mg Tsai could not support herself financially, so she was forced to stay with the relative and silently endure the abuse.

The housemate she was living with saw this abuse and quickly introduced Mg Tsai to a man from Macau, Mr. Law, hoping he could pull her out of her situation. Mg Tsai and Mr. Law soon got married, but he abused her as well. By the grace of God, her friend Ah Yee discovered her situation; when Ah Yee found a different job to support her daughter, Mg Tsai took her place. Mother liked Ah Mg very much. As she became a part of our family, her bond with mother grew; when she became a Catholic, my mother became her godmother. We were Mg Tsai's first job ever, but she worked with our family for her entire career; she helped me raise my elder daughter, and worked for my godmother and her friend for a few years. When Mg Tsai retired, she settled in her orchard in Macau, until she injured her foot and moved to the nursing home in Lou Wan.

Every day, when mother awoke before dawn, Ah Mg awoke with her and made sure to keep our house quiet and not to stir up any noises while mother prepared for work. Mother was a stock record clerk, which required her to work with figures constantly for a few hundred workers to get paid every two weeks. This meant that she needed to be well rested and alert every morning. She also needed time to prepare and perfect her appearance in order to maintain her authority. The high esteem and respect in which mother was held made it necessary for her to have an orderly and crisp appearance, which included everything from her clothes, to her hair and makeup, right down to her shoes and accessories. When mother walked out the door of our home every morning, Ah Mg would smile her encouragement of mother's trendiness and spotless, polished demeanor. From head to toe, mother was the image of grace, elegance, and beauty.

In the 1950s, women were still not allowed to wear pants to work; yet mother still found a way to look authoritative and elegant all at once. Every day for work, she would wear a special Chinese gown called a Cheung Sam. A Cheung Sam forms perfectly from neck to knee, with slits on both sides, and has a high-raised collar with two to four buttons, and a zip on the waist. They are not the dresses you would be able to buy at stores; they are custom-made by Shanghainese tailors, the most skilled tailors in the world for these kinds of dresses. After 1949, when the Communists began to occupy China, people from the very wealthy and modern city of Shanghai came over to Hong Kong to establish their businesses, and this is how the Shanghainese tailors' reputation grew among the people of Hong Kong. Their origin increased not only their value and significance, but also their beauty, as mother was well aware. Yet even the specialness of the gown was not enough for mother. She made sure that she matched these gowns with beautiful handbags and colorful high heels.

Mother's hair also always matched the orderliness and perfection of her clothes. Not a hair was ever out of place, and she was always in trend with the latest styles. Ah Mg reminded me of a time when I was in grade school and I wanted to get my hair done to look more fashionable, and mother went with me to get my first perm at her hair stylist. In those days, perms were the way all the fashionable male hair-stylists from Shanghai were styling women's hair. My mother's hair stylist put a first layer of rollers on, added papers with clips, then added perm liquid, and finally put on electric clippers. It was very heavy, weighing down like a ton of bricks on top of me. It took a long time to complete, not only because it was my first time getting one, but because my hair was thick and straight, making it difficult to style. By the time the perm was done, and the stylist had removed all the rollers, paper, clippers, and wire, I felt as light as a feather and looked very fashionable, just like my mother.

It was amazing how much mother was able to keep up with the latest styles in fashion and hairstyles when we had so little money to spend on things like clothes and trendy haircuts. It was not until I was older that I discovered she had managed to do this because she was incredibly frugal. She could bargain for as low as twenty to sixty percent at any place she shopped, from street hawkers to the big department stores. If she didn't find any clothing to her liking to bargain for, she would buy plenty of yarn for knitting her own clothes, a hobby that she loved to do. I could barely remember a time when she did not have her knitting in her hands.

Her diligence to her hobby gave all of her four children all the clothing that we would ever need. She knitted us vests, jackets with lining, shawls, hats, mittens, short skirts and long skirts, in wool, yarn, or mixed yarn. She sometimes made us tighter knit clothing that we wore under our clothes next to our underwear to prevent dirtiness. Mother did not even use a measuring tape when fitting us; she simply used her hands to measure our bodies. Usually, she was more accurate than the measuring tape; our clothes always fit each of us perfectly.

One of her favorite things to make us was sweaters. She could craft a sweater in any style; from V-neck, round-neck, turtleneck, complicated designs in cable crewneck, opened with big button-holes, or zip-front with small openings, she knitted all types of sweaters for us. As we grew older, she allowed us to help in any way we could; when she began knitting a new sweater, I used to help her to spin the yarn with my two hands, moving from the right and left sides alternately. She taught us to appreciate the

71

clothing she had made us, and how to take care of it properly. Our sweaters were only washed by hand after the winter was over, and she taught us to use special wool detergent in lukewarm water and rinse them many times until the water had no more bubbles. We could not place them in the sun to dry, because they would shrink. Instead, we would take the sweaters out of the water and hold them straight, squeezing but not wringing them out, so any excess water had drained. We then placed each sweater flat on a towel and rolled it up, so the sweater was inside, and then squeezed again. Any remaining water would be absorbed in the towel, and the sweater would not be shrunk or wrinkled. To this day, I still use this tactic on my children's and my own wool sweaters.

Mother was keenly aware of how much work went into crafting an excellent piece of clothing, and that was why she always took the utmost care in her appearance. As she examined herself critically in the mirror every morning, she made sure her Cheung Sam was fitted perfectly, and wrinkle-free. She would look over her hair and make sure every strand was combed and shined to perfection. When she stepped back and checked her appearance, she looked respectable and beautifully elegant.

Mother not only had a sharp eye for detail and trendiness, but she had a world traveler's perspective for clothes and looks. It was not just about looking good; it was important for her that her clothes, her hairstyles, even the food that she ate out at restaurants were diverse. On Sundays, when us children were often rowdy and wanted to enjoy the day off from school, Ah Mg would help us get ready for Sunday Mass in the Rosary Church in Tsui Sha Tsuen, where we attended Mass regularly. After Mass, mother would always invite us and Ah Mg to have Chinese tea. One time, we went to a European restaurant to have our tea. When I looked at the menu, I found out the dishes were very expensive. I murmured into my mother's ear, "Mom, the price is very expensive—are you sure you've got enough money?" Mother told me that if she did not have enough money, she would not have brought us here. "This is a once in a lifetime chance," she said. "Eat all you like." That was all my two brothers needed to hear. "We will untie our belts, Mom!" they said hungrily. Ah Mg had looked on with horror at my brothers' naughtiness, but my mother just laughed. After that meal, our stomachs were full and satisfied, and we were happy that mother had taken us to such a delicious meal. Mother's intention was to allow us to try more than just the typical Chinese cuisine we were used to.

It was a joy to talk about all of these wonderful memories of mother now with Ah Mg. After we finished our tea, we went back to Ah Mg's home to bid our goodbyes to her. As I gave her a big hug, I thanked her for sharing the stories about mother I had forgotten. Larry and I enjoyed the rest of our trip; on our last day in Macau, traveling on the ferry back to Hong Kong, I was so grateful for the time I was able to spend going back through my old childhood places. I knew that in mother's mind, some of these memories were just as bright and alive as I had experienced them today.

When Larry and I arrived home, I felt refreshed and invigorated. Happily, I gave mother a hug, and before telling her about my trip, I asked how things went without Larry and I around.

Mother paused. "It was quiet," she said. "Without Larry around, I had to tease Linda all by myself!"

Linda rolled her eyes like a good sport. I grinned widely. Nothing had changed. No major catastrophe had suddenly happened in my absence. Linda showed me the logbook and how there had been no change in mother's vitals. I breathed the biggest sigh of relief possible. I had made the right decision in taking that short vacation. We all needed some time apart, and now we were all happy to be back together.

Mother had clearly missed our company (Larry especially of course), and our first few days back with fun, with lots of conversation. I took mother through her photo book and pointed out places I had visited in Macau. She nodded and listened as I spoke, sometimes adding in details and missing pieces.

After Larry and I shared all of our stories with mother and Linda, it was time to get back to work. I was eager to see how mother had been while I was gone. When Linda updated me on the recordings in our logbook, we noticed something very clear. Our numbers showed that although mother was remaining steady, she was not showing any significant progress. Although our routines maintained mother's health, now that mother knew what to expect every day, her mind and body had become too used to our daily tasks, and they were quickly losing their initial impact.

I was glad we had recorded all of this information so far in our logbook, because this told us something very important about mother's health. Mother had now reached a threshold. If she simply remained steady like this, it was very likely that she could slip backwards and regress instead of progress. Therefore, we were at a crucial point in our efforts; it was time to do more now to help mother move forward instead of risking sliding backwards.

Enhancing mother's fine motor skills became my first task. I recalled that Ms. Mok had said that stroke victims often have the greatest difficulty gaining back their fine motor skills, and things like picking up small objects or even holding a pen in your hand to write might never again be possible. I planned to do this by incorporating more small but challenging tasks for mother to do directly into our daily routines.

I came up with a very small activity that would help mother quite a bit. I would have mother write down both the prayer she had been saying at mealtime since last year, and the names of all the food on her plate. This was an easy way to strengthen her hand coordination, writing abilities, and her memory all at once.

So one night at dinner, very early in the year, Linda and I were each sitting next to mother, with our folding table spread out between us all, our dinner steaming in front of us. Mother had just recited her usual prayer. From across the table, Linda pushed a piece of paper and a pen toward mother and asked her to write the prayer.

Without a word, mother grasped the pen confidently in her right hand. Her grip on the pen was firm as she carefully wrapped her fingers around it. Slowly, she touched the pen to the paper and began to draw the traditional Chinese characters of the prayer.

I could see her mind working hard. When she wrote, mother knew only the traditional forms of Chinese writing that had been set in place since colonial times, before the rise of Mao Zedong in the 1950s. Beginning with Chairman Mao's desire to simplify those traditional forms, and more recently with so many mainland Chinese tourists coming to Hong Kong, these characters are adopting more contemporary forms that are easier to write. Mother of course wasn't accustomed to these new forms, and wrote only what she knew and had grown up with. This would give her even more practice in using the strength of her memory as well her hands; in the traditional form, the Chinese spoken language differs from the written characters.

But even translating thought to paper, mother wrote the prayer with no problem. Linda and I looked at each other and smiled. The strength of her fingers was a fantastic sight to our eyes.

Linda turned the paper over and asked her to describe the food on her plate. This was no problem for mother; she always inspected her meal carefully with her supreme x-ray vision. She furrowed her brow and studied her plate carefully, peering at every morsel on it with the concentration of a scientist.

Her plate was a colorful blend of fresh foods, rich in healthy vitamins and omega-3 fatty acids, following the diet I had placed her on last year. Ah Fan had been cooking mother a nice variety of these healthy foods in traditional Chinese dishes since last year. In the morning, mother would usually have fresh juice, and any combination of sesame pudding, oatmeal, egg whites, and raisins. Sometimes, she would have "thousand-year-old eggs," a Chinese dish that is either preserved duck, chicken, or quail eggs made in a mixture of clay, ash, salt, and rice hulls and preserved for several weeks. These were a delicacy, and were a real treat for mother. Three times a week, we fed her black fungus soup to prevent blood clots. We also gave her plenty of pumpkin soup and other pumpkin dishes to maintain her vitamins.

For dinner, mother would always request her favorite dish: delicious, tasty fish. Mother loved all types of fish; dried oysters were a favorite, as was eel; she usually consumed eel with other meat like lean pork, or vegetables, like carrots or beans, or sometimes just on its own without any other meat or vegetables. The fish that I always had Ah Fan buy was fresh, meaning it was still alive when she brought it home. Ah Fan would steam it in a wok and prepare it with fresh ginger and scallions, which would remove the fishy odor, and leave us with nothing but a delectable feast. When we ate, mother took her time in eating every single bite. First, she ate the fresh steamed fish by itself, then her vegetable, and only about two mouthfuls of cooked rice. Every bite to her was a delicacy; every taste bud on her tongue savored every morsel that danced in her mouth.

Most of these foods were easy for mother to eat. They were beneficial to get her used to chewing and swallowing normally again after her feeding tube and the congee. But now that she had improved so much, to challenge her motor skills further, we began to give her more complex food that she would need to work at. We had first given her a delicious treat: chicken wings. Chicken wings in China differ greatly from American chicken wings; in America, chicken wings are gobbled up by people at fast food restaurants on a daily basis. In China, however, they are a delicacy to have. We don't eat the tip or drumsticks, but rather just the middle portion. When mother devoured these wings, her hand held them firmly as she brought them up to her mouth, and her mouth and tongue worked together to take in every bit of the wing she could.

We had then given her one of her favorite foods: sugar cane. In China, there are two kinds of sugar cane: one that has a thick, green skin that is commonly used for juicing, and another with a deep brown skin that is often used for skin moisturizer. Mother used to have the green-skinned kind when she was a young girl, but it took quite a bit of time to eat, since you had to peel it and use the strength of your teeth to get to the juices inside. Now, at eighty-five years old, mother could take a piece of peeled sugar cane and use her strong teeth to chomp on it and suck all the juices out with the muscles in her mouth, just as easily as she did when she was young. It was a joy to watch her smile with delight as she enjoyed every last drop of juice from the sugar.

Seeing mother advance to eating these new foods now made me happy that we had come a long way from that terrible feeding tube dangling from her nose. With these new challenges to her diet, I made sure that we regulated everything that she ate and drank, in order to see how it affected her temperature, blood pressure, and all her bodily systems.

Tonight, as mother finished examining her food and wrote everything down, she signed her name to the paper, and smiled at Linda and me. Linda and I exchanged satisfied glances as we looked over what mother had written. Her penmanship was good, and she had accurately recorded all the correct names of her food. We knew that we could successfully incorporate this activity into our routine at every mealtime.

I was beyond pleased with the success mother was showing. The next step I wanted to take was to do something now that rewarded her for all the hard work she was doing. I didn't want to do anything too big, just something a little out of the ordinary to stir up a little enthusiasm and make mother feel confident and happy, and boost her spirits. This type of environment for mother would actually help to stimulate her brain function.

So I came up with another idea: I decided to celebrate every Chinese holiday on the calendar. This would be a great way to give mother some pleasure without breaking our daily rituals. Not since my childhood had we celebrated the traditional Chinese holidays; back then, mother had made every holiday fun and exciting for us. Now it was my turn to do the same for her.

I told Linda about my idea, and she nodded happily in agreement. I grabbed a nearby calendar and began flipping through it, circling the dates of all the holidays we had celebrated when I was a child. The first was easy, because it was right around the corner. On January 22, we would celebrate the Chinese New Year. The New Year was one of our favorite holidays we used to celebrate in my childhood. There was so much involved in the holiday that we would have plenty of opportunities to put some fun into mother's daily rituals. I had a lot of planning to do, so I immediately set to work.

The Chinese New Year is well known throughout the world for being a wonderful and extravagant celebration. It sets itself apart from other New Year's celebrations around the world for many reasons. First, we do not celebrate the New Year on January 1, because unlike other countries in the world, we do not follow the 365-day Gregorian calendar, which has 365 days a year. Instead, we follow a lunisolar calendar, meaning each month follows one cycle of the moon, which in total lasts about 354 days. A new year in the Chinese calendar begins on the second new moon after the winter solstice, and for this reason, the New Year does not fall on the same date every year.

The lunar calendar also matches to animal signs—the year of the monkey, the year of the tiger, and so on. This is called the Chinese Zodiac, and it is based on a twelve-year cycle with twelve animals rotating - the rat, ox, tiger, rabbit, dragon, snake, horse, sheep, monkey, rooster, dog and pig. Traditional Chinese belief is that the characteristics of each animal are the characteristics that most people will have during that year, including both strengths and weaknesses. The ox, for example, is a persistent, simple, and honest animal but is also stubborn and poor at communication; people born in the year of the ox will embody these same good and bad characteristics. I noticed on the calendar that 2004 was the year of the monkey. Positive traits for people in this year are cleverness, intelligence, and liveliness. I took this as yet another positive sign for us; mother certainly had all of those qualities.

Another difference in our New Year is the length of time we celebrate. Our New Year does not last for a single night, like many other countries around the world; in Hong Kong, we officially celebrate for three full days. Mainland China, however, spends ten days celebrating, and for some, the festivities go on for one full month. Traditionally, the whole country shuts down to host all the festivities, though in recent years many businesses some of the restaurants, and movie theaters have remained opened to increase their income.

There are many New Year traditions that every family takes part in. First, before the New Year, every household has a good cleaning to get rid of all the bad luck collected in the past year. Once the cleaning is done, on the first day of the celebrations, no one sweeps the floor, in order to prevent sweeping away all the new luck. Next, enough food must be prepared to last three days; according to Chinese tradition, using a knife during the first days of the New Year "cuts off" good luck. The large meal that is eaten on New

Year's Day is composed of dishes with names that will bring good luck for everyone at the table, such as "Broth of Prosperity" or "Silver Threads of Longevity." On mainland China, some families have meat dumplings as their traditional food, and some cook the dumplings with copper coins right in them to bring luck.

On New Year's Eve, across every city, firecrackers, loud drumming, and clashing cymbals welcome in the New Year. In the streets, lion dancers, which are major symbols of ushering in good luck for the coming year, perform exquisite shows. Young men from a local martial arts school hide under an elaborate lion costume and through their movements make the lion jump around, lie down, roll over, and rear up on its hind legs. As they are dancing, other people from the school beat on large drums and gongs. Many people invite lion dancers to come to their homes or shops to perform; per tradition, some will hang a bunch of lettuce or some fruit, as well as a red-colored packet, high up on a stick. As the lion "eats" the food and the red packet and spits out the peel of the fruit, the owner of the home or shop will throw firecrackers at the lion; the cracking fire makes the lion jump or dance to avoid the firecrackers.

While the celebrations are going on in the streets, people gather at the homes of friends and relatives to indulge in their succulent feast. Older or married couples give children and unwed adults red envelopes with money inside called "lay see." By the end of the holiday, the children will get quite a bit of money from parents, grandparents, aunts, uncles and other relatives. People also give certain fruits or candies that symbolize peace and goodwill. The apple is our traditional symbol of peace; the orange is our symbol for gold; and candies symbolize love. At home, each family prepares a tray of symbolic goodies, including watermelon seeds dyed red, to represent earning more money (and which are very hard to open); sweet lotus seeds for newlywed couples, to symbolize hope for conceiving a child in the coming year; candied kumquats, also symbolizing gold; and candied lotus root, representing the connective power of love.

After all gifts are given and bellies are full from the delicious dinner, everyone will gather together to play games. The most popular game played is the ancient Chinese tile game of Mahjong. Many Americans may be familiar with the game through computerized versions, but the history of the game can be traced well back to the latter part of 1890 in the area of Ning Bo, China, from where it soon spread throughout China, with different regions adopting its own unique set of rules. Mahjong is a game that involves skill, strategy, and calculation, as well as a certain degree of chance. The basic Mahjong set consists of 144 tiles in total, plus a wind indicator and 3 dice. The 144 tiles have different designs on them in different categories; the first categories include types of bamboo, different circles, and words, and each of these three categories have ten tiles each. There are also tiles with the four winds, east, west, north, and south; lastly, there are tiles with flowers for spring, summer, autumn, and winter. Four players sit at four corners of a square table and put the 144 tiles upside down on a square table, so that no one can see the descriptions. Then, players roll the dice on the table to see who has the east wind; whoever has it will be the first person to make their move. Although the game is ancient, it is still very popular in Asian countries today, especially on New Year's Eve. Families will sit at large tables and play long into the night until the New Year comes, adding the noises of tiles and laughter to stir up the celebration.

Our own small celebration this year would not be as loud or lavish as the ones on the streets of the cities, but they would be just as significant. I was going to do my best to uphold all the Chinese New Year traditions that we had all grown up with to keep mother's spirits high. Linda and I worked hard to scrub and clean and make our home beautiful for mother. Linda and I decided to forgive mother's healthy diet for the celebrations, and Ah Fan prepared a delicious feast. On our New Year's Eve, after we had finished dinner, the look on mother's face told me that she couldn't wait to play Mahjong. Mahjong is mother's favorite game; it was one of the few games that challenged mother's high intelligence. When she was younger, in between working and taking care of her four children, playing Mahjong was often the only enjoyment she had. She would occasionally play with her colleagues, or get our family members and guests to play it at weddings and birthday parties. Most of the time, however, she played with my seventh, fourteenth, and sixteenth aunties at the home of my seventh auntie. I remember that they would play so late that I would fall asleep on the couch in the other room and wake up to the sound of mother's cheerful voice as the tiles clicked and clacked on the table. Not surprisingly, then, Mahjong had become one of the most frequent games Linda and I played with mother every afternoon to help improve her memory. Tonight, as we played, the celebrations went on with loud cheer outside our window; when I looked at mother's happy expressions, I knew there was just as much joy inside our cozy and comfortable little home.

The following morning, of the first day of the New Year, mother awoke with a smile. The first thing that each family member says to each other on the day of the New Year are good wishes and wise words. There are different good wishes and words of advice for different relationships; we wish different blessings on adults than we do on children or older couples, or even businesses. The most common wish, "kong hai fa choi," is for people to have lots of money. When I was little, I rarely heard this come out of mother's mouth; her wishes for others were always of good health, happiness, peace, and love. Today, when we awoke, I wished mother all of those wonderful things. She grinned and wished me the same. Shortly after breakfast, we received a festive call from my thoughtful daughter Iris, who never missed calling on birthdays or holidays. I smiled to myself as I watched mother chat excitedly on the phone with Iris.

The New Year's had been a soaring success. It had stirred up wonderful excitement in our household, and over the next few days, that excitement lingered and did exactly what I was hoping it would do by giving us all an extra jolt of energy as we returned to our daily life. Mother had responded positively to all of our celebrations, and she seemed exhilarated by it all, responding now to her exercises and other activities with increased vigor and an incredibly upbeat spirit.

On January 28, during her usual visit, Ms. Mok provided me with more excellent advice. She said it was a good idea to decorate the room with more colors to help mother pay more attention to her surroundings. She also advised me that our conversations should be soft and not loud around mother to make sure she is not overstimulated. Also, if our weather was cold, we could give mother a warm small towel to make sure she was comfortable. I took note of all of this advice, and immediately began to plan ways to make mother's room more bright and colorful.

A few days later, on February 3, we had a wonderful surprise: Larry's son Mark came to visit us all. We were so happy to see him. It was a short visit, but we took him sightseeing all around Hong Kong, and we had a great time.

On February 4, mother was scheduled to attend a party at the Ming Sum Lau Clinic. The party was specifically for dementia patients. To make sure mother felt festive and special, we had custom designed a lovely red and green apron and hat for her to wear, just for the occasion. Linda and I made sure to complement mother more than usual as we dressed her that morning, to make sure she knew it was a special day. At the party that afternoon, I was happy to see that mother's true personality immediately came through, just as it always did when she was in a large group of people. She was incredibly upbeat, laughing and talking with everyone around her. She participated with joy and vigor in all the activities. It was a wonderful afternoon for all of us.

As the party came to a close, the clinic workers announced they were handing out some prizes to each patient. To our delight, mother won a prize for dressing festively for the party. As the clinic workers brought the prize over to us, before Linda or I could take it, mother immediately extended her good arm and firmly gripped the prize in her hand. She beamed widely and held the prize up, while the clinic workers clapped for her.

For the first time since her diagnosis of dementia, mother was demonstrating a genuine sense of self-awareness of her own progress. As she held up her prize and smiled, mother displayed not only full recognition but pride in herself of her achievement.

Linda and I both whooped for mother, and clapped hard alongside everyone else in the room. When I told Ms. Mok about how proud mother looked that day, she reminded me what an important step this was for mother. One of the symptoms of both stroke and dementia patients was a denial of their illness. But now, mother showed full recognition and even personal pride in her progress. After all we had done, all of our routines and activities, our encouragement of mother, it was finally becoming clear now that it was all working. I was so ecstatic at mother's progress; our efforts so far this year were succeeding beyond my expectations.

In the days and weeks after the party, the new change in mother was now evident. She continued to work through her exercises daily at her own pace, but the difference now was that confidence in herself was skyrocketing.

In every one of our daily activities, she began to show more and more awareness and pride in her accomplishments. Linda and I encouraged mother all along the way, knowing that our encouragement continued to fuel mother's motivation. Some days I could not believe that mother had reached this threshold and then surpassed it; then I reminded myself who mother was. I knew that true to her character, mother would continue to exceed all expectations set for her, like the extraordinary woman she was.

A little over one month later, on March 23, Linda frantically called to me from the living room. I rushed in to see what was happening.

Mother was stretched out on her bed in the living room. She was shaking uncontrollably from head to toe. Her mouth was shut tight, and her lips were bleeding. Her eyes were wide open, but she showed no recognition of anything in front of her.

I knew what this was. This was the same type of convulsions mother had experienced after her stroke.

"Linda!" I said firmly. "Get the water bottles."

In the blink of an eye, Linda rushed to the kitchen and grabbed bottles of frozen water we had stored in the freezer. She brought them to me, and we stood by mother, firmly placing every bottle against her exposed skin.

I gritted my teeth, holding the bottles as determinedly as I could against mother's shuddering body. Linda did the same. Gradually, mother's body stopped shaking. Her eyes closed, her fingers unclenched, her mouth opened, and all the muscles in her body relaxed. Linda and I removed the water bottles and waited for a moment. Mother opened her eyes. She could not speak for a few moments, but I could see in her eyes that she had no recollection of what had just happened.

I had known what it was the minute I saw mother's poor body shaking uncontrollably. I knew that there was always a chance that the convulsions could return, but this still came as a shock to us. Mother had been progressing so well; this convulsion had come upon her with no warning. But I had also been prepared and knew what to do immediately, thanks to an Indonesian woman I had met. She told me that her husband suddenly had a convulsion one day while they were sitting behind their house. The woman had been washing clothes with very cold water from their well. All of a sudden, her husband's body began shaking uncontrollably, and when the woman immediately ran over to check on her husband, she put her cold hands on him, and the convulsion suddenly stopped from the shock of the cold. Because of this reason, she shared her experience so that others could benefit. When I had explained this method to mother's doctor, he told me that it is actually a good idea, and it was important to use whatever method it takes to stop the convulsion, as long as it can be used wisely. I then stocked frozen water bottles in our freezer, just in case we would have to use the same tactic on mother.

I couldn't believe we now actually had to use it. Even though this was the quickest and most effective way for us to stop the convulsion, I felt

80

as though Linda and I were cruelly giving her electro-shock therapy. I wondered if the one convulsion was simply an isolated incident; perhaps it was simply a freak delayed effect. Over the next few days after the convulsion, mother returned to normal, almost as if nothing had happened. She showed no signs of remembering it; her vitals did not change over the next few days, and she showed no lasting effects either physically or mentally. I hoped that that was it.

But, two weeks later, on April 6, it happened again. At 4:20am, mother had a big one. On this early morning, Linda was sleeping next to mother, just behind her bed, and Ah Fan slept on the other side of the room. When mother's convulsion began, Linda awoke immediately and turned mother sideways, removing her pillow. Linda yelled to me; Ah Fan and I awoke and went without delay to get the icy bottles. We patted these on three areas of her body, from her face, down to her hands and legs. It was hard to see mother suffering, with her teeth grinding together with an awful grating noise; her body sweat profusely and urine went uncontrollably through her diaper.

In total, that convulsion lasted twenty minutes, making it one of her worst convulsions she had ever experienced. I wrote down everything that had happened in our logbook and took the book to mother's next two follow-up appointments, one on April 13 at 9am at Ming Sum Lau for updates on her neurological condition, and one the following day at 3:30pm at Tuen Muen Hospital for updates on the continued effects from her stroke.

The doctors examined mother at length in both appointments. I showed them every recorded number and vital in our logbook, I was hoping they could find a pattern that I had somehow missed, some clue that would have let us know that this would happen. But the doctors told me that there was simply no answer. It was just a common occurrence in people who have had strokes.

The effects after this big convulsion were long-lasting. Mother became exhausted in a way I had never seen before. Her doctors put her on convulsion pills for four days starting on April 15, which added to her tiredness. For the next two whole weeks, she spent her days mostly laying on her bed sleeping. When Ms. Mok came for her visit, we discussed the convulsion, and she showed us how to put a wooden stick into mother's mouth to help stop her from biting her tongue. Mrs. Cheung also came to inject her with vitamin B6 and B complex in the hopes of energizing her a bit.

Mr. Lau, the occupational therapist, and Mr. Chan, the physical therapist, continued to come twice a week to help continue mother's exercises, which she still needed to do as she recovered. Since mother slept so much, we now had to wake her up every time it was time to do her exercises. Getting her awake was the easy part; when it came time to do the exercises, mother was now very sluggish. Sometimes it was as if she had never done them. This entire process took much longer now than it had before; since we exercised five times per day with mother, almost immediately after we finished one round, we would move on to the next one.

81

This was the worst possible setback for us in what had been otherwise a steady several months of progress for mother so far this year. It was as if we had been pushing a large boulder up a steep hill very slowly, only to reach the top and have it begin to roll backwards again. This instantly brought down the entire dynamic of our household. What was a bright and lively environment only a few days ago suddenly once again became a place of slow clockwork. As positive as Linda and I were trying to be around mother, it was difficult when everything that was once fun and lively suddenly seemed fatigued.

The weather did not help either; it was a very hot and humid summer that year in Hong Kong, and all of us seemed to be drained of energy. However, there were some days when the weather would cooperate, and the humidity would drop. On these days, Linda and I would take advantage of the weather and would take mother out for walks in her wheelchair around our building after breakfast, just like we had done last year. We wanted to coax mother slowly out of her exhaustion and let the sunlight hopefully renew some of the energy she needed.

At this time of the year, the shady paths outside our apartment were filled with beautiful flora, lined with tall purple flowering trees also called Bauhinia blakeana, or the Hong Kong orchid tree. This is a tree with large thick leaves and striking purplish red flowers, usually ten to fifteen centimeters across. They bloomed most vividly from November to late March, and were very fragrant. Mother loved these flowers, and as we strolled along the paths, we often took pictures with mother in her wheelchair sitting in front of these trees and their beautiful flowers. The sun would shine very brightly at that time of day, so I always put a black hat on mother to prevent the sun from getting in her eyes.

In the nicer weather now, the young families with children were out and about playing around. As we walked along, mother would always want to stop and watch them play. As the weeks passed, slowly she became more active, talkative, and happy; sometimes she would want to stop and talk to the parents and compliment them on how cute their children were. The more we took these walks, the more mother gradually became animated.

A couple of weeks later, on Easter Sunday, when Linda and I took mother outside for our usual walk, I noticed that she seemed more energized than usual. There were plenty of children and families outside, some all dressed up in their Easter best, presumably going off to church. As I pushed mother along, she grinned at nearly every child, and said hello to all the parents. Mother even stopped to have a conversation with a few young couples, and told them their children were absolutely adorable. They all thanked mother and wished her a very happy Easter, which pleased her greatly.

Next to Christmas, Easter was mother's favorite holiday. Much like the New Year, Easter is a very important holiday in Hong Kong, and everything shuts down during Easter Holy Week, or the week before Easter, while everyone celebrates. Catholics, like us, would go to church daily to remember how Jesus suffered, was tortured, and died on the cross for us, and was resurrected on the third day. On Maundy Thursday, we would go to church to commemorate the Last Supper, and on Good Friday, we would go to commemorate the crucifixion and death of Jesus. On Pentecost Sunday, we would go to church to celebrate Jesus' rising and His life everlasting. Mother always made sure we went to church, but our favorite part of Easter was after church on Sunday, when mother would take us to go visit her godparents, Mrs. Ho and her husband, Dr. Ho Tin Sung, who lived in a big, Western-style house on top of a hill on Homantin Road, overlooking Mongkok City. They had eight children, all of whom were highly educated, and spoke both English and Cantonese. We would arrive at their home in the afternoon after attending church in the morning, and would first have tea and delicious biscuits with them. Then, all of us children would grab a basket and go outside to hunt for well-hidden Easter eggs. We would have a blast, running around wildly in the yard, searching behind the bushes, under the trees, and around the outside of the house. My sister Agnes always came with me, so I usually let her find the eggs. After we removed the silver or colored wrap, we found that the eggs were chocolate underneath! After our hunt, Mrs. Ho would give us each a large chocolate bunny and other gifts before we headed home. I was close to Mrs. Ho's youngest daughter, who was almost the same age as me; sometimes, if we stayed very late, mother allowed me to stay at their home overnight, and she would pick me up the following day. It always warmed mother's heart to see her wonderful godparents and her own children all in the same place.

These walks and conversations with other people outside in the sunny weather did their job by renewing some of mother's energy. As the summer months came upon us, her personality began to come through again; now, when we saw our neighbors out along the pathway, she had no trouble immediately striking up a conversation with them. This cheerful mood also helped boosted her physical health; her heartbeat and blood pressure were stabilized. She was not at the level in her health she was at before she had the convulsions, but all of this positivity was still a very good sign.

When it became too hot to take mother outside for a walk and talk with people every day, I tentatively began to allow a few more visitors to our apartment. I knew I would have to monitor each visit carefully, watching how mother would react; I did not want to do anything that would cause too much overstimulation and possibly trigger another convulsion.

Mother was very excited to see her nieces and nephew from her number six and seven twin sisters, Suk Ching and Kit Ching. On June 19, Suk Ching and her husband Law Wing Kwong's children Yan Wai and Yan Chi visited my mother at 8:30pm. They both worked long hours, and lived far away on the other side of the New Territories; it was gracious of them to drive such a long distance after a long, tiring day after work to see mom.

83

The next day, mother had a visit from her nephew Moses, Kit Ching's son, and his wife Kin Chun. Moses and Kin Chun came to visit quite often, which showed just how much Moses cared for mother, since they lived in Kowloon, quite a long journey from where we were. Whenever Moses visited, mother's smile would light up the room as they chatted happily. Moses would jog mother's memory by reminding her of when she used to bring them to get ice cream and toys when he was young, and he always thanked her for her generosity. Before they left, they would pray a very short but effective prayer in front of mother, which pleased her greatly. Their visits were always too short for mother, but they were very busy with their own active life in Kowloon, so it was always a special treat when they came.

Kit Ching and Suk Ching were wonderful women, always very friendly, smiling, and very happy. I remember Kit Ching as being shorter than my mother; but she made up for her lack of height in her outgoing personality. They would always tell me that when my mother and I lived with her parents in Tai Po Market during the Japanese War, the two of them would always help out my mother in caring for me (even though whenever she picked me up, I always pulled at their long braids). Kit Ching married a kind, gentle young man named Daniel (Chan Chak Kai). He was blessed with good hands, and could fix anything electronic with his magic touch. Their love was pure, and they were very frugal in saving money for their future. They didn't mind living in a 200-square-foot room, sharing a bathroom and a kitchen with other tenants, when they were a young couple. Since they were so frugal, they soon had enough money to make a down payment for an apartment at the National Court on Nathan Road in Kowloon. From there, their family flourished, and they had three children altogether: Moses, Paul, and Patricia. We always called Patricia "Lung Ngai," the name of a fruit that had big black seeds, because her beautiful eyes resembled this seed.

Mother was happy and energized seeing her twin sisters' families. After their visits, mother continued to show encouraging signs of better health. In the mornings, she now awoke with more alertness, showed a good appetite throughout the day, and completed her exercises with greater energy.

I wanted to maintain this progress, so I decided to celebrate another upcoming holiday. We hadn't celebrated anything since the New Year, which seemed like ages ago. The Dragon Boat Festival was coming up quickly on June 22, which was perfect; we could celebrate with lots of food and quiet fun.

The Dragon Boat Festival honors the life of the ancient Chinese poet and statesman Wut Yuan. During his life, Wut Yuan was a loyal minister of the King of Chu, but was falsely accused of conspiracy against the King because of his intelligence. The King betrayed Wut Yuan's loyalty, and exiled him, during which time he composed many poems expressing his sorrow for the Chu villagers who lived under such tyranny. In 278 BCE, at the age of 61, Wut Yuan attached a large stone to his chest and drowned himself in the Miluo River. The villagers were devastated, and took their boats onto the river and attempted to find him. They also threw cooked rice into the river to dissuade the fish from eating Wut Yuan's body. They also began the tradition of making dumplings in the hopes that the dumplings were heavy enough to sink to the bottom of the river and reach Wut Yuan's body. The Dragon Boat Festival celebrates all these rescue efforts. Today, people eat rice dumplings and insert meat, salty egg yolk, soy beans or green beans during the festival in remembrance of Wut Yuan. The highlight of the celebrations is the dragon boat races, in which up to eighteen rowers paddle together in long, narrow boats with a carved dragon's head at one end and a tail at the other. A leader shouts directions and sets the rhythm for the rowers using a large drum, making the races very noisy and exciting.

Of course, we could not attend any of the very loud races, but we would celebrate in our own way by making delicious homemade dumplings with salty pork, salty duck yolk, soaked green beans, and raw sticky rice. I took the opportunity to put mother's fine motor skills to work: we put all the ingredients out onto the table, and mother, Linda, Ah Fan, and I sat at the table to put them together. Mother would use her good hand to pick up the yolk with a spoon, and would remind us only to use half of the egg yolk to reduce cholesterol. She even had the motor control to use chopsticks to pick up the beans. Then we would wrap them together in narrow leaves that we bundled and tied together with few straws, would cook them on high for three hours. The dumplings were so delicious that we finished most of them even before the festival began!

I could tell mother really enjoyed our small but fun celebration. Her mood remained upbeat and her health steady and stable, and the atmosphere in our home remained alive with energy in the days following the festival.

Then on June 27, as I was getting mother ready for her exercises, I noticed that something seemed different in her. While she had been slowly gathering more energy with every passing day, today she seemed to have even more energy than usual. I suspected she was still feeling great after our festivities. As we went through most of our normal exercises, mother did everything perfectly. When it came time to exercise her legs and toes, I decided to try something a little more difficult. I asked mother if she wanted to try something new today, and she agreed easily.

Immediately, I called Ah Fan in to help us out. Linda stood on one side of mother and Ah Fan on the other, both of them supporting mother under her arms. Quickly, I scanned the room and made a mental pathway for us.

"Are you ready, mom?" I said.

She nodded.

"Let's go, then," I said.

Slowly, mother moved her legs off the bed and put her two feet flat on the floor. Linda and Ah Fan helped her rise, holding her gently but

85

firmly. Mother lifted her back as upright as she could; soon, she was standing up! As soon as she was standing as straight as she could, mother put one foot out in front of her. Then another. Then another.

There, in front of our eyes, the impossible had happened – mother was walking!

I let out a whoop of joy. I couldn't believe it! What an amazing feat!

Slowly and steadily, with Linda and Ah Fan right by her side and me in front of her, mother walked straight across the room. When she reached the doorway of my bedroom, we turned around and mother walked right back again. Gently, Ah Fan and Linda helped mother sit back down. Mother had barely sat down again when we all hugged her and congratulated her. She smiled back at us, fully aware and proud of her accomplishment.

Linda and I were so overwhelmed with joy at this miracle that afterward we marked a record in our logbook as an incredibly special day. I snapped a photo of mother as she walked to remember how amazing she was.

This was simply extraordinary. A year ago, mother had been paralyzed on the entire left side of her body. Only a few months ago, she had convulsions that had set her progress back significantly. Both times, the doctors had not held out much hope for any recovery. But they did not know my mother's intense strength and determination. I recalled that one day back in March of last year, when Mrs. Tsang, the special physical therapist, had told me for the first time that mother might someday be able to walk again. Well, that day was here! It had happened.

The following week, on July 2, mother's occupational therapist, David Lau, brought his boss, nurse and others to witness mother's outstanding progress. It was incredibly rare for a recovering stroke victim to improve from losing all ability in one half of their body to being able to move and walk again with two people supporting her. And yet, mother had done it. After every bit of work we had done, all the therapy mother had undergone, the exercises we did with her every day, our prayers, all the ups and downs that we had gone through this year alone—all of this was living proof that hard work, patience, personal encouragement, and sheer resilience really paid off.

CHAPTER 6

As the summer went on, the weather became too hot and humid to go outside much. In between her daily exercises, I needed other indoor activities to keep mother busy. Sometimes I would take her downstairs if our building was having any events. If there were no events, mother liked to stay in our cooler home and watch television. Watching television was not wasted time for mother; while typical dementia patients have difficulty following storylines, mother had improved so much that she could easily follow everything on the programs. She would usually tell the characters on television who had a lot of life struggles that she had been through much worse. If the programs got mother too riled up, I would shut the television off after only one or two shows.

When the television was off and no events on the calendar, I would do my favorite activity with mother: look through old photographs in her photo books and let her tell me the stories of her past. To my mother, her past was not collected in photographs and scrapbooks; these were only the reminders that signaled the greater story. My mother's past was real for her, alive and vibrant, replaying over and over again in her mind every day, like a film that never ended. The stories that she remembered could not be shut off with the flick of a switch; they were ingrained in the deepest parts of her heart, like roots to an old tree. To the visitors dropping in, her stories and recollections may have served only for entertainment, or their own brief remembrance of a different time, soon to be forgotten again as they left and would go on with their own busy lives. For mother, though, these stories served as her lifeline to the people who cared deeply for her. These stories and memories gave us brief glimpses into the parts of her mind and heart where only her deepest emotions lay—the loss, sorrow, and, most importantly, her bold, unbreakable love.

My mother, Chu Yi Ching (Anna is her baptized name), was born on August 28, 1917, in Tai Po Market in Hong Kong. Her father was Chu Tak Hing, a respected Clerical Officer in the Hong Kong government's Land Department, and her mother was Wong Lai Ching, a kind and generous midwife.

My mother's parents placed a high value on education from an early age. Raised in a strict yet caring Christian household, my mother in her youth showed signs of exceptional intelligence, and was well-prepared for her schooling even before she entered formal education. She was fortunate enough to attend an average school for a period of time in Tai Po Market, but it soon became clear that her sharp intelligence distinguished her from the other boys and girls in her class.

After she completed primary school, she was one of the few students accepted by St. Mary's Canossian College, a Catholic girl's school in Tsim Sha Tsui, Kowloon, which prepared its students to advance onto university. During that time in Hong Kong, school tuition was very expensive, taking up about one-third of a family's income. Many parents could not even afford to send their children. Parents who did pay for school were not usually very wealthy, and sacrificed a great deal to afford it. Young girls had an even more difficult challenge; it was rare for girls to attend school at all, and those who did would sometimes have to travel long distances to attend a good school. Some parents only allowed their daughters to study at a local school for three to five years before getting married. In many cases, girls married before they even graduated high school.

My mother luckily was not one of those girls. She learned at an early age to be self-sufficient and the importance of sacrifice. St. Mary's location was far away from my grandparents' home. Every morning before dawn, my mother took the first train from Tai Po Market to the Tsim Sha Tsui train station by herself and after a lengthy train ride, she walked half an hour the remainder of the way to school. Very often, she traveled on an empty stomach, having no time or means to eat breakfast in the morning, and thus was forced to wait until noon to have her lunch from the cafeteria. Though she often went hungry, she never once complained to my grandparents. She was smart enough to know how fortunate she was.

It was during mother's daily travel from her home in Tai Po Market to St. Mary's that she met her friend Kwok Wing Shui. Both of them were about the same age, but Wing Shui was studying at one of the famous Chinese schools, Lai Chack, founded in 1929. Although they attended different schools, they would talk with each other every morning on their way, and a solid friendship soon formed.

Although St. Mary's was a far travel for mother, she knew how lucky she was to attend. At this time in the 1930s, Chinese values were beginning to change. The increased exposure to Western culture challenged many Chinese traditions, especially the role of women. Mother came of age in this exciting time of transitions; all around her, the clashes between older and younger generations were slowly becoming apparent, in everything from fashion to music to education. Mother was lucky to have such fair-minded parents. Although they were still traditional in many aspects, they believed in education above all else. New, progressive values at high-ranking schools would allow mother's high intelligence to be fully recognized. Mother therefore became part of the first generation of Chinese women who were educated at top-rated, Westernized schools, like St. Mary's.

While at St. Mary's, my mother excelled in all her subjects. She became fluent in both Chinese and English, as all subjects were taught in both languages. Her best subject, was math. Her mathematical skills developed far beyond the level of her classmates, and her diligence was noticed and respected by both her teachers and her peers. Mother's teachers allowed her to often become a substitute teacher to correct her classmates' homework.

St. Mary's progressive embracing of Western culture also allowed mother to try activities that many of her peers at different schools could not.

While her female friends spent hours in front of the mirror leaning how to apply make-up, mother was outside partaking in the recreational activities that allowed her to use all of her bright energy. She played Westernized sports, like soccer, right alongside the boys outside of school, and taught herself how to swim; she loved the thrill of adventure in sports, and once even dangerously dove off a very high cliff straight into the water.

While mother still embraced many of the traditional Chinese activities for girls, including dancing and playing the piano, which she taught herself, these new activities allowed her bold, curious, and courageous personality to shine through. She was a multi-faceted woman: her skills were wide and varied, and her intelligence was balanced by her broad imagination. She was creative and artistic; she could dance exquisitely, draw beautiful sketches, and could play piano very well. My mother had a sharp ear, and a gift for music. When she was younger and attended church services, her memory and listening skills were so keen that she would memorize the notes she heard on the organ during the service and then practice playing the same notes at home, without a single lesson or guidance from anyone. Not only could she play the notes, but she would switch them around and would create a new song of her own. Her creativity was a gift that not many people had.

It was this wonderful spirit that made my mother so attractive to the male friends she played with. But mother was not interested in any of them—none of the young men she knew could match her strong persona. That changed when she was introduced to a young man named Wong Pui Lai in 1932.

Born on November 18, 1913, Wong Pui Lai, or Joseph, was a strong, handsome, intelligent man. Like my mother, he came from a progressive family who believed in education above all else. Although as a male he was offered more opportunities to continue his schooling, his sheer intelligence allowed him to enter and excel at one of the most prestigious schools in Hong Kong, King's College, the oldest government secondary school in Hong Kong. An esteemed, government-funded school founded in 1862, it was known not only for its exceptional, progressive, Westernized academics but also its modern, fully equipped buildings. When my father attended the school, the facilities for students were state-of-the-art; there were twenty-nine classrooms, two science laboratories, a library and museum, a photography room, and a gymnasium.

As a man gifted in both intelligence and natural strength, my father took full advantage of all these facilities, both inside and outside the classroom. His broad shoulders, solid stature, and high posture allowed his talent for sports to flourish, especially in swimming; like my mother, he was an excellent swimmer, and in 1934, he even won a competition in swimming across the Victoria Harbor.

The similarities between my parents were all too obvious: their exceptional intelligence, their embracing of progressive ideas, their love of adventure, and the strength of their kind, generous hearts, seemed to bring them together like two stars under the sun. The two of them were young when they had been introduced to each other by a family friend—mother was only fifteen and father was nineteen—but from the moment they met, mother knew that fate had brought them together.

They began dating almost immediately after they met, and spent as much time as they could together. As they began to get closer to each other, one week turned into one month, one month turned into two, and two months turned into six. Before they knew it, they were in love.

Yet, the only time they could spend together was outside of school, since all Chinese schools at that time were still separated by gender (allowing both genders to attend the same school was one Western value that unfortunately had not yet reached China). They also lived quite a distance away from each other; they would have to take a train if they wanted to visit each other. So on the weekends, my mother and father would finish their schoolwork as quickly as they could and prepare to spend their lovely afternoons together.

On the weekends in my parents' area of Hong Kong, one of the most popular places for young people to go was Lai Chi Kok, a fairgrounds and beach in Kowloon. The fairgrounds themselves were built just above the beach, in several high wooden buildings; they were equipped with restaurants, bingo tables, and other fun activities. On weekends, the beach and fairgrounds would be crowded with young couples whose sweet adoration for each other slowly began blossoming into love, and my parents were right there alongside of them. After a fun night of dining on a delicious dinner and playing games, young couples could hold hands and take a stroll on the beach, where the sun would set like a golden globe over the horizon. The beach over time grew to hold many wonderful memories and a special place in mother's heart, from her time dating my father all the way to when she had her own children. I remember when I was a young girl, mother would take my siblings and I there and we would chase the crabs on the beach, dig for clams, and play the American game called jacks, which we called stones.

Oftentimes, on the weekends, my grandfather would take my mother and her siblings to go have Chinese tea in Yuen Long, a city west of Tai Po Market. After the bus stop in Yuen Long, there were many large cotton trees along the street on both sides. The children loved to play with the cotton trees' skin because they had layers of white bark as thin as tissue paper. My mother told me how much fun it was to peel off the bark of the trees, layer by layer. Even up through our generation, we did the same whenever we came across the cotton trees; it was soft and thin to peel. Of course, we did not peel too many layers, because it would hurt the cotton tree.

It was on these magical weekends that my parents really got to know each other. Sometimes, they would listen to modern pop music on 33-inch records on my father's record player, which had a cumbersome handle that needed to be cranked and turned in order for the music to play. (Compared to today, such a music player seems outdated, but in those days, it was extremely modern – my mother did not have that kind of technology because she lived outside the city). They squeezed every moment they could out of the dipping sunlight on those weekend nights; it was painful to separate and to know they would have to spend their days apart. But my mother's faith that fate would keep them together never faltered; no matter how long they were apart, when they embraced again, it was as if it was for the very first time, and all the stars had aligned again.

Before they knew it, five years had passed since they first met in 1932; my mother was now twenty and my father was twenty-four. My father had graduated from King's College, and was studying Radio Engineering at the Technical Institute of Britain. He graduated from there on July 17, 1937, and soon after, he received a position working as a radio engineer on board a ship. This was an excellent opportunity for someone with his background and intelligence. But the position meant that he and mother would be apart from each for quite some time. This was not like being apart from each other during the week; he was no longer a short distance away from mother, and they could not meet up on the weekends to rekindle their love. They would be spending much time far away from each other. It was in these next two years, with my father far away from my mother, that their young love quickly blossomed into a strong, vibrant, and unconquerable energy.

The longer the days dragged on without my father, the more my mother felt a growing pulse in her heart—she knew that she could not live without him. Mother was still in school at St. Mary's at this time; she graduated in 1939, the same year my father returned. Upon his arrival, they didn't want to wait any longer. They knew there was no one else in the world for either of them—and they didn't want to waste any more time being apart. On August 26, 1939, after seven years of dating, my father proposed to my mother. My mother happily accepted, and they were officially engaged.

Their families were delighted. They, along with everyone else, could see how perfect they were for each other. They had known that it would only be a matter of time for their young love became a legacy. Now they had a full year to prepare for the wedding.

My parents had to consider many things when planning the wedding; they knew they wanted to embrace much of the new, Westernized customs they had been exposed to in their education, but their strong connection to their families had them still upholding a few Chinese traditions. They decided ultimately to have a good balance of both—to please both themselves and their families.

First, they chose October 12, 1940, as the date that their love would be recognized and celebrated by their closest family and friends (and many, many more guests!). Much like American culture, many Chinese couples get married in the fall, because the weather is perfect. They also kept the tradition of the bride's family sending out special cakes called "bridal pastries" to the bride's extended family and friends as an announcement of the wedding, two months before the actual ceremony. Bridal pastries are breads packed with

91

either savory or sweet fillings, and signify good wishes like ever-lasting prosperity. With such a large family and so many friends, my grandfather Chu had to hire a truck instead of regular cars to deliver all the pastries!

My parents also kept the traditional color of red for everything in the wedding, right down to the wedding invitations, wedding gift boxes, and envelopes. In China, red is the common color of weddings; it signifies love, joy, and prosperity.

But on the actual day of the wedding, it was my parents' true embracing of both Western culture and Chinese tradition that was on display everywhere. In contrast to Chinese tradition, the wedding ceremony took place within the church—at St. Theresa's Church, the biggest in Kowloon. They also had both bridesmaids and bridegrooms and flower girls and boys. Both sides of the family wore traditional, formal Chinese garments that were embroidered with gold. My mother's bouquet was the roses at the front, and gladiolus flowers at the back; these flowers had longer and stronger stems, and supported the roses—just like the strength that would be supporting my parents' precious love. Above the entrance of the church hung a huge bell that was covered entirely with flowers; from each side of the bell, long ribbons were strung from each side of the bell, and the ends of each ribbon were held by their best friends as a symbol of their blessings for a lifetime of happiness.

My parents' love was witnessed by all of their closest family and friends; after they declared their love for each other, they walked down the aisle of the church, surrounding by those who loved them. The room radiated with pure love and energy, and my parents were glowing as if they themselves were stars brought together to shine brightly as one light in the sky.

In the Chinese tradition, my parents held a tea ceremony directly after the wedding and before the reception, attended only by the couple's immediate families. The bride who honors tradition will serve tea to her in-laws first, and then serve those who are older than her. After the tea ceremony, my parents held their reception at the Peninsular Hotel, one of the most prestigious hotels in the world, in a large hall called the Rose Garden. All guests in attendance at the wedding were seated at round tables that sat twelve each, and were served many courses of succulent foods, all of which held symbolic meaning. Extravagant delicacies such as bird's nest soup, shark fin soup, and abalone attested to the bride's family's generosity. Whole fish symbolized lavishness, as the Chinese word for fish, "yu," resembles the word for "abundance." One of the most important dishes served was noodles; they hold high importance in Chinese culture because their length signifies a long life, perfect for a new couple. Desserts that contained lotus seeds were served as a wish for the couple to have many children. All of these foods symbolized the hope for success the bride and groom will have together.

My mother also followed the tradition for a Chinese bride to change outfits at least three times during the reception. I still have one of my mother's Cheung Sam gowns from her wedding, looking only to be about a size one for my mother's tiny waist, made from a pink lace material. Mother also had a lot of dowry when she married, some of which I still have today. Mother told me that her father gave her many beautiful pieces of jewelry, which included jade, emerald, sapphire, and gold; my mother asked me to give one of these pieces of jewelry, a jade brooch, to my own daughter Iris when she got married.

My parents' wedding day signified everything that their love was about—energy, strength, purity, and the exquisite things that could happen when tradition and progressive ideas came together. The day was perfect— and so were my parents.

They were eager to begin planning for their own family almost immediately. Not long after their wedding, they rented a two-story house on Fuk Lo Tuen Road near Lion Hill in Kowloon City. The house was not much, but the love my parents filled it with would plant the seeds for their future happiness.

My father was earning one hundred and sixty Hong Kong dollars per month, an excellent income in those days, and more than enough to cover their finances. Twenty dollars went towards the rent, five dollars each was given to their two servants, and twenty dollars went towards food and other spending. Mother had just enough left over to start saving for the future—but first, she needed to make their first home look warm and inviting. She planted two rows of her favorite flower, the dragon flower, along the sides of the walkway of the house. The dragon flowers symbolized my parents' love: vibrant, colorful, full of life, and always blossoming.

Like the dragon flowers blooming, my parents' family bloomed as well. Mother became pregnant with her first child, myself, only two months after she and my father were married. My parents were overjoyed; the seeds of their humble beginnings were now beginning to grow, and would soon develop into a full and beautiful family.

Although her first pregnancy was a blessing, it was a hard experience for mother. She did everything she was supposed to for her first pregnancy; she followed every tradition and rule that her mother had taught her. But it was still difficult to tolerate, as it is for most first-time mothers. During her first two weeks straight, she vomited every day, from morning until night, and could not keep any food down. Then she continued vomiting almost daily for seven months. She was concerned she would have to endure this for the remaining two months of her pregnancy. But nature had other ideas. I was ready to arrive at only seven months instead of nine.

Mother was extremely worried that I would not be healthy when I was born. But when I came into the world, with the help of my mother's cousin Yip May Chun, a midwife, on September 1, 1941, I was perfectly healthy, arriving crying and kicking like any other newborn baby. My name is Wai Yu; my baptized name is Seraphina. Because we were Catholic, within two weeks I was baptized with an English name. In our Chinese tradition, we have both Chinese and English names. Chinese names are family names given by our grandfathers. When we studied Chinese in grade school, we used our Chinese names with each other. In high school, we used our English names. Relatives chose to call us in either name. If we immigrated to a foreign land, we used English names.

When mother held her tiny, five-pound baby in her arms, seeing me staring back up at her, all the physical pain she had endured washed away. I was the light of her life. When my father saw me for the first time, he embraced my mother with pure joy. My parents were living the fairy tale they had always dreamed of. They were happy, financially secure newlyweds now blessed unconditionally with their first child. Theirs would be a life of eternal peace and prosperity.

Then, three months later, everything changed forever.

In December of 1941, the Japanese began to occupy Hong Kong as part of their military strategy during World War II. After eighteen days of fierce fighting, on December 25, 1941, the unthinkable happened: Governor Sir Mark Young was forced to surrender the territory of Hong Kong to Japan.

This occupation was a sorrowful time for the people of Hong Kong. It would eventually last for three years and eight months, a term that would later leave many survivors to call the occupation "Three Years and Eight Months." The Japanese military were cruel and inhumane, and merciless in their tactics of torturing the good people of Hong Kong. They first cut off our most valuable resource: food. They robbed any food bank they discovered, and allowed citizens only a half a pot of rice for each family, forcing them to line up each week to receive it. If there was no rice left, those who went without were forced to eat grass, roots, or anything edible they could find along the road, reducing our proud people, who had worked so hard all their lives, to poor beggars.

We had enough food for the time being, but sooner or later, all the resources were going to run out. My mother was no stranger to sacrifice, but she now had two mouths to think of; if she was malnourished, her baby would be too.

But this was not the biggest of mother's worries. My father had returned to work two and a half months after I was born, as a wireless operator on board a ship, a British-owned vessel called the SS Henry Keswick, to continue earning money for his new family. He had begun work again right before the occupation began; if he had known this was going to happen, he would have stayed with his family. Mother therefore was all alone at this point; it was just her and her brand-new baby. Mother wasn't sure what was going to happen, but she had faith that my father would return safely.

But nothing could have prepared mother for what would soon happen.

Right after Christmas, only a few days after the invasion, mother received a phone call. She believed it was a family member calling to make

94

sure she and her baby were all right. Instead, it was my father's ship company.

Mother's heart started to pound. Why would they be calling her?

The company told mother that on Christmas Day, the day of the invasion, my father had been on board his ship. Without warning, the ship had suddenly lost contact with its base, and disappeared completely from the radar. No one knew where the ship had gone, if it had sunk or been bombed. No one knew whether anyone on board had been captured, were even alive, or ever be found again.

It took a moment for this news to sink in. It was too horrific to hear. Mother simply could not believe it. In an instant, the fairy tale that my parents had been living became a nightmare. Their beautiful love celebrated only a year ago at their wedding had now been torn apart—perhaps forever. How could my mother go on without her dear Joseph? How could she raise a child by herself during wartime?

At this critical crossroad in her young life, my mother faced challenges that many people have not faced in their entire lives. No one had taught her how to raise a child, let alone raise a child without a father or family, and in the midst of wartime. At twenty-five years old with a newborn baby, no husband with her, and the close threat of death nearby, my mother had to learn to live and survive every day completely and utterly alone.

In her infinite wisdom and bravery at her young age, my mother decided that she could not waste time directing her energy toward worrying about things she could not control. Instead, she put her own fear aside and focused all her attention and strength on protecting her child. Not only would she have to accept the possibility that she might never see her husband again, she had to use her sharp intelligence and hard work ethic to learn how to survive on her own with her newborn baby. In such a fearful time, she remained courageous, and embraced every day with faith and a fierce, determined strength.

The dangers and threats that faced women in Hong Kong were especially horrific. A certain set of Japanese soldiers, called substitute soldiers, had been recruited as part of Japan's unofficial military, and were untrained and uncontrollable. They often robbed and raped women at random. The official Japanese soldiers that had been trained were more respectful than substitute soldiers, but it was almost impossible to tell the difference between each type. This made it more difficult for Hong Kong women to hide from them. Every day my mother and every other Hong Kong woman faced the threat of being discovered, harmed, or killed by these soldiers.

One afternoon, my mother was taking a nap with me in our home when she had the sensation that someone was staring at her. She woke up suddenly. When she opened her eyes, she saw a Japanese soldier standing in front of her bed, holding open her mosquito's net and staring down at her.

Mother stopped breathing. She didn't move a muscle. She could not tell what kind of soldier this man was, but she knew the danger that both she and I were in, she lay as still as she possibly could in our bed with me curled tightly beside her, simply staring at the soldier, not even daring to blink.

After a few moments, the soldier closed the mosquito net and left silently. Mother let out her breath; he had been an official soldier.

After that, every morning before the day began, she, like other Hong Kong women, carefully applied black ashes on her beautiful face in order to look unattractive, so the soldiers would not approach her.

Even that incident was not enough to make mother panic. I cannot imagine the courage she had in laying perfectly still; even when faced with extreme danger; my mother had remained calm and prevented us both from being harmed.

But although mother's courage kept us alive, the chaos finally became too large to hide from. It was only a few days after mother encountered the solider when she suddenly heard loud explosions outside our home. Rushing outside, she saw the unthinkable: above us, low-flying planes were buzzing, dropping thick black masses. Mother saw only one quickly before it fell out of the sky like a black teardrop. Suddenly, a building was aflame. It was the Hong Kong Kai Tak Airport, which was very close to our house.

The most extreme threat had finally come. We were being bombed.

Mother did not panic. She knew instantly what she had to do. She immediately went back inside and packed only one can of milk powder, water, a few cotton diapers for her baby, and a few nuggets of gold to tie around her waist. Mother rubbed the ashes on her face to make sure she looked unapproachable, gathered me in a bundle, and then set out, alone and on foot, to safety at her father's home in Tai Po Market—over one hundred miles away.

If I had been older, I might have begged mother to stay where we were in Kowloon. It was a ragged path to Tai Po Market, through thick woods, steeps mountains, and rocky trails. With zero shelter, mother and I were completely out in the open—we were never shielded from the Japanese warplanes overhead. Any one of those bombs could have hit exactly along our path at any time.

No one in those circumstances had any good chance of surviving; indeed, many people who took the same route she did perished, some from bombs, some from the cruelty of the soldiers. As mother walked, she saw the dead corpses of those who had lost their lives lying around the hillside. Still, she walked on, holding her baby in her arms and her head held high. Sometimes, if the bombings sounded too close, she hid in surrounding shelters with others who were fleeing. She never had to be afraid of her baby crying to expose her; I was a good baby, and most people believed she was simply carrying a parcel.

Mother walked for three days and three nights straight. By the end of the third night, as the dark gave way to morning, mother could hardly stand. She didn't know if she could go on anymore. Her journey had taken her down perilous twists and turns, and dark, unfamiliar roads; she barely knew where she was anymore.

And then suddenly, like the North Star, off in the distance, my grandfather's house came into view.

My mother gazed at it in wonder. It was like a castle in a fairy tale. We had made it. I was unharmed; she was unharmed. It was a miracle.

As she trekked the final steps of the most treacherous journey of her young life, she fell to her knees at her parents' doorstep. She let a single cry of relief escape her and thanked God that we had finally reached our safe haven.

My grandparents were overjoyed to welcome their daughter and granddaughter safe and sound. My mother of course was ecstatic to see them too. But after a bath and a full day's sleep, mother awoke the following morning with a fresh vision. She was still aware of the circumstances: she was twenty-five years old, married, with her own child and own home. My mother wanted to remain faithful to strict Chinese traditions she had been brought up with; she did not want to disrespect her parents by moving back in and simply giving them two more mouths to feed. Wartime and the threat of death were obvious exceptions to traditions, and my grandparents were only too happy to have mother and I stayed with them. But mother was firm; she did not want to be their burden. She thanked my grandfather for allowing us to stay with them, and promised him that she would not seek any special attention or extra assistance. We would stay with them only until it was safe to go back to our home, or we heard any news about my father.

Days passed. The war was not ceasing, and we still had heard nothing about my father. Days turned into weeks. My mother's anxiety was beginning to grow. My grandparents comforted my mother, but she knew there was still the real possibility of the worst outcome. She didn't know if she was ready for it. But she couldn't sit around and wait for much longer. She wished with all her heart that the war would end and she and I could go back to our home and wait for my father's return.

Everyone else in my mother's family knew the struggles she was facing. But not everyone embraced her with open arms. After a few weeks of living with her parents, some people decided my mother did not deserve any more help. One day, my mother's sister-in-law, Chan Cheung Kiu, angrily confronted her and said, "A married daughter shouldn't come home to rely on her father. It is shameful." Cheung Kiu had no right to talk to my mother in this manner; after all, she was not even blood-related, just a sister-in-law. It was a hateful comment made out of spite and jealousy.

But mother took her insult to heart; she had been brought up too well to break tradition. Even despite her extreme circumstances, she did not want to disrespect her parents or dishonor her family. To her, braving the open air space and risking her and her child's life did not mean that she deserved to move back with her parents. So in early 1942, mother decided to move on. She took her small child and left her safe and secure childhood home in Tai Po Market and went to Macau to stay with her elder sister Lily.

Auntie Lily, in her kind and generous manner, was only too happy to have us. When we went to live with her, she was teaching at the Sacred Heart Catholic School in the afternoon. She knew mother needed to begin earning an income to start providing for her child; the money that she and my father had saved that she had taken with us was not lasting forever. Auntie Lily immediately helped my mother receive a job teaching at the same school in the morning. The schedule worked out perfectly; since mother worked in the morning and Auntie Lily worked in the afternoon, the two of them took turns taking care of me when each was at work. As a young baby, I would often confuse them, and early one morning, when I was first beginning to learn how to speak, I called out "Ma!" to the first person I saw. Instead of my mother, it turned out to be Auntie Lily! This was the relationship we kept up all throughout her life; she was like my second mother.

We stayed safe in Macau with auntie Lily for several months, until Auntie Lily left to join the convent in late 1942. But she was kind enough to let mother and I stay and live in her apartment. Mother and I would often take trips to visit our other family members who lived nearby, including that old building in Macau where my father's second sister, Wong Shui Kwan, lived with her husband, Mr. Cheung Fai, and their seven children, including Rosie. This was the same building in which I remember mother gripping my hand tightly as we ascended the long and narrow stairs with no handle. Even as a young child, I still remember feeling safe and secure; I never felt lost or in danger during this time. Somehow, mother had suppressed all of her own emotions –the fear from travelling alone and exposed with her child, her never-ending anxiety over my father's disappearance, and the dishonor she felt in moving back with her parents. Somehow, she never showed any of that—she only concern, ever, was to make sure that her child, above all, was protected.

Mother and I were still living in Macau in Auntie Lily's apartment when the Japanese were finally defeated by the United States in September 1945, ending World War II. Hong Kong had been desecrated; there was nothing to go back to—no home, no life. We had also still received no news of my father.

My mother had not been sitting around worrying for three years while we waited for the war to end and my father to return. She had been thinking and preparing to continue her life for the time being with no husband or home. She had made an arrangement with the Ko brothers, who owned the Star Hotel on Nathan Road, to supply mother with a job and a place to live. The Ko brothers were a part of our family—their mother was my grandfather Wong's sister, who had been widowed when she was young with seven children to take care of. My grandfather had taken care of her and all her children. To return the favor, the Ko brothers now showed my mother the same kindness by giving her a job at the hotel and allowing her and I to live there.

It was a family hotel in a commercial area reserved strictly for tourists. There was a living quarters at the back of the hotel for its employees, which was where we lived. Mr. Chan Bing Kwong, the grandson of my grandfather's sister, and his wife lived there as well, and we became good friends with them. During the day while mother worked, I would stay in our quarters, and mother divided her time between working and coming back to the room to check on me. Occasionally, to make it easier for her, she would have me accompany her around the hotel. To have a four-year-old child at her side as she was trying to do her job was a lot of responsibility and took a lot of strength of mind and emotion for her. Luckily, I was a good girl for her, and I never injured myself or got in trouble.

It was while we were here at the Star Hotel when mother received the phone call she had been waiting for. It was news about my father.

Mother didn't know if she wanted to hear it. There were only two options; mother did not know if she could handle the worse one.

But the news was extraordinary—after four long years, my father had been discovered alive and had been rescued by the Red Cross!

When World War II broke out and the Japanese invaded Hong Kong in December of 1941, my father was working on board a ship in the South Pacific. My father had no knowledge of the war or the dangers that it posed for him on the open waters. Then suddenly, one day, the inevitable happened: my father's ship was bombed. The ship was devastated, exploding into a million tiny fragments as the bomb rained down without warning.

With the ship gone, the seawaters turned black. Pieces of the ship were floating everywhere. It was almost inconceivable that anyone could survive such a trauma. Then suddenly—my father's head appeared amidst the floating fragments. He was alive!

By the grace of God, my father had survived. Looking around, he realized that if he wanted to stay alive, he would need to get to land—fast. His instincts kicked in, and he began swimming through the howling seas. My father was able to do this because of his talented swimming abilities; he was a swimming competitor, and had won a competition to cross the harbor between Hong Kong and Kowloon in the Victoria Bay in 1934.

It was not long after he had been paddling that he suddenly spotted a nearby island. The island was named Ryukyu Island. Out of breath and on the brink of drowning, he immediately swam towards it. He had no idea what was waiting for him; he knew that he just needed to get to dry land. As he kept swimming, finally reaching the island, pulling his tired body up onto the shore, he collapsed on the soft sand. Land had never felt so good to him.

But as his breath slowly returned to him, he heard someone walking on the sand, close to his ear. He looked up. In front of him stood

Japanese soldiers—the enemy. They had been there waiting for him. Immediately, they took him for a spy and captured him.

My father's capture lasted for four years. Four years he was stuck on that island with the enemy. The most inhumane experience my father had as a prisoner with the Japanese was their torture method. He was not slashed with knives or shot with bullets; instead, the Japanese demanded my father be tortured slowly and painfully. A tube was inserted into his mouth, and heavy loads of water were pumped through this tube into his stomach and, eventually, his lungs. The pain from this bloating was unbearable. Flour was also popped up into his mouth to add to the pain. After four years of this torture, my father was on the brink of death. And yet, he still survived against all odds. He was sustained by a hope and strength that seemed superhuman; he was a man who lived life on the edge of endurance.

By the grace of God, the war ended, and the Japanese were defeated. After their defeat, the Japanese were forced to leave the island, so they left him there on the island with the other prisoners, lying on the beach, bloated and severely ill. My father had survived the torture so far, but with no food or proper water, he had no chance of surviving for more than a few days if he was on this island.

It was around this time that the Red Cross began making rescue missions to all the formerly Japanese-occupied territories. Miraculously, they arrived at the island my father was on not too long after. The solders had pulled all prisoners on the beach close to the water, and let the waves pull them into the water. When the Red Cross came, they discovered water already covered half of my father's waist. That was where they found him. When they pulled him out of the water, they asked him where he came from, and he managed just enough breath to tell them. The immediately brought him back to Hong Kong.

When my mother received the call, they told us that we could go immediately to see him at Kai Tak Airport. She hung up the phone, dried her tears, gathered me quickly, and left for the airport.

When we met him there, I will never forget how he looked. Two men were holding him up on a wooden stretcher. His skinny body lay there, almost lifeless. He was all skin and bones. Mother held my hand, tears streaming down her face, leading me gently up to him, telling me he was my father, how much he loved me and couldn't wait to hold me in his arms when he got better.

After his examinations at the hospital, his doctors discovered that he because of all the water that had been pumped into his lungs, he had contracted tuberculosis, a terrible and painful disease in which the dangerous tuberculosis germs spread throughout the lungs like cancer, forcing the individual to cough up blood persistently. If the disease was inactive, the germs would calcify in the lungs, and the individual would appear healthier. But my father had a very active case of it, and so instead of being able to come home with us, he was taken to Lai Chi Kok Tuberculosis Hospital to receive treatment and to recover. As he slowly improved, his tuberculosis became less active, and by early 1946, he was allowed to leave the hospital.

While our family was complete again, it would be a long while before the three of us could all begin rebuilding our life and love together. After my father was discharged from hospital, his parents brought him back to their home in Siu Kiu, Nam Hoi, Canton, China to continue to recover. The transportation between Hong Kong & China was quite difficult between two lands. It took one day to travel back there; first, they took the train from Kowloon Bay, which arrived in Canton. Then took a long ride in a car to the river bank, then took the ferry across the river. Once my father was settled, he needed his wife. So mother and I went to Siu Kiu to live with him in my grandfather Wong's home, though in a separate section of the house from my father while he continued to get better.

My father came from a large family, and many members were still living at my grandfather's home when mother and I went to live there along with my father. Although allowing us to move in with him was a generous gesture, my mother again faced the challenge of living in a home that was not hers. Because there were so many other people living there, mother would not often reap the benefits. My grandfather was kind enough to let us eat with his family in the dining room at his two round tables that sat twelve people each. But with so many people in the house, servants had to prepare two meals with limited portions. My mother always let me eat before she did to ensure that I had enough. By the time I finished my meal and mother sat down to have hers, she often found no food on the table except the fish head, and leftover sauce on the plates. She usually either went hungry for the rest of the night, or she would buy food on her own.

My mother was not going to complain about any difficulties. She was clever enough to take the obstacles that faced her and use them to her advantage. In one case, one afternoon while she was out shopping, she passed by a hawker who sold fish-ball and noodle soup in the street every day. This hawker challenged my mother to a contest with a coolie—a strong male laborer whose job was to carry hundreds of pounds of products and goods daily to different locations—to see who could finish ten bowls of noodle soup first. Each bowl of soup had five fish balls in it, much more than my mother was used to eating for her small meals. Of course, those watching the contest all bet the coolie would win instead of a young, weak woman. As they began the contest, the other person started to eat one bowl at a time, including all five fish balls, the noodles, and soup, all at once. This was not a wise decision; by the seventh bowl, he started to vomit. My mother, however, had used her mind and come up with a strategy; first, she ate all fish-balls in each of the ten bowls slowly, totaling fifty fish balls. Then she ate the noodles in each bowl, and lastly drank the remaining soup. Using her quick mind, my mother easily won the contest. The people watching were amazed; they could not believe a small woman had eaten all of that food. They did not know that she was already underfed.

101

My mother soon became pregnant with her second child while we were staying in my grandfather Wong's home; by the final two months of her pregnancy, although she appreciated my grandfather's generosity, her lack of food and crowded living space were not healthy for a pregnant woman. Although it broke my mother's heart to be away from her husband, she had no choice but to go back to the only place she knew she could carry and deliver her baby safely—her parents' home in Tai Po Market. Despite not wanting to dishonor her family, she had nowhere else to go, and she wanted her child to be born healthy. So she decided to return to them.

Mother was able to give birth to a healthy son, Tai Chi (Paul) on October 14, 1946. My grandmother delivered Paul in her own bedroom. It was not easy in those days to give birth; my mother lived through three days of labor with Paul, yelling and shouting through her suffering, with no medicine to aide her. When Paul was finally born, he was a big baby, over nine pounds. Mother used to say that he had already begun sucking his thumb at birth. It was difficult for my mother to breastfeed him because he was such a big baby. He required feeding every three hours, and my mother had to feed him regardless of her own needs. One day, Paul sucked too hard and injured my mother. It was painful for her, and she could no longer hold enough milk to feed him anyway. She then switched to feeding him formula.

To make sure that my father was close to his growing family, my mother rented a house in the Kam Shan area, about a ten to fifteen-minute walk, or a five-minute bicycle ride, away from my grandparents in Tai Po Market. She hired a part-time servant to take care of him. Sometimes we would visit him as well. I recall witnessing one time how he ate slowly and seldom talked when he ate. After he finished his meal, he would use tissue paper to clean all the utensils, and put those tissues in a paper bag, repeating this process many times until all the utensils were spotlessly clean. He would then go downstairs and carefully burn the paper bag of tissues in a special burner. This way, my father eliminated all traces of germs. Thanks to his carefulness, none of us ever became sick with tuberculosis.

With a new baby to take care of, my father needed to support his growing family. He had recovered enough to return to work as a private English tutor. His English was exceptional, and he specialized in tutoring students who were preparing for university. He was recovering steadily as he worked, and by late 1946, he left his job as a tutor and returned to work full time as a radio wireless operator on board a ship. The ship's company allowed the executive officers to have their family to stay with them. My mother naturally accompanied him.

The time that my parents spent together on board the ship became one of the most celebrated and joyous times in my mother's life. There was no war to keep them apart, no danger or menacing threats, and no long, arduous journeys necessary to undertake. On board this ship together, my parents could rest in the peace and happiness they had once dreamed of having. They traveled through China and Southeast Asia, and he and my mother took time in between his work to enjoy the beautiful sights around them. My mother felt as though she was a newlywed again, exploring the world with fresh and spirited eyes, ever cheerful and blissful with her husband safe by her side.

My mother became pregnant with her third child, and returned from sea back to Tai Po Market in late 1947 and gave birth to a second son, Tai Yan (Stephen) on November 7, 1947 in my grandmother's bedroom again. Because of mother's pregnancy on board the ship in a foreign land with a different climate and different food, Stephen's complexion was a bit darker than an ordinary Asian baby. He was a cute, healthy boy, over nine pounds, with two big black eyes I remember looking straight up at me. These dark features made him look Indian, and we nicknamed him "Ah Cha." My mother said that he was an easy baby to take care of, and always slept through the night. My mother did not have enough milk to feed him, and Stephen always drank the formula that was given to him immediately after he was born.

There was a very specific way to clean and sterilize the baby bottles in those days. When a baby was first born, it was easy for him to suck out all the formula from the tiny nipples at the tip of the bottles. As the baby grew older, however, and his strength grew, he would naturally want to suck out greater amounts of milk in one gulp. If the hole was small, he would have a difficult time getting all the milk he needed, but my mother could always sense the greater effort that her baby was taking to get the formula, and she just made the hole bigger for the baby to suck down more formula. Mother would first sterilize a safety needle by rubbing alcohol on it and burning it over a fire. This killed all the invisible germs that were on the needle, and prevented the baby from becoming ill. Mother had to be quite skilled at this, however; if she made the hole too big, the baby would receive too much formula in one gulp and choke.

To clean and sterilize the bottles after feeding, the bottles would all be placed in a large boiling pot with the top nipples removed. The bottles would be boiled, and the nipples would be added in the last five minutes, so all parts of the bottle were fresh and sanitized for the baby. It was a painstaking process to go through, but my mother was always thorough and always made sure her children's bottles were cleaned completely.

My father had remained at sea when Stephen was born, but not long after, his illness acted up again, and he left his ship to return to Kowloon to stay in the hospital off and on. When he was better, he moved back into the apartment mother had rented for him. We were still living in my grandparents' home in Tai Po Market, and we would often visit him. It was difficult for mother to manage her family this way, between two places, but at least it was still better having my father close rather than at sea.

My mother became pregnant for a final time, and her second daughter, Wai Ling (Agnes), was born on a cold day, February 12, 1949. Like her siblings before her, Agnes was also born on my grandmother's bed. With her experience and knowledge, my grandmother fed her formula immediately instead of my mother's breast milk. Agnes was a cute, timid baby; she barely made a sound as mother allowed me to hold her in my lap. She was absolutely adorable, all wrapped up in a wool blanket, her beautiful eyes staring curiously up at me. Sometimes mother would let me hold her in my arms as we sat on the swinging chair, but only for a short while, because mother was afraid I would drop her. Agnes was a precious bundle of joy for all of us.

My parents now had four beautiful, healthy children. Our family seemed complete. But we were still not altogether. My father's illness still prevented him from living with us; from Agnes's birth in 1949 through early 1951, my father remained living in his apartment while mother and her four children remained with her parents in Tai Po Market. Then, finally, in July of 1951, my father was well enough to return to work full-time again, and he quickly received a job working as a consultant of a radio school to generate a steady income for us. That money allowed him to build what would become our first home together as a family.

My parents bought a piece of land measuring around 10,000 square feet at 59 On Luk Tsun, Fan Lan, the town next to Tai Po Market. In a letter from District Office in Tai Po dated August 28, 1951, written by my father's friend Mr. T.B. Low, who worked on the Marine Department in Hong Kong said that my father had requested to build a wooden structure added on this property of D.D. 51 Lot No. 1B/4433 On Lok Village and hoped the application would be granted. A letter dated Sept. 17, 1951 letter came back, saying that my father was not approved to build a wooden structure there. In October, Mr. Low wrote a letter to the land office again; he explained the situation about my father needing a place to live in this location after his many stays in the hospital and being in and out of work, also mentioning that my grandfather was a wealthy and reputable gentleman in Tai Po Market. The request was then granted, and they built a one-story, 3,000 square foot duplex. This would be our first home all together as a family.

After construction was completed, at long last, my parents and their four children moved in under one roof for the first time in their lives. Exactly ten years had passed since my parents' young and blossoming family had been ripped apart. But now, the perfect life that my mother and father had dreamed about was finally a reality. We had come a long way from the modest home outside of which my mother had planted dragon flowers; now, my parents had lived through a war, and had paid for and built their own home for their family to plant our roots firmly to flourish. Love, my parents firmly believed, always won out in the end.

My mother and father had planted their new roots in our new home in Fan Lan in 1951, fully expecting to live our lives as a complete family. But we had not lived in Fan Lan for not that long before my father became sick again, and had to return to Kowloon to stay in Lai Chi Kok Hospital.

Perhaps it was the fact that we had all just moved in together for the first time that made this separation much more difficult for my father.

He had endured his illness for quite some time, but this latest separation from his family pushed him over the edge. He had tolerated unsanitary conditions during all of his admittances to the hospital over the past few years. But he was not a man to sit idly back and complain about unjust situations, even in his physically weakened state. In 1951, he wrote a strongly-worded letter to the hospital administration of the conditions in which he and other patients were living, and his dissatisfaction with the lack of authority the hospital was displaying.

In his quarters at the hospital amongst other tuberculosis patients, the conditions were dirty, unhygienic, and certainly not up to par with what a major hospital should offer. In my father's ward, the patients were loud, rude, and obnoxious, treating their recovery stay in the hospital as a holiday, even taking advantage of the lack of authority to instigate fights. The bathroom facilities were unsanitary: there was a single bucket, about a foot in diameter and depth, for thirty patients to use every day. The facilities were located on an upper floor, so patients who were located on the lower floors, even if they had difficulty walking or other ailments, had to use that single facility, running the risk of exposing themselves to other patients or inclement weather when the doors to the stairs were open.

The hospital also lacked an X-ray lab; patients had to be transported by ambulance to Kowloon Hospital, several miles away, every time they required an X-ray screening. Since there were so many patients, they were herded into the ambulance like cattle in unhealthy conditions. My father related in his letter one such experience he had in one of these ambulances. The stretcher on which he was placed was slid into the ambulance beneath a bench on which lay another sick patient. There was no more than six inches between my father's face and the bottom of the bench. When the doors closed, the stench became unbearable, and my father realized that he would be packed in this small enclosure full of germs and disease and no circulating fresh air for the entire ride.

My father did not withhold any detail in his letter to the hospital administration; the more details he provided, the more the hospital would know exactly how unclean their living quarters were. For each of his grievances, my father also proposed a solution. For the rowdy patients, he suggested signs, posters, lectures, and a set timetable to educate the other patients about the risks of their behavior, and to keep them on a schedule that would prevent such behavior in the future. He proposed the addition of several bathroom facilities for his ward to halt the use of the single bucket and reduce the risk of fragile patients going up to another floor. He also recommended the addition of X-ray labs at the hospital to stop altogether the need for the unsanitary ambulance rides. Even while ill, my father found the strength to make the situation around him more livable for everyone involved.

With my father back in the hospital in Kowloon, my mother could not rely on the income my father had made from his jobs before to take care of her four children. To retain our income, she received a job as a Stock

Record Clerk at the Hong Kong & Whampoa Dock Co. Ltd. in Hung Hom. This meant that we would be leaving our family nest that my parents had planned and worked so hard to build, and we would have to relocate to Hung Hom. But mother still kept our apartment in Fan Lan and rented it out to generate further income for us, and we kept it in our hearts as the brief but precious time we were altogether.

In Hung Hom, mother rented us a first-floor apartment at 20 Wuhu Street. My mother would sometimes be home around lunchtime from her work, depending on the day. It was easy for her to come home, since the distance between our apartment and the dockyard was very close; the dockyard was at the beginning of our street. Every day in the morning, mother walked to work, passed through the entrance and was greeted by the guard. The dockyard itself was huge, but her office was near the mid-section of the front yard. At lunchtime, mother walked back home to have a quick lunch and nap, and then went back to work. A good lunch and speedy nap allowed mother's mind to rest and refresh itself before going back to work; mother needed to work with figures constantly for a few hundred workers in order for them to get paid every two weeks.

Mother was working hard every day at work, and very quickly, her diligent work ethic and excellent math skills allowed her to be promoted to a Punch Operator in the Mechanical Accounting System. It was in this department where she met Mr. Wong Koon Kou, a very kind and honest man whom mother liked immediately. A strong friendship grew between them, and he soon became one of mother's best friends. He was two years younger than mother, and was very bright and hard-working. Unfortunately, during his childhood, he had polio on his left leg, which gradually crippled him for life. He remained a bachelor for a long time, but my mother, seeing his kind and honest nature, introduced her number five sister, Suk Ching, to him, in the hopes of them finding happiness together. They dated for a while, but eventually grew apart, so their relationship ended.

A few years later, however, Koon Kou dated and married a kind, gentle woman named Li Sin Woon. Mother was ecstatic that her friend had found a lovely woman to settle down with, and was even more ecstatic when they were blessed over the course of their marriage with two sons. The two of them were excited as well, but Koon Kou told my mother that they felt as though something was still missing in their lives—they desperately wanted a daughter. My mother knew how kind-hearted they both were, and decided that they could become my godparents in order to have a "daughter" of their own. It was an honor for me to become their godchild, and I still remember the day of the official ceremony like it was yesterday. In Chinese culture, the ceremony for receiving your godparents is similar to wedding banquets; we invite our friends and relatives on both sides, and we celebrate in abundance afterward. I had to follow the tradition of kneeling down on the floor to serve them tea, just as my mother had knelt to serve tea to her parents-in-law, and my mother also gave them a gift. As I served them tea, and the ceremony continued, the look on their faces during the ceremony was something mother would never forget; her simple act of kindness had changed the lives of her friends forever.

I was growing older now, and I was beginning to realize just how important mother was to so many people. My godparents were a perfect example. They adored my mother—just like I did. I began to see what everyone else saw in her: how she treated everyone that she met with equal kindness and generosity. One of her favorite teachings was that if someone gives you one foot of a favor, you give them one yard in return. I remember that one day, mother and I went to visit my number seven auntie, Wong Yui Kwan. They lived on Chatham Road in the same district with us, not far from Wuhu Street, about a twenty-minute walk up two streets. After mother finished her business, my auntie prepared to have their lunch. Since auntie asked me to eat, I went to sit on the chair, but mother pulled me away. She said we already had a date with a friend in a restaurant, and we would eat there. By the time we went down the stairs and walked back to the road, I asked, "Are we going out to eat?" Mom said, "No, we are going home." Mom explained that Wong Yui Kwan had not prepared enough food for two extra people. If mother and I sat there to eat, they had to sacrifice their share to feed us. It was just one of the many times mother taught me to put others before yourself.

As it became clearer to me what kind of a person my mother was, I began to realize then how special our time was together. We did not get to spend too much time together because of her work, but I remember that when we did, it was like the whole world stopped, and it was just the two of us. One of my favorite things to do with her while we lived in Hung Hom was to take rickshaws as taxis to travel around to places. A rickshaw is a two-wheeled cart that usually sits one or two people that is pulled by a person. They were first imported to Hong Kong from Japan in 1880, and were very popular from the 1920s through the 1940s. However, their popularity declined after World War II, when motorized taxis began to replace them. I cherish the memories I have with mother riding in them in the last of their glory days. Mother and I would take them to any location, but she especially would take them to visit her cousin Yip's family in mid-level Hong Kong, where there were many hills made from cobblestones. There was no way my mother could walk through those streets in her high heels and her Cheung Sum.

My favorite times traveling in the rickshaw with mother were on rainy days, when we would sit close together, tucked snugly underneath the canopy, and watch the rain trickle down the sides of the rickshaw while we stayed dry. I can still remember the smell of the rain and mother's soft skin. One of the most common places we would travel to in these rickshaws was Shanghai Street, a street bustling with business, where mother used to bargain shop. Mother could always get the bargain she wanted; she was firm in her debate with the salespeople, and she could always get the most beautiful things for the cheapest possible price. We would then take the rickshaw back to our home, with mother and I snuggling up together.

These times I had with mother were precious to me. Since she worked so much, it made every moment I had with her all the more treasured. By 1953, my mother was earning the company's top salary in her position at Whampoa Dock Co. Though her position and salary not bad, it did not offer her any benefits; there was no opportunity for advancement, and she would not receive a pension. With a husband who was ill on and off, she needed a job that would give her benefits and allow her the chance to advance her salary gradually. At that time, a position happened to open up in the Preventive Service. The job was for a Revenue Custom and Excise, Class II, and it offered full benefits and the opportunity to advance throughout the service. The starting salary, however, was half that of my mother's earnings at her old job. This did not concern her. She immediately applied. Because of the salary cut, her decision to leave the dockyard was not an easy one; but she had the support of both my father and Koon Kou. My father at this time was back from Okinawa, Japan, where he had been for half a year, and wrote a letter to Mr. Low asking for a recommendation for my mother. Mr. Low had an excellent job and was a very respectable man; and my father knew that a recommendation from him would be very favorable to my mother. It certainly proved to be an asset to her; she eventually received the job. She was assigned to work shift duty in the Kowloon train station, supervising eight to ten female staff members working under her. People coming into the station from China were smuggling illegal products into Hong Kong, and since my mother was the boss of her staff, it was her responsibility to catch the criminals, which she did with ease.

She also worked at the airport to catch criminals, which gave her the opportunity to buy exotic fruits from her friends who ordered fruits from Southeast Asia and air flights to Hong Kong. Very often, mother brought home a basket of Philippine mangoes. This particular mango had a yellow color on the outside and a potent fragrance when you cut into it, and its pulp was sweet and juicy. Another kind of mango she brought home came from Thailand; it was green on the outside, but was also sweet and tasty inside. She also brought home Thailand papaya, star fruit, and lai chi, and many more that I could not remember. My mother always made sure her entire family, including the servant, enjoyed the fruit. I always wondered how, with such a difficult and important occupation, that mother remembered to bring a small piece of happiness home to her children and servant. She was under a tremendous amount of pressure every day, but she always thought of others.

To further contribute to our income, mother rented one bedroom to my grandfather Wong's first concubine, Yeung Wai Fan. She had nine children, but most of them had already married and moved on, except her youngest daughter, Yuen Kwan. Yuen Kwan loved to sing; when I was a teen, I learned most of Patty Page's songs from her. It was lovely to have her in our new apartment with us.

108

Having my second grandmother living with us meant that my grandfather Wong would often come over to visit us. My grandfather had left China in 1949 during the communist occupation and came to Hong Kong, where he established a few businesses with friends. One of his jobs was working as the manager of the Wing Luk Movie Theatre, which was located about a ten-minute walk from our apartment. Once a week, on a weekday, after my siblings and I finished our schoolwork, we would rush to the theater and go straight up to our grandpa's office to get a coupon to bring down to the ticket counter to see movies for free. (My grandfather only allowed this to happen during the week, since the weekends were usually very busy.) Since the theater was only a short distance away, he used to come about four times a week to have lunch with Yeung Wai Fan. I went to school only in the morning, from 8am to 12:30pm; by the time I returned home from school, around 1pm, my grandfather was usually in our living room. He liked to listen to the radio when he visited us, even when he was alone in the living room or having lunch with his first concubine. Our radio was on the windowsill in our living room, and when I came home from school, I would usually turn it on to the popular music station; almost immediately, my grandfather would just switch it to a news station without asking. He told us that listening to the world news was the most important thing we could listen to, especially since the radio news station only broadcasted the world news twice a day at 1pm and 6pm. We would not question our grandfather when he switched the station on us; this was a typical way of my generation interacting with our grandparents. As children, we would simply obey our elders blindly; nowadays, children can challenge and ask questions to their parents and grandparents, and adults have to be quick on their feet to answer.

In between working many long hours, mother found joy in taking us back very often to Tai Po Market to visit her parents. To travel there, we took a two-hour train ride; in those days, trains ran on coal, and sometimes, if we put our heads out of the window, our white shirts would become stained from the all the coal dust. We would hardly look presentable when we reached my grandparents' house. We would stay there for an entire day, and sometimes we would stay for an entire weekend if they were holidays, the New Year, or birthdays.

When we arrived for our visits, by the time we walked halfway up the long stairs of the entrance, our grandmother was already standing there to greet us. I would be amazed every time we visited at how beautiful my grandfather Chu's home was. It was quite a large house, composed of two stories and a loft. When guests came, they passed through an iron gate, a few front steps, and into the large room on the first story called the main hall. Nowadays, the equivalent of the main hall would be the living room. Off of the main hall were three bedrooms: my grandfather's, which was first on the left, one bedroom beside his and another behind it. The kitchen was further in the back towards the right on the first floor. The food was cooked in a large wok with a wooden lid and placed on the cement block on right-hand corner, and a big hole situated in the middle on the top side. Below the

109

block was a fire-pit, and in the pit were the hay and branches used to fuel the fire. The left-hand corner of the kitchen held a built-in cement cistern for the water with a cover, next to which there was always a ladle. The bathroom was next to the kitchen, and was so small that it only had a long hole for a toilet, a single water tap, and one wooden bucket.

There were two sets of stairs to get up to the second story and the loft; one of these sets led past the bathroom and kitchen, and were called the back stairs, or fire stairs. The loft itself was quite large, and divided into three sections. The front sections were used by the second grandmother's children. The other part was used by my mother's sister-in-law Cheung Kiu and her children, Pui Ying, the elder daughter, and Cheung Wai, the younger son. Pui Ying and I were very close. Sometimes I slept with her, but she always wanted me to sleep on the outside of the bed. The bed was just a simple bed, two wooden saw horses supporting two twenty-six-inch-by-six foot wooden planks. The mattress they used those days was an old thick comforter made from cotton, with four bamboo poles, one at each corner to support the square mosquito netting, which had an overlapped opening in the center. The mosquito net in my bed was different; it had cone-shaped netting. Getting in or out of the bed was not that easy; we needed to act very fast, so as not to let the mosquitoes get into our beds. If so, those mosquitoes would suck our blood. I must have tasted the most delicious to them; my mother would always say, "We all sit here, and no one ever gets bitten except for you; your blood must be delicious." I think my mother was right; my two legs were full of mosquito marks for several decades.

When we arrived and had walked up the path and passed through the iron gate and entered the main hall, we all gathered downstairs and greeted our grandfather first. In our impatience, the children would be eager to play around the house, so while my mother would often stay downstairs with my grandfather to discuss some important issues, we would go upstairs to see our grandmother, and then explored the house to see if there were any activities we could participate in. I usually went to see my cousin Maria.

With such a large family, my grandfather's home was still a flurry of activity, and as children, we would love every wonderful moment we spent there. Once it was time to leave, our day would not be over; my mother would then take us walking around Tai Po Market. This was a thrill for us, to be walking around in the busy marketplace, with all the fascinating people and stores. One of my favorite places to go was a small store that sold delicious marinated foods, like vegetables, plums, ginger, olives, and pickles in large, glass jars. Since there were many lanes and buildings in Tai Po Market, I knew how to get there from my grandfather's house the quickest by landmarks. I would look first for a temple near the end of a street, and then I would see a set of long stairs; those stairs took me directly down to the store, located in the market area, and I could bypass all the pesky streets. Every time I rushed down those stairs, I couldn't wait to get a piece of scrumptious food from the store. When I walked in, the kind, friendly owner knew exactly who I was; my grandfather owned many of the buildings in the area, so mother and her children were like royalty!

From that store, I would usually go across the street to a Chinese herbal store which my grandfather rented to them. The parents of the store, had several children, the youngest girl was my best friend Cheung Ching Po. Ching Po was a boy's name; she was named so because her parents wanted a boy badly, and by giving her a boy's name, they believed it might bring a boy to their family in the future. (It actually worked; they got a son two years later.) Ching Po studied at St. Rose of Lima School with me, and took a train to school daily. After we graduated high school, she studied as a nurse in England. Despite the distance, we kept our friendship throughout the years. When her mother was sick, she came back from London to live with us while she worked in Hong Kong; when she was not working, she went back to Tai Po Market to stay with her mother until her mother passed away. Then, she immigrated to Vancouver, Canada. Her friendship means just as much to me today as it did back during our childhood days in Tai Po Market.

When these lovely weekends in Tai Po Market would end, we would all bid goodbye to our grandparents and walk back through the iron gate to catch our train back to Hung Hum. As children, we all missed our grandparents and the fun times we had in their home every time we had to leave them, but I think mother missed those most of all. Every time we left, I would catch a brief, wistful look in her eye as we walked away and their home faded out of sight. The look would then disappear as quickly as it came, and her stern, motherly expression would return to her face as she began thinking about her work week ahead.

While we were going about our daily lives at work, school, and travelling frequently to my visit my grandparents, my father was still recovering in the hospital. In 1953, he was well enough to return to work again, and took up a part-time job as an Assistant Manager of one of his father's businesses, the Mei Lee Kin Ice Cream Factory, located at 192 Prince Edward Road. My mother and I and my siblings used to go to visit him all the time and enjoy his delicious ice cream; the mango and chocolate flavors were my favorite, and mother love the red bean popsicles. Later that year, he received another full-time job, this time as a wireless operator on board a tramp, the S.S. Ameise, in Formosa, Taiwan. A tramp was a cargo boat running on no regular line or schedule, the equivalent to a commercial hauling-truck on land. It was out for hire to carry things from one place to another. The ship was owned by Panama, and carried the Panamanian flag on it as it sailed. After several years of enforced idles due to his ill health, my father was pleased to come across this job. The pay was reasonably well. But he had to leave his wife and children, and had no idea when he would be back to Hong Kong. All of us went to Kai Tak Airport to see him board the plane that would take him to his new job; his departure was yet another tearful goodbye for our family.

111

During his long days at sea on board the ship, far away from his family, my father needed something to keep him occupied. He was a very educated man, and he loved to read. His travels had taken him to Japan often, and in 1955, he taught himself the Japanese language. From his readings, he also learned the ukulele. The ukulele is a Hawaiian guitar with four strings. It was introduced to Hawaii from Portugal around 1879, and has been a popular musical instrument there ever since. My father could play it very well. He also studied English through mail correspondence, and his writing became excellent. My father became an asset to all on board because of his writing abilities. His illness prevented him from providing any physical assistance, but he always offered to help with tutoring English and writing documents for the captain.

His business took him all over Southeast Asia. In 1956, he traveled to Balikpapan in Indonesia, Colombo in Sri Lanka, Dungun in Malaysia, and Saganoseki in Japan. The following year, in 1957, he traveled to Singapore, Saigon, and Calcutta. Yet despite his travels and all the wonderful and exotic sights he saw, his family was the only thing on his mind. One letter written to his brother Anthony, dated June 14, 1958, stated, "Our ship goes back to Hong Kong every few months on the average, and stays there for a few days each time. It means to say that in one complete year I'll be at home for not more than fifteen days. Worst of all, we do not know when we are going back. It is this waiting, this suspense that saps most of the spirit and joy out of our lives as sea-farers on board a tramp." My father's life at sea was disheartening to his spirit; he missed his family, and he longed to be home with us again.

At home, my mother was having her own difficulties. Her two sons were growing older now and showing signs of not having a father to raise them as they were growing up. They were very active and difficult during this time, and were trouble-making. Once, in 1956, they purposely hit a passer-by with a water balloon while there was a riot marching down the road. Two men came up to bang on our door; mother opened the wooden door that was separated with a closed iron gate. One of the men shouted to mother about her son throwing a paper bag filled with water smashing over them. Mother had no idea what was happening and called her two sons to come out to apologize. Later, the two men scolded her with a few words and left. Because of the situation of the riot in the streets, they were suspicious that some people deliberately were out to harm them instead of simply the naughty boys playing.

This had not been the first time they had acted up. They were known as the "wild children," or the "naughty boys." Another incident was when they both had laid down in the middle of the street in protest of not getting money from their nanny to buy snacks. My mother didn't mind allowing her sons to have a little bit of money to buy snacks to eat with their friends, but she did not want them to eat so much they would not eat their dinner. It happened so repeatedly that my mother had to talk to the servant to tell her not to give them any more money. When my brothers asked the

112

servant for money this time, she did not give any to them. My brothers then came up with a strategy. They laid down in the middle of the busy intersection near the docks entrance in protest and would not get up. Their behavior was a large burden and an embarrassment for my mother. They did not have the structure and discipline of a male figure to follow with my father away at sea, and my mother was exhausted and frustrated with their behavior.

But she didn't have the time to fully address their behavior. She worked long hours to ensure our financial survival, and most of her energy was spent on her responsibilities at work. The benefit of working so much, though, was that she was rising steadily in her job. She was promoted to Class I in 1957, and to Revenue Sub-Inspector in 1958. When she was promoted to Sub-Inspector, her job was to oversee 38 women stationed of all Custom's ports – airport, ship wharfs and train stations. Part of her job was to ensure these ports were free from crime. Once, while working, she spotted a young man wearing a nicely tailored suit and who was smoking constantly, one cigarette after another. Although the airport was cold with its high air-conditioning, this man was sweating a lot. This behavior immediately made mother believe that this man was nervous for some reason. Mother's sixth sense kicked in, and she knew instantly that this man was up to no good. She asked two of her staff members to bring him into the questioning room. What a shock when it was they discovered that he was taped, neck to toe, in clear, plastic bags filled with opium! Mother's instincts were far superior to most people; she could look at you and notice immediately if there were any problems. Her skill had no exceptions. There was a reason she was well-respected among her colleagues; in a job where people frequently attempted to persuade her to let certain items pass, she remained uncorrupted, never accepting any bribes and never turning a blind eye to any illegal activity.

On December 17, 1959, the big building, Kimberly Mansion, at 15 Austin Ave, Kowloon was officially settled, and we moved in happily together, along with my father, to H Flat, 10th Floor. There were fifteen floors in total, and each floor had three big apartments in the front, facing the street, and five smaller apartments facing the weather reservation in the back. We lived in one of these smaller apartments. It was considered mid-sized for a family of six; it had two bedrooms in total, and my father slept on the left side of the room. The bathroom was situated in the between of two bedrooms. Four of us in bulk bed slept in the other, mother slept in the living room, and Ah Mg slept in the servant's room. There was also a half bath behind the kitchen. Our apartment was facing the weather reservation separated by a hill across. Since this was a busy district, most of the buildings were facing each other, but we were lucky to enjoy the open space; the sun faced this way, and because of this area, they planted trees & flowers with only one low building to work instead of looking across all high rises. My mother was clever in choosing the back because our view was much nicer than the street. (It brought to mind an old Chinese saying: "even if you have money, sometimes you can't find an apartment facing south.") St. Mary's Canossian College was right across the street, and the land investments were wonderful; my mother was very clever and smart to move here to this high-class, residential area with excellent schools.

At Kimberley Mansion, our lives picked up right where we left off back in Fan Lan in 1951. We were altogether as a family again usually, until my father would leave for a time to continue working on board his ship. When my father was home, I would proudly show him what I had learned in my piano lessons from my cousin Pui Ying, who traveled from her home in Tai Po Market to our house to teach me. My father loved to listen to his favorite piano pieces, "Blue Danube" and "Fur Elise," and he would often ask me to play for him. Sometimes my parents asked me to play a waltz for them, and they would dance together. When we had visitors, we would play the piano for them, and make my parents proud. It was very important for my parents to make sure their children were well-educated, both in school and extracurricular activities.

Now that we had moved into a new place, my parents were both working, and the apartment in Fan Lan was still a rental property for us, my parents had enough income to send my brothers to boarding school. My father and my mother had discussed at length my brothers' behavior. Enough was enough; their behavior as children was unacceptable as it was, but they did not want them to grow into unruly and discourteous adult men. They enrolled them in Salesian Catholic Boarding School in Hong Kong for one year to give them the structure they were not receiving at home. The school only allowed their students to come home every three months, and during their first visit home, we could see that mother's decision had paid off. Paul and Stephen behaved very well; when we were at the table for dinner, they were not picky and ate anything that was handed to them. They told us that during their school dinners, food disappeared quickly; when they would finish their first bowl of rice, and went up for a second round, there would be no food left on the dishes on the tables when they returned to the table. Paul told us his strategy: "You need to play smart before you turn your back to get the second bowl of rice. Make sure you scoop food in your empty bowl before you get up. For one meal, that is not much food on the plate, so I put the fish head or fish tail and sauce in my bowl before I get up for more rice." Just like my mother had enacted her own strategy in the fish-bowl soup eating contest years ago, Paul had devised his own strategy.

With my brothers off at school, Mother remained a busy woman every day. She worked hard on shift duty, taking different and difficult hours every day, and she took care of my father and her two daughters at home. On Sundays, if she was not required to work, mother and I would go to visit my brothers at school. It was quite a long distance; from home we took a twenty-five-minute bus ride to Star Ferry, and then took a ten-minute ferry ride. When we got off the ferry, we caught a bus at Sau Kai Wan, then took another tram to Chai Wan and walked up the hill to where their school was located. We always brought soup, delicious dishes, and lots of fruit for my

114

hungry brothers. We spent the entire day doing this for the full year they attended that school.

Mother was so busy at work and so used to taking care of things herself at home every day that she rarely had time or cause to have a good conversation with any other adults. She was used to being self-sufficient, and did not have anyone around her to share her difficulties and anxious emotions with. No one had been through what she had, and she did not want to burden anyone with any of her stress, so she kept her feelings to herself. There finally arrived one person, however, who understood my mother's hard work. Her lovely younger sister Theresa had arrived in Hong Kong when she learned that her mother, the second wife of my grandfather Chu, had become sick in the hospital with tuberculosis. Now, she had come back to Hong Kong to be by her mother's side while she was working in the Kowloon hospital. Mother understood what she was going through, and invited Theresa to stay with us for several months. While both my father and Theresa's mother were ill, Theresa offered my mother the comfort that she needed. She was the only one who understood mother's situation and deep emotions.

Theresa stayed with us through early 1960. The start of a new year brought my mother the hope that we would be able to stay together for good now. Although my brothers were off at school, mother still had the job of having my father recovered as best as he could be and living with us in Kimberly Mansion.

My father had begun feeling slightly ill again, enough to prevent him from working on his ship. Now, he worked in the side business he had had since 1956, reselling medical, electric and other enterprise products to the local stores to make as much money as possible for his family. He wanted to work as much as possible to provide for his family if his illness returned.

In early 1960, that's exactly what happened.

My mother was not usually outwardly worried about my father. She never let her emotions show. This time, though, things were different. The doctors had told my father in 1952 that he only had three or four years to live. God was good to him and gave him more, but my father knew he could still become ill again at any time. Now, the doctor told my mother that if her husband entered the hospital again, there wasn't much else they could do for him.

My mother kept this news hidden from her children. Every day, she worked hard to keep her emotions in. She continued going to work every day as if life was normal. At this time, she was sleeping in the living room while my father was sleeping in his room. She never slept through the night. I remember hearing her get up in the middle of the night, tip-toeing around, so she wouldn't wake anyone, checking on my father to see if he was all right. She checked on her children too, tucking up the blankets to my brothers, who had kicked them off. During the day, you could not tell that she had not slept well. She remained smiling and outgoing, always willing to go out of her way for others. You would never suspect that underneath her warm persona, she carried a stressful burden that no one but her could understand.

In mid-September, my father entered the hospital again. He had no words, no more letters to write; he was done fighting. He was helpless at the hands of his illness.

Mother was by his side every moment she could be. She knew this was the end. One day, she saw lines of ants marching up to his bed's legs and frames. No explanation needed.

My father's brother, my uncle Ambrose, came quickly when heard about is brother. He was very close to my father, as they had had the same mother, Chiu Hung Yee, my grandfather's second concubine. At that time, Uncle Ambrose was a director of China Airlines in Taiwan, flying between Hong Kong and Taiwan very often. He knew my father had only one hope: that his young wife and four children had someone in the family who could offer some help. Standing beside his bed, he promised my father that he would take care of all of us.

It was on September 21 that my father was holding one hand with his beloved mother and the other with his wife, when at long last, God set him free. At the age of forty-six, my father, Joseph Wong Pui Lai, died from pulmonary tuberculosis.

My mother was only forty-two years old when her husband died. His illness had already prepared her for his death, but her strength and determination allowed her to pick up the remains of her life with her four children and accept her new responsibilities with no tears or complaints. It had not been my mother's fault; she was a victim of an unfair tragedy. The Japanese war destroyed our family, destroyed my father, and destroyed so many people's lives in Hong Kong.

Mother told us that she could not allow herself to have time to grieve. The loss of her husband was devastating; nevertheless, she'd rather see her husband relieved of this painful battle with his long-term sickness. I never saw her shed her tears, except the day my father died and the day we were in the funeral home; perhaps she carried her grief in her solitary place. Instead, she held her head high to allow the tears in her eyes to roll back down into her heart. Gone was my mother's true love; their perfect love and promises were eternally vanished in the mist of the air.

I did not have a lot of memories about my father's funeral. I only remembered that my mother picked his favorite suit, tie, shirt and shoes. He was holding a rosary, and next to him was a Bible. Mother ordered a western-style coffin with nice fabric lining. The ceremony was held in Kowloon Funeral Home, and he was later transferred to Cheung Sha Wan Catholic Cemetery. Mother told us that this plot was permanent, as the cost was expensive. If she bought one temporary plot, after eight years of being buried, my father's bones would be dug up to put into an urn. She believed that after my father died, his burial in the ground allowed him to turn into ashes and soil, and his soul could ascend to heaven.

116

I don't know how long it took my mother to heal her wounds; she kept her rollercoaster emotions inside her. Instead, she went about her daily routine without being interrupted or distracted. She picked up what was left of her life and continued to nurture her children, taking on the new responsibility of providing all financial resources for her family. Somehow, she sacrificed her grief to make sure our lives went on as usual.

We had no life left at Kimberley Mansion, so we moved back to Fan Lan for the second time. I remember that our new house had three bedrooms lined up on the right side, with a bathroom between Paul's bedroom and my bedroom that I shared with Agnes. Mother shared the other bedroom with Stephen. The living room and dining room faced opposite the bedrooms on the left side of the house, and the kitchen was near the servant's quarters where Ah Mg lived. Between Paul's bedroom and Ah Mg's quarters, there was a big open square that was usually used as a working area for washing and hanging clothes. Outside, a big porch with a roof made an overhang in front of the building, and one big cement path lay in the middle of the yard, usually used as a parking spot for cars, but leaving plenty of room for people to walk through. There was also one big tree that we called "Tai Hung Fa" on the left side of the garden that Paul liked to climb up. (One day, after he was scolded by mother, he was stubborn and did not come back to sleep in the house, and the next morning, mother found him sleeping on the tree.)

Our lives continued on as usual, almost as if nothing had happened. Mother and I took the train in the morning to go to work and to school; and my two brothers studied at the local school. In Fan Lan, people ate their dinner earlier than in the city, around five and five-thirty. Before six, almost all families had finished their meal and would sit outside to relax. On one particular Sunday, mother's friends' teenage sons came in from the city and stayed until dinnertime. Our servant had not prepared their share of food, but mother insisted they stay for the meal. She pretended she was not hungry, just picking here and there at the food to accommodate the guests. Paul and I heeded mother's actions; we tried to eat until we were only half-full, and Ah Mg did not show up to the table at all. This was the lesson of giving that my mother taught us; four of us sacrificed our supper to them. Mother always said, "To give is much better than to take."

It wasn't until 1962 that we would finally find a permanent place to live. That year, my mother's department at work, the Hong Kong Government Custom & Exercise department, finished building a series of high rises for their higher ranking officers to live in, so we moved again from Fan Lan back to Hung Hom at 3 Lee Kung Street on the tenth floor. From the high rise, we could see the whole view of the playground where the children played and all the flowers and trees below our eyes. Transportation was convenient and shopping was not that far to walk to the market.

With all that had happened in the past few years, mother wanted nothing more than to plant her family's roots somewhere safe and solid.

117

Our new apartment finally felt like an actual home for us; mother bought a color TV, and a music player with round plates. She introduced us to listen to soft music like semi-classical, which I fell in love with and am still in love with now. We all adjusted to our new lives well. Mother did everything in her power to make sure that we had the most normal upbringing possible— never once thinking of herself.

It was around this time, however, that extra attention needed to be paid to mother's youngest daughter, Agnes. My mother was thirty-one years old when she brought Agnes into the world. Agnes was my mother's last child, the beautiful, final blessing that completed my parents' perfect love. I was eight years older and would eventually grow to be four inches taller than Agnes, but as we were growing up, the gap in our ages didn't matter; I loved spending time with her. She remained quiet and easygoing as a child; no matter what I asked of her, wherever I asked her to go, whatever I asked her to do, my obedient baby sister would always toddle along after me, without a whisper or complaint.

As we grew older, however, our age difference began to show; after school, I would be busy with extracurricular activities or out somewhere with my friends, and our brothers were often playing together, so Agnes was usually left to play on her own. But Agnes didn't seem to mind; as a child, she began to show an incredible aptitude for activities she could do alone. My mother decided to let her try playing the piano, and immediately discovered that Agnes had inherited my grandmother's gift. Mother gently encouraged Agnes to practice playing as often as she could, which allowed Agnes's talent to soar. She practiced whenever she could, touching each key with grace and beauty, and she grew to be wonderfully skilled. Somehow, the songs always sounded better when Agnes played them; her playing was one of the few things in life that could bring tears to my mother's eyes.

In school, Agnes was a dream to her teachers— obedient, pleasant, and well-behaved. From a young age, Agnes also showed that she was very bright. Her academics were consistently near perfect, and she always received the highest grades in her classes. Mother encouraged Agnes to continue working hard at her studies, but she didn't want to push her too much. As proud as she was of her daughter, she wanted to make sure Agnes enjoyed a balanced, normal childhood, so she focused on making sure Agnes stayed the happy, easygoing child she was, while still working hard in school.

Agnes remained quiet and well-mannered as her talents were nurtured. She never showed any signs throughout her childhood that would give my mother cause for concern. Mother knew she had a wonderful, promising future ahead of her.

But things changed when Agnes entered her second year of high school at St. Rose of Lima's School. As the school year began, Agnes's grades suddenly begin to slip. Mother knew it was not laziness; instead, she thought perhaps the harsh pressures and high demand of the rigorous school was putting too much stress on Agnes. So she took Agnes out of St. Rose of Lima's and enrolled her in a different school, hoping to relieve some of the pressure.

But Agnes's performance still did not improve. Mother then tried a different school, and another one after that, each time trying to pinpoint the difficulties Agnes was having. The standards were lower at each of these new schools, and yet Agnes's grades remained poor.

As her academics declined, Agnes's health began to change too; she started to lose a lot of weight, and often she couldn't sleep at night. Mother knew then that something was very wrong.

Confused and concerned, mother took her to several doctors, trying to figure out what was wrong. Each one failed to give her a sufficient explanation. Mother became increasingly frustrated at seeing her daughter's health continue to deteriorate with no proper diagnosis. She did not know what path to take or what options she could even offer Agnes for recovery or treatment, since the doctors could not establish the problem.

In 1967, the doctors finally determined that Agnes suffered from a mental illness. Satisfied that she had received a formal diagnosis, mother began to seek treatment for Agnes. Mother wanted to ensure Agnes would be treated like a human being, not simply a medical patient. She decided to enroll Agnes in private psychology sessions with Dr. Lau, a kind and patient man. His office was in Causeway Bay, very far from our home in Hong Kong; mother and Agnes had to take a ferry and a bus to get there. While the sessions were only a half-hour long, mother and Agnes spent over two hours traveling to get there and back. But it was worth it; mother was gratified with the way Dr. Lau treated Agnes with kindness and humanity, not simply as a patient.

Eventually, the sessions, along with the proper medication prescribed, began to have the desired effects, as Agnes began to show visible signs of progress. Mother firmly believed that this was only a small bump in the road for her daughter; her illness did not mean she would have to stop her studies or activities, or that she could not live a normal life. With the proper treatment that she was receiving, Agnes was well on the path to successfully managing her illness and returning to her studies. Mother was beyond grateful for these treatments, and was glad that her beautiful, intelligent daughter would be able to resume her normal life. Mother knew that Agnes would be able to live up to her full potential with all the support she had now.

But all of that would soon change.

Unbeknownst to my mother at the time, the chance for a normal life for Agnes would never come. All the while that mother had been seeking answers and help for her daughter, a terribly bitter family battle had been brewing for years. Mother knew about it—but she did not know the effects it would soon have on her. She had no idea what would soon be stolen from her and her children, and the terrible events that would follow.

CHAPTER 7

It had begun with my grandfather's will. My grandfather's will and estate was of much interest to all of my mother's family, since he had such an abundance of property that he had been accumulating throughout Tai Po Market since he was a young man. Back at the turn of the twentieth century, Tai Po Market was a small cluster of streets and market stalls and not much else. This was essentially the situation found by the British when they took over the New Territories lease in 1899. It may have been small, but it was still significant enough to make the British want to use Tai Po Market as their administration center for the northern New Territories.

This was perfect for my intelligent grandfather to begin building his own wealth. Over the years, as Tai Po Market grew, so did my grandfather's estate. My grandfather worked as a senior clerk in the District Office in Tai Po Market, where he had foreseen the important land soon to be developed. That was why he purchased much of his land at only a few cents per foot. All of his property he gradually accrued was not strictly housing; he had mountains, lands, and full or empty lots. Eventually, he had so much property that he always had at least six or seven containers full of deeds. If it was very important property, he would put the deeds in his safe.

His most prized property was of course the piece of land he bought for him and his family to build their nest at 1 Yan Hing Street, the first house next to the small hillside of the train station. This was very convenient for his grandchildren whenever we needed to take the train; when we heard the train whistle, we would simply walk up the steps and get on the train without waiting.

My grandmother also worked at a local clinic. At that time, in Chinese culture, however, men were the master of all family property and finances; although my grandmother contributed all her salary into the same account as my grandfather, she did not have any power or authority to act in financial matters.

This tradition also meant that my grandfather would need another son in order to pass on his wealth and property, because only the sons could inherit all property rights. Since his first son, Yam Wah, had died in World War II, my grandfather decided to take his first wife's maid, a fifteen-year-old woman named Tsui Sau Ha, to be his first concubine. At that time in Chinese culture, and up to 1962, it was legal for a man to have multiple concubines, in order to produce sons to pass on the family name. However, any man who took concubines would also have to be wealthy enough to support and house them financially, which my grandfather certainly was. Sau Ha eventually had six children; one child died at an early age, but she eventually had two sons, Yam Kwan, born June 3, 1931, and Yam Ko, born December 27, 1946.

Unfortunately, Sau Ha soon contracted tuberculosis, and my grandfather wanted more sons. He then married his second concubine, nineteen-year-old Yau Sun Dai, in 1949. I can still remember the day of their

120

wedding: it was around early summer, a sunny day with lots of people cheering in and outside my grandfather's house. I was standing in the middle of the street with my cousin Pui Ying, when we saw the "Bridal Sedan Chair" coming towards us. This ancient bridal sedan chair, painted bright red, was one of the main vehicles used in Chinese wedding ceremonies. There were several men walking in front of the chair, blowing music instruments. There were four carriers, two in front, and two in the back. The "good luck woman," as she was called in Cantonese, walked beside the sedan chair and accompanied the bride all the way to the bridegroom's home. Traditionally, the bride was not supposed to walk into the bridegroom's house; the bridegroom would come out to open the curtain of the sedan chair, and the good luck woman next to the chair would carry the bride all the way back to the bridegroom's house on her back. But since Sun Dai was the second concubine, she walked on her own, accompanied by the good luck woman, and stepped in the main room, and then to my grandfather's bed where she waited with patience.

I always remember how beautiful she looked that day; she was wearing a pink-beaded bridal suit to match her fair complexion. She was also wearing a pretty embodied large handkerchief that covered her face. She was a lovely woman, and my grandfather was lucky to have her. After their wedding, their marriage yielded six children, three of whom were sons, Yam Hong, Yam Ki, and Yam Cheung, so my grandfather got his wish.

With such a large family, my grandfather continued to work over the years to accumulate more property that he would eventually pass on to all his sons. Beginning after 1946, my grandfather placed all new property he bought under different made-up names: Heung Chi, Nam Yeun, Yi Fong, Wai Chi, and Tak Yam Tong. Anything that was purchased in any of those names all belonged to him. It's similar to how authors use pseudonyms to write books, or how actors use stage names. He used these aliases to purchase property for himself. The names were different on every purchase, but the signatures were all undeniably my grandfather's – they all had the same handwriting. All of his property together, collectively under all these names, formed what is called a "tong."

Regardless of what name he used for each piece of property, everything still belonged to my grandfather. With such a large estate, my grandfather hired managers called "sze lei" to help him collect all the rent. Chu Sut Hon, my grandfather's nephew, was his first sze lei. Sut Hon had lost his parents when he was six years old, and my grandfather had raised and educated him, to which he was always very grateful. In return, when he became older, although he had a permanent job as a postman, he still helped my grandfather after his office hours and during weekends and holidays.

But my grandfather accumulated more and more property, so he assigned his daughter-in-law, Cheung Kiu, the wife of his son Yam Wah, to be a sze lei as well. He also hired Yam Kwan, his son with his first concubine. Yam Kwan had already tried his hand at several jobs that did not work out. He had gone to Hong Kong University to study sociology; after he graduated, he wanted to work as a social worker, but he was turned down from such jobs because he was told that he was not aware of the state of the poor. After that, he taught high school for a year, but did not have the proper work ethic yet to deal with all the responsibilities. So he finally began working for his father as a sze lei. Still, Yam Kwan showed laziness and irresponsibility in his position.

It was not long before their new positions as sze leis allowed greed to overtake them. Soon after he hired them, my grandfather discovered that Yam Kwan and Cheung Kiu had been pocketing the rent for themselves. Not only that, but he also discovered one day that Cheung Kiu had signed an important document about a property behind his back. Legally, she had no right to do so in her position as a sze lei; she had done this in a clear attempt to undermine him.

Upon this discovery, my grandfather could not believe that he had entrusted two members of his own family with such responsibility, and they had belittled him like that. He became so stressed and angry that he had to enter the hospital. When Yam Kwan and Cheung Kiu found out that my grandfather was in the hospital, they didn't realize how wrong they had been or attempt to apologize; instead, they were hoping that he would die in the hospital! All they wanted was more power, money, and property. When my grandfather discovered this was their intention, he knew they were capable of doing much worse than stealing the rent.

At that time, my grandfather's second concubine and her seven children were very young, and the elder son was only fifteen years old, so my grandfather wanted to protect them as best he could. So to protect his family in the event that anything should ever happen to him, or if anyone ever tried to steal again from him, in 1960, my grandfather made a will that dictated what would be given to each of his sons when he passed away. This way, all of his property that he had worked all of his life for would fall into the rightful hands.

The will was very simple. First, no females were allowed to participate, according to Chinese tradition. Second, all sons were to be equal beneficiaries; this was what my grandfather called "one son, one share." My grandfather had six sons in total to which his property would be given. This meant that Cheung Wai, Cheung Kiu's only son, who was already fully grown, the first concubine's two sons, Yam Kwan and Yam Ko, and the second concubine's three sons, Yam Hong, Yam Ki, and Yam Cheung, all received one share each of my grandfather's property. However, that also meant that my grandfather's second concubine and her sons would receive more of his property in total because she had more sons than his first wife and his first concubine.

After my grandfather made his will official and public, many family members saw that this division of his property was unfair. But the key person who protested was Cheung Kiu. It would have been improper for her to protest even if she was blood-related; she was still only an in-law, and yet she still had the nerve to complain about property that did not even belong to her. She immediately enlisted Yam Kwan in her complaints as well, and together, their relentless protests began to form a harsh rift in my mother's family. The fighting became so bad that my grandfather remained in the hospital more frequently.

One day, he called my mother to come and see him in the hospital, so he could explain to her what was going on. What my mother saw him, she became frightened; he was crying bitterly. This was out of character for her normally strong-willed father.

Before she knew what was happening, my grandfather took my mother's hand and knelt down in front of her. Mother was stunned; the elder parent in Chinese tradition never knelt down to their children. She immediately knelt down as well.

My grandfather begged my mother to help him and his third wife's children, asking her to keep honor in his family's name. He also gave mother a handwritten letter, stained with tears on it. He trusted my mother so much that he knew she would keep this promise.

My mother didn't hesitate or ask questions. She looked straight in his eyes and promised him that whatever happened, she would be there for all his young children. She would keep the honor of her family's name and her father's hard work.

My mother had no idea what this would entail in the coming years, and neither did my grandfather. After he had my mother's promise that she would help him and his third wife's children, my grandfather took extra steps to make sure his estate would be safe. On March 16, 1964, my grandfather appointed four volunteer trustees to ensure that his will would be followed when he died. One trustee was a minister named Chu Yee Shun from Church of Christ at 22 Sui On Street, Tai Po Market where my grandfather attended; one trustee was his first concubine's brother, Tsui Chuk Shan; one was his second concubine, Sun Dai; and the last was my mother. All the trustees had no benefits; they were strictly volunteers, performing their duties only to protect my grandfather's wishes.

After he appointed these four trustees, he gathered them all together to explain to them why it was so important that his will be carried out. He told them all about the property he had through the years, to give the trustees a good picture of everything he owned. When he died, he wanted to make sure that all of his sons, especially the second concubine's three sons, were provided with benefits. Those three sons were young children at the time, with the eldest being only fifteen years old. My grandfather was very responsible, and wanted to make sure these children would be cared for.

The trustees all agreed and promised my grandfather they would protect his will and wishes. My mother especially, recalling how her father had kneeled before her in the hospital, promised with all her heart that she would do whatever it took to make sure my grandfather's property remained in the right hands.

123

While my grandfather and his trustees were working hard to secure all of his estate, the situation in our family became more and more tense. When my grandfather passed away on July 3, 1964, only four months after he had appointed the trustees, he left behind a bitter, unresolved battle between his honest trustees and two resentful family members.

At the time of my grandfather's passing, Yam Kwan and Cheung Kiu were still legally employed by my grandfather and were allowed to continue to collect all the rental properties each month without giving anything to the second concubine and her six children. Now, however, and unsurprisingly, they decided to put their full evil plan into action. They decided to override my grandfather's will and divide his property into two shares only. Out of sheer spite and greed, they refused to allow the second concubine to receive anything to support their six children.

When my mother discovered this, she knew immediately what she had to do. As she had promised my grandfather, my mother convinced the other trustees to bring this bitter conflict to court to defend my grandfather's will and divide all of his property the way he had intended it. They had no other choice; if the four trustees didn't go to court, the second concubine and her sons would receive nothing, leaving them penniless. It was up to my mother and the other three trustees to honor my grandfather's will and wishes and place his hard-earned money and property into the right hands.

As each side met with their lawyers and prepared for court, my mother assumed this would be an open-and-shut case. There was really no question who was right and who was wrong here; there was an official will that stated exactly what my grandfather had wanted; there were four honest trustees that my grandfather had appointed to defend this legal will; and there were two greedy people with a history of disrespecting and challenging my grandfather, one of whom was not even a blood relative. My mother figured this would be an easy decision for the judge.

As the trial began, my mother had no idea what she was in for. From the very first day, Yam Kwan and Cheung Kiu presented a horrific case of lies in court. In one of the property documents under the aliases presented to the court, Cheung Kiu lied and said she had signed her name legally. My mother knew, however, that she had signed her name behind my grandfather's back, since my grandfather had made every attempt to keep her away from such documents. When asked about how she had earned all the money that she now had, she lied and said that she and Sau Ha, my grandfather's first concubine, who died in October 1961, had both worked hard for that money that was used to purchase the property. But with only having the job of manager, with a low income, it was clear that there was no way they were able to save or contribute anything to the purchases.

On one of the other property documents, the alias Yi Fong was also listed; Yam Kwan lied and said that this was the alias that grandfather had given to him, rather than his own alias. This was impossible, because Yam Kwan was too young at the time to even own property. One of their

124

witnesses, David Akers-Jones, the deputy district commissioner of the New Territories, said that he had never heard of the names my grandfather had used as aliases before; under the certain section of which my grandfather's properties were purchased, Mr. Akers-Jones stated he believed they were actually clan and family properties, rather than personal properties. His evidence stated that if this was the case, the property was rightfully left to any living male descendants, regardless of what was stated in the owner's will. His testimony was simply incorrect.

My mother's side had plenty of evidence to refute what Cheung Kiu and Yam Kwan's witnesses stated. On November 8, 1961, my grandfather had made a written declaration that the three relevant names were his aliases. My mother's lawyers argued that my grandfather had given all the properties under the aliases to his only two sons living at that time. One of their witnesses, a Tai Po village elder, Lam Tsap Choy, who had known my grandfather for about forty years, said that grandfather did indeed have these aliases, and according to the law, if a person buys property in the name of these private "tongs," the property belongs to him.

For four years, the two sides, one honest and one deceitful, fought long and hard in court. Back and forth, the testimony was given and refuted; lies were spoken with no sense of conscience. After all of the testimony, and with all of my grandfather's life savings and the future of his children at stake, the verdict soon came down to what the one judge presiding over the court believed.

It was not until May of 1968, four years after my grandfather's passing, that the judge declared his final ruling. My mother and the three other trustees were ready. They knew they had the truth on their side, and with all the bold-faced lies that Yam Kwan and Cheung Kiu had presented, mother felt confident that the judge would see right through them and rule fairly, logically, and justly.

As the judge began to read his ruling, my mother's face changed. Her eyes widened, and her mouth dropped open. My mother never shows her emotions—but this was a clear exception. After hearing all the evidence, presented, the judge somehow believed that grandfather's intention in creating the aliases was to create a trust for his living male descendants, and not dividing the property not by "one son, one share." This meant that every son was an equal beneficiary. Thus, my grandfather's will was overridden; this meant that the second concubine and her sons would only receive one third of my grandfather's estate rather than half as my grandfather had originally intended.

In one swift motion, on that day in May 1968, a lifetime's worth of my grandfather's hard work, a representation of the morals, ethics, and values of our entire family, was gone.

My mother actually didn't believe the judge at first. There was no way that with all the evidence presented to him that he could possibly rule in favor of Yam Kwan and Cheung Kiu. Even if all the trustees' evidence was not enough to match the opposing side, any logical judge would be more inclined to trust four people that my grandfather himself had trusted—not two people that he had tried to keep away from his property.

The judge also didn't even stop to think about this from my grandfather's perspective logically; if my grandfather had lived, and had left all of his properties and estates to his descendants, as the judge believed he did, he would have nothing left for himself, his wife, his concubines, or his young daughters. With this ruling, Yam Kwan and Cheung Kiu, as sze leis, controlled all my grandfather's property—every piece of land and building that was in his name. This meant that my grandfather's first wife, my own grandmother, and his second concubine now had no rights to their own property anymore. How was there any logic in that?

My mother soon found out why the judge had ruled this way. She discovered that this particular judge was from England, and was not at all familiar with Chinese estate law history. My mother was dumbfounded. The court was leaving the fate of her entire family and generations to come in the hands of someone who was not sufficiently prepared to rule. How could someone like that be approved to rule on a case like this? Where was the justice?

But that was not the end of the tragedy. After hearing their case of lies in court, mother knew that Yam Kwan and Cheung Kiu were capable of truly horrible things. But she did not yet know how far they could go.

In addition to winning this case and overriding his will, all of my grandfather's property and taking away my grandfather's dignity and everything he had worked hard for, Yam Kwan and Cheung Kiu decided that they were not going to pay the court fees. The judge's ruling also allowed them to forgo the court fees in favor of the losing side—the four trustees then were forced to pay all the court fees for the entire trial. That included everything—including the extremely expensive fees for the lawyers on each side. There were many defendants; each of them had one lawyer to represent them each, including the most expensive, Mr. Brooks, the barrister on Yam Kwan's side, who charged $2000 per day.

There was nothing the four trustees could do about this, according to the judge's ruling. It was either pay the fees or go to jail. The total cost did not have to split evenly among the four of them; Yam Kwan and Cheung Kiu just wanted the money any way they could get it from them.

My mother was yet again astounded. She knew that Yam Kwan and Cheung Kiu were bad people, but she did not know they would take it this far. But she had no choice but to pay. She believed that the money from my grandfather's estate would pay not just her share, but for all the trustees. But the money was no longer hers to give out; it all belonged to Yam Kwan and Cheung Kiu. Mother would have to pay the fees using her own money.

Here she was, a widow with four children, barely surviving with the little expenses she had. At least, she reasoned, there were four trustees altogether, so they could split the entire cost.

But after all four trustees were notified that they would have to pay the fees, two of the trustees, Tsui Chuk Shan and Yau Sun Dai, grandfather's second concubine, suddenly disappeared. They were simply gone without warning; mother could not get a hold of either one of them again after the trial. The only honorable people left to pay were my mother and Chu Yi Shun, the minister.

How could Sun Dai do that to my grandfather? How could she do that to my mother? Mother was a war widow with her own children; how could Sun Dai simply disappear and force mother to take on the whole financial burden?

After a week, mother was still figuring out how she and the minister were going to pay all the fees. One day, without warning, she was working in her job at the head office as usual when two policemen suddenly marched in and presented a warrant for her arrest.

My mother was shocked. The policemen explained that Yam Kwan and Cheung Kiu were no longer waiting for the court fees from the trustees; they were demanding all the money now. They didn't care which one of the trustees would pay it; they just wanted the money.

My mother explained that she didn't have the money. The cost had equaled out to $85,000 in total (an amount equal to over one million dollars today); she didn't just have that kind of money. The policemen then told my mother that they had no choice but to take her to jail.

In front of everyone at her office, everyone who respected her, my mother was forced to walk in shame and humiliation down the hall escorted by these policemen. Here was my mother, the picture image of honor and authority, put to shame in the eyes of her esteemed colleagues over a price she did not have to pay.

Without giving her time to even change her uniform, the policemen marched her right from her work to the detention center, where she was forced to stay until she could pay all the court fees for every plaintiff involved.

Mother remained in that detention for a week while she scrambled to think of something. She had no idea how she was going to pay; she had believed that her father's money would suffice, but that was clearly not the case. We certainly did not have the money saved up in our family to pay such a high cost; mother was still supporting two of her children on her income alone.

After five days in the detention center, she came up with the only solution she could. She called her younger son Stephen to get the two deeds for our rental properties at Kimberly Mansion and Fan Lan in her first drawer on her tall dresser in her bedroom. Stephen had to break open the drawer by force in order to take the deeds. She instructed him to hand over the deeds to Cheung Kiu's lawyer. This was the only option she had.

Once Stephen handed the deeds to Cheung Kiu's lawyer's office, mother was released that very afternoon. That was it; the homes that my mother and father had worked so hard to build and pay for were now going to be gone in the blink of an eye.

127

Mother had no choice but to sell all her property at very low prices in order to attract the buyers quickly. Kimberley Mansion was an apartment located in one of the best residential building in Kowloon; she sold it to her tenant for the low price of $43,500 on June 26, 1969. The house of Fan Lan on a 10,000-foot lot sold for only $30,000. In 2000, our flat at Kimberley Mansion and the house at Fan Lan were each worth almost one million dollars, a staggering amount.

Still, after selling her properties, mother could not pay off the entire court fee; she still fell $19,000 short. It didn't matter to Yam Kwan and Cheung Kiu; they wanted it all. Once they knew that mother had nothing else to give, the two of them then demanded the remaining money from the minister. He certainly did not have the money saved up, so he too was forced to sell his only apartment for the money. This poor man, who had no relation to my grandfather and who had only been a volunteer and doing his duty as a man of God, now had no home to go back to. But it didn't matter to Yam Kwan and Cheung Kiu. They had their money, control of my grandfather's property, and all of my family's pride. For them, it was now over.

Just as the dust settled, suddenly, after all the court fees were paid off, the other two trustees mysteriously reappeared without notifying mother. Just like that, out of thin air, they were back. When mother found out they were around again, she was livid; their intentions were crystal clear.

Mother and I went to see Sun Dai at her home in Shum Shui Po, Kowloon, with her sons, Yam Hong, Yam Ki, and Yam Cheung, and her daughters, Lai Kin, Lai Yung, and one other young daughter. She confronted her angrily; where was her mindset? How did she have a conscience, to leave my mother like that?

Sun Dai told us, "Don't you worry; once we got the money, we will repay you with interest." We visited their apartment many times during the year between May 1968 and August 1969. Each time, Sun Dai assured mother that she would pay her back. But the money never came. On our final visit, the eldest son, Yam Hong, who was fifteen at the time, assured my mother yet again that once they got the money they would gradually pay us. But with all the millions they had from the court case, it should not have been a problem—right?

But no. Once they had the money, they disappeared, and we never heard from them again. The years passed, and my sister and mother moved from place to place because Hong Kong housing was very expensive and mother couldn't afford to rent an individual apartment. I later found out that Yam Hong became a minister at the Chinese Alliance Church on Shanghai Street in Kowloon. When I discovered where he worked, I went to confront him one day. As a man of God, where were his morals? How could he live with what had happened to mother, knowing he could have done more to help her? Yam Hong told me he was too young to remember what his mother had promised my mother. I knew that my mother had fought for her younger male siblings, and Yam Hong was the eldest, so it should have been his

128

responsibility. How dare he spoke such ungrateful words to us? As a minister, where was his conscience? There is a saying in Chinese: "hanging the lamb's head is actually selling the dog's meat."

In everything that my mother had been through—in risking her life in the Japanese war, losing her husband, raising four children on her own—this was, up to this point in her life, the most trying time for her. It was not simply about her; the case was about my grandfather, her family's history, and their honor. It was not about the property; it was about mother's dignity and her bloodline. The sheer greed and evil that Yam Kwan and Cheung Kiu had created and spread like a poisonous snake had left an aftermath of rubble and dust.

Mother still couldn't understand the logic the judge had used; he was just as guilty as Yam Kwan and Cheung Kiu. How could he ask the trustees to pay so much for the court fees—to take everything from a minister and a widow who had four children? How could the judge approve such a thing for regular people who had worked hard all their lives? Who has the power to make such an evil ruling? How can you face your conscience and face the world? What kind of a man of God could live with himself after what he did to us? This was not about justice—it was about humanity.

The only solace my mother had was that most everyone else aside from Cheung Kiu and Yam Kwan agreed that the judge had not been fit to rule on this particular case—including the Hong Kong government itself. While the case was finished and could not be challenged, it soon became well-known as one of the most bitter and inaccurate rulings in the history of the Hong Kong legal system. It was written in large headlines in the Hong Kong newspapers in May 1968, and it is now studied extensively in Hong Kong law courses.

Still, textbooks cannot explain the sheer travesty that Yam Kwan and Cheung Kiu spread across my mother's family. Mother thought about the case and her losses all the time. She did not complain about what had happened, but only mentioned it when she had difficulties, when the money could really be used, like in paying tuition or rent. But still, even after all these years, no one thought to repay my mother—not one cent. All her brothers flourished into millionaires, especially Yam Kwan. For the first few years after the case, Yam Kwan still controlled all the assets. He cooperated with Sun Hung Kee developers to build a building at #1 Yan Hing Street over twelve stories high. Gradually, they sold more of my grandfather's houses in Tai Po Market, and with each sale, all the males in the Chu family became richer and richer. Their consciences were long gone and replaced by greed. They never returned anything to my mother, ever, in her lifetime.

Being the saint that she was, mother did forgive all of them. But she never forgot. She often told me that if it wasn't for her religion, she would make them pay. Once in 1994, mother went to see Yip Shek Yan, a Hong Kong senator, to see if there was any chance for some justice in reopening the case. Shek Yan told my mother that she could help her if her case was no more than ten years old, but it was too late, and the case could not be revived. My mother had no hope of ever gaining back all that she had lost – her property, her dignity, and everything my grandfather had worked so hard for.

But it was not just my grandfather's land and money that was lost in this case. The effects on mother's own children were immediate. Without our finances, my brother Paul could not enter his seventh year of medical school at Portland University in Portland, Oregon in America. He was nearly finished with his medical degree, and now he had to drop out. Luckily, because of his high academic performance, he received a full scholarship to Notre Dame University in Nelson, Canada as an analytical chemistry major, and because of his medicinal background, he only needed to study one and a half years before his graduation.

While Paul was lucky to receive the scholarship, mother's much larger concern quickly became Agnes. Agnes had just begun receiving the proper treatment from her doctors she needed to maintain her mental health.

It was at this point that mother knew she needed to make a major change in her life. She had spent years fighting for her father's hard work and her family's dignity, and had been left with nothing. It was time for mother to rebuild her life anew.

My brother's scholarship to study in Canada opened a brand-new world of opportunities. For my mother, Canada began to represent a distant, bright light, one that promised the hopeful prospect to depart the deep hate and evil surrounding her in Hong Kong and seek a new life.

Since my brother was studying in Canada, my number ten uncle, Father Bernard, suggested that mother stay with Mrs. Hartman, who lived in Vancouver Island, as her personal assistant. My mother immediately accepted and was very grateful for Mrs. Hartman.

Only for a short while, Agnes did not adjust well to her new environment and her condition significantly worsened since she had stopped her medicine. Mother had no choice to bring her to see a professional, and Agnes entered a hospital, which was located in mainland Vancouver.

Mother then began working as another personal assistant for a Mrs. O'Toole, who lived closer to the hospital where Agnes was. Mrs. O'Toole treated her very well, giving her a private cottage that was fully furnished and even air-conditioned. Mother loved working for her, and especially enjoyed being around her five, white, fuzzy, very playful poodles.

At this difficult time, mother met a wonderful woman named Verna Poling. She was an angel sent to my mother by God. She was incredibly kind and thoughtful. Later, she invited my mother to her church's service. Mother was amazed at their sincerity and genuine friendliness of the people she met there. Immediately enticed by how untied their community was; every member of the church genuinely cared and looked out for one another. Mother was pleased to see that they followed through on their kind words with action; if someone needed help, others would jump to offer their

130

assistance. Everyone was sincere in their beliefs. Mother was blessed to have her friendship and compassion for the rest of her life.

Mother found the comfort she had been looking for in this community. It seemed as if a broken piece of her had begun to heal itself. On May 30th, 1970, she was officially baptized into the Church of Jesus Christ of Latter-day Saints by elder George Leopold Lambert. Once mother embraced the Mormon religion, she changed completely; the church became the sole, driving force in her life, and she became very active and involved with the church.

Still, my mother still missed being home in Hong Kong. I missed her too. She called often, but it was not the same as having her there by my side. I especially missed her on her birthday, a day I cherished because it meant a day completely dedicated to mother without her having to worry about others for a change. In one of our phone calls, I told mother how disappointed I was that I would not get the chance to honor her. Upon hearing that, mother decided to create a new tradition. In her absence, she told me that if she wanted to honor me on her birthday, I could honor my grandmother instead. "If you want to pay your love and respect to me," she said, "you should honor my own mother to repay her for giving birth to me. Since I am not there in person, you represent me. This is how you will honor me." So when mother's birthday came around, I did just that; this became a tradition that I passed down to my own daughter, who now calls me on her birthday.

I knew that this tradition was motivated by my mother's own excellent relationship with her mother. While mother's relationship with her father had often been temperamental, mother always got along well with her mother. Most of mother's good qualities she had inherited from my grandmother, including her unwavering faith in God and her commitment to her health. When my mother moved to Vancouver with Agnes, she missed her own mother greatly. On my grandmother's birthday, mother would call me and ask me to visit her mother to represent her love. I did so with love, proud that I could give my grandmother my mother's love.

The bond between my mother and grandmother was one that could not be broken. All of my grandmother's knowledge and best traits were living on in my mother, and would live on in future generations. It was then in October of 1971, while my mother was living in Canada, and I was still living in Hong Kong, I received a startling phone call about my grandmother.

My grandmother had fallen in her living room. Even though she was healthy for a woman her age, a fall still had dire consequences. My grandmother only had a servant who took care of her; everybody had left their large house to build their new nests. Now there were just three of them living in that house: my grandmother, the servant, and my grandfather's relative Ah Mook.

On this day, her servant had gone to a job interview and Ah Mook was also out. My grandmother had intended to take a bath; she put her wooden clogs on, when she would sit on the wooden stool and pour the warm water on herself, and after she finished, she walked back to her bedroom. On this day, she had gone into the living room; with her wet feet, she fell and hit her head.

When Ah Mook came home, he had forgotten his key, and when he knocked, nobody answered. Usually, my grandmother was always home to answer the door. He had to get a stool to look into the ground window because it was high off the ground. When he could see into the window, he found my grandmother lying there on the floor. He immediately called the paramedics.

My heart sank at this horrific news. The first thought that ran through my mind was to call mother. But there was no time for that. Ah Mook called Yam Kwan, who came and picked up my auntie Lily and me and rushed us to Tai Po Market. Immediately, when we arrived, we saw that the Emergency Medical Technicians were placing my grandmother into what we call a black box in Hong Kong.

I gasped when we saw her. My Auntie Lily grabbed my hand. We knelt down beside the box. My grandmother's eyes were open. Auntie Lily swept her hand over her face and closed her eyes.

We went all the way back to Kowloon to a governmental morgue for people who died accidentally, where people need to be examined for the cause of their death. When we arrived, my uncle signed the papers confirming her identity and her cause of death as the fall.

My grandmother's passing was quicker than the blink of an eye. There was no time even for mother to fly back. I think if mother had come back, even with her immense emotional strength, it would have been too difficult for her to handle. Instead, my Auntie Lily absorbed all the grief for her sister. Auntie Lily was satisfied at least in knowing that her mother was at peace.

Meanwhile, mother was still checking often on my sister in the hospital. At this point, she didn't realize that Agnes's tourist visa had expired. Agnes had accumulated too many hospital fees for a tourist visa, and mother would need to pay money now to keep her in Canada and receiving treatment. The only way they could stay in Canada would be if mother could pay for Agnes's hospital expenses.

Mother was incredibly disappointed with this news. She of course did not have that kind of money. Therefore, they would both have to leave Canada.

I was living with my family on Tsing Chau Street in Hung Hum back in Hong Kong at the time, and when I learned what had happened, I wanted to accommodate mother and my sister as best I could while mother decided what to do next. In 1971, they returned to Hong Kong, and after much planning, I arranged to have mother stay with my family and I, and my sister to enter into Castle Peak Hospital to continue her care.

Mother was not confident that my sister would receive the same treatment at Castle Peak as she did in Canada. Mother knew that being here in Hong Kong was only a temporary pause. She was determined to go back to Canada in the future.

It was only a short time after mother and Agnes had returned to Hong Kong that mother received more shocking news in February 1972: Cheung Kiu was in the hospital with a fatal cyst in her brain.

When mother heard Cheung Kiu was in the hospital, she went to see her immediately. Mother held her hands, despite everything she had done, told her that she forgave her. Cheung Kiu became apologetic in her condition, and told my mother that if she was allowed to live half a year more, she would pay my mother back. God did not allow her to live, and she died on March 1, 1972.

I never understood how mother could forgive her, after all the pain she caused our family. But mother followed God's commandments, and loved her neighbor as herself. She told me later that "no matter what, we need to thank God with gratitude, rely on Him, ask Him for direction, and forgiveness." Somehow, she found the strength in her heart to surrender all her pain and anger to God and allow Him to deal with it. Mother had always told me, "There is no point to getting revenge. There's only a purpose in forgiveness. If I forgive the people who wronged me, I relieve my own pain and will not have any suffering in heaven." She truly was, I began to realize, a true Saint on earth.

After Cheung Kiu's passing, a great opportunity came up that would help keep mother busy. It just so happened that Mr. Chan, one of the owners of Pearl Island Development, and the brother of mother's godchild Mrs. Ho, had a big development project that he needed assistance with: he had bought an entire island, which he named Pearl Island, and was planning to build a hotel there. First, however, he needed to build a road connecting to the main land. Mr. Chan hired my mother for a one-year contract to help his company manage this project, since she had a background and skills as an inspector. She soon became the right hand of Mr. Chan; she oversaw the blueprints, spoke with the contractors, and organized meetings.

Once the projects were finished, and mother's contract was up, Mrs. Ho did not want to lose mother. She deeply valued and respected mother's intelligence and hard work ethic. So in 1973, mother became a private tutor for Mrs. Ho's children, Victoria and William. They were very smart, and were enrolled in two of the top schools in the entire Hong Kong school system: Victoria was in grade three at Mary Knoll Convent School and William was in kindergarten at Diocesan Boy School.

Mother was grateful for the continued opportunities she was receiving. Every day, mother would travel the lengthy distance from our home in Hung Hum to Mrs. Ho's home in Mongkok. She would take two busses and from there would still have to walk about two miles from Argle Street to Perth Street where Mrs. Ho lived. It was getting harder for mother to do this, since she was now in her late fifties. It was also especially hard in the summer, since the temperature could reach up to one hundred degrees with one hundred percent humidity. By late afternoon, it would be

133

sweltering, so Mrs. Ho usually asked mother to stay for dinner, so she could wait until the sun went down to make the long walk to the bus station.

Mother oversaw all of Victoria and William's subjects in both Chinese and English. The children were very bright, smart, and diligent; their school reports came back with all "A pluses," leading to a proud tutor, as well as proud parents. Mr. and Mrs. Ho were very grateful to have mother and treated her respectfully.

Mother worked tirelessly, like she had all her life, and saved every penny she had from these jobs, and never spent one cent on something extravagant or unnecessary. If she threw away one item, it meant it was really useless. One thing I remember her always saving were the small things on clothing: lace, pins, rubber bands, elastics, and, most of all, buttons. She gave me plenty of buttons that she had been saving for ages. There were snap buttons, gold or silver, wood, metal, plastic, cotton, wool, pearl, some with designs or different shapes, some as big as a cookie and some smaller than a dime. I still have them in a drawer, all in my mother's favorite jar. I still clearly remember one event when I pulled my favorite wool sweater accidentally on the front near the button area. I told my mother, and she immediately looked into her drawer, pulled out a bag of wool threads with all sorts of colored threads that had collected from old wool sweaters, and mended it perfectly. No matter how many saved, scattered threads and buttons she had, mother always seemed to find just the right one.

I wished that mother and Agnes's journey was mended and sewn up as easily as my mother had sewn up my old sweater. But it was more like the jar of buttons; there were too many pieces and not enough thread to hold it together. No amount of paper money in the world could ever show just how hard mother worked for her youngest daughter; the evidence was not in numbers, but in heartache and sacrifice. Mother would have sacrificed every last penny she had for her daughter, and all she ever wanted was to get that chance. So she continued to save while she waited; but she never knew if that chance would ever come.

Still, while mother was living with me in Hung Hum and my sister was in Castle Peak Hospital, mother had been worried that the shift from one continent to another would cause her to significantly regress. But fortunately, that was not the case; while mother had been working diligently tutoring Mrs. Ho's children, Agnes's symptoms eventually began to subside, and she seemed to be progressing with every passing day. Mother was incredibly relieved; she prayed and thanked God every day for Agnes's continued improvement.

By 1976, my sister had made wonderful progress. Her doctors determined that she was well enough to continue her studies again, as long as she remained on her medication. Immediately, Agnes applied for academic programs; with her intelligence, it was certain she would be accepted into a college.

Sure enough, a letter soon arrived. The news was fantastic—Agnes had received a nearly full scholarship to study Advanced English at Dixie College in Provo, Utah, in America.

Mother wanted to jump for joy. She was so proud of her daughter! After all of Agnes's treatments, she would now have the opportunity to have a new start by studying abroad. Mother was hoping that Agnes's studies in college would continue the progress Agnes had made and have a positive effect on her mind.

This was also a window of opportunity for mother. Mother was certainly not going to stay in Hong Kong so far away from her daughter; although Agnes had made tremendous progress in handling her illness, she still needed care and comfort, and mother couldn't bear to be a long plane ride away from her.

So in late 1976, mother and Agnes set off once again to the other side of the world. Mother helped Agnes make the transition into life at college. Agnes seemed to adjust well, and after a few weeks, mother felt comfortable leaving her.

Mother then moved into an apartment by herself in Vancouver, Canada. Vancouver was over one thousand miles away from Provo, but at least it wasn't halfway across the world. On her visa, mother couldn't go visit Agnes whenever she wanted to. To do that, mother had to achieve the status of permanent resident, which would allow her to travel in and out of Canada at any time. To become a permanent resident, mother first needed a sponsor. My brother Paul, who had graduated with a degree in analytical chemistry at Notre Dame University in Nelson, Canada, and was working in a high-paying job in the pharmaceutical industry, was in excellent standing to sponsor mother.

The process to achieve the status of permanent resident was not lengthy; as soon as her status changed, mother was on the first plane out to Utah to see Agnes. When she arrived, she was pleased to see that my sister was perfectly fine; she was adjusting well, was receiving very good marks in school, and showed no signs of relapse in her illness.

Mother was incredibly relieved. Perhaps this would be the start of a major change. For the next year, mother flew out every so often to see Agnes. Each time, she was happy with how well she was doing.

However, in her third semester, my sister suddenly began to show familiar signs of distress. The adjustment to a new environment and the pressure from school soon caught up with her and caused her to relapse. She entered the hospital again to recover. This time, however, something happened; no one knows for sure what caused it, but for whatever reason, Agnes slipped into a coma.

Mother flew out to see her immediately. When she arrived, she found her youngest daughter lying in a hospital bed, unmoving, and completely unconscious.

135

She rushed to her daughter's side, collapsing in tears next to her. The doctors told mother they had examined her thoroughly, and they did not know what had caused the coma—or if Agnes would ever wake up.

This stopped my mother's heart cold. With every fiber in her being, my mother gathered every bit of strength she had and told the doctors that there was no way God would take Agnes from her. She knew that she would wake up, and she was going to be right there when she did.

My mother did not leave Agnes's side all day and night. The following morning, Agnes awoke from her coma. Mother looked down at her daughter, her face filled with love. But Agnes stared right back up at her, her face showing no recognition. She did not know who my mother was.

The doctors examined her completely, but they could not figure out what had caused the coma or the memory loss. This memory loss was not permanent, however; soon, Agnes showed signs that she recognized my mother, but she still had no recollection of being in the coma or how it had happened.

It was obvious that Agnes's illness was becoming more serious. She needed to receive the proper treatment before continuing with anything else. She withdrew from her college and remained in the hospital.

Mother stayed with her to help her transition out of college and back into the hospital. Once mother was satisfied that Agnes was comfortable and all of her treatments had been set up, mother flew back home.

The moment she returned to Vancouver, she began to plan for her future trips. Mother knew she was going to need to fly out to see Agnes more frequently now, and she needed to do two things: earn money to pay for her flights, and figure out travel plans to get to and from the airports.

This is where she was fortunate enough to have good friends from her Mormon church who helped her. The people at her church knew about my sister's situation, and once mother told them what had happened now, they offered to help in any way mother needed it. So whenever mother flew from Vancouver to Utah to visit Agnes, she always had people from the church bring her to the airport and pick her up and drive her back home when she returned. When she was in Utah, she would usually stay with one of her many church friends who lived in Salt Lake City. This is why mother was so firm in her Mormon beliefs; their community was genuine, and believed in the simplicity of helping others in need, no questions asked.

To save up money for her plane tickets, mother quickly obtained a job working as a store detective in Vancouver. With her immaculate background with the Custom and Excise Department for the Hong Kong government, this was an easy job for mother, and put her sharp intelligence to good use. She devised her own methods of observing and then catching the criminals was an easy catch, simple and fun. One of her favorite techniques was when she would disguise herself as an old lady, wrap her head with a scarf, and pretend to shop around the store in order to better observe thieves. The thieves sometimes stuffed things in their underclothes or baby carriages, or went in the dressing room to wear the new clothes and put the old ones in a bag. The law was that a staff member could not pursue the thief who was in the store with the merchandise, but once the thief stepped out, then it became a crime. Mother's clever method allowed her to catch the robbers with swiftness and precision.

Mother spent some of the money she made from this job for her own sparse living expenses, and saved the rest of it to travel to see my sister as often as possible. Mother never mentioned to anyone that she was ever short on money. She never asked her other children, or anyone else, to pay for anything, ever. It was mother's hard work ethic and firm belief in personal responsibility that allowed her to sacrifice her own comfort to be by her daughter's side.

As mother traveled back and forth between the two countries, Agnes made some steady progress. But knowing that this could happen again, mother never allowed herself to become overly hopeful. Turmoil had become mother's constant; she had grown used to the travel and the perpetual possibility that my sister would relapse. Mother was always waiting for the next problem to show itself and challenge her heart and spirit.

By 1979, after enduring three years of continual work and travel, mother was getting tired of waiting. Agnes was still progressing, but she was certainly not ready to return to school or endure any major changes yet. My mother was now sixty-two years old; she knew she could not continue this lifestyle forever.

In the fall of 1979, however, a key part of mother's unfinished dream finally fell into place: mother officially became a Canadian citizen. This was a day that mother had waited for so long.

When she called me in Hong Kong with the news, I was overcome with happiness at how excited she sounded. I hadn't realized how deeply mother had truly believed that Canada was her place of hopes and dreams. Throughout all her hard work and pain, it seemed now as if the gates had opened and mother only had open waters in front of her.

Immediately, I booked my first ever trip to Canada to visit her. When I arrived, I barely had time to put my luggage down before mother excitedly whisked me off into the city to show me around.

The first place she took me was to her Mormon church. This was when I saw how deeply mother was involved with the church; all the parishioners knew her well, and told me how lucky I was to be the daughter of such a strong woman. Mother beamed with pride to show off her daughter to the parishioners.

True to her character, mother refused to let me pay for anything during my trip. She took me shopping in a thrift shop and bought me quite a few clothes. We don't have thrift shops in Hong Kong, so I had no idea what they were. This is when I saw mother's frugality and fashion sense meet; somehow, mother had the keenness to select only the most beautiful and trendiest clothes that were somehow also always the least expensive.

Instead of going out to expensive restaurants every night, mother cooked wonderful meals for us both. She never formally learned how to cook, but she never needed anyone to teach her; everything she made was delicious. That week, she made us fish soup; even when we went to shop for the ingredients, mother had her own unique way of selecting only what she needed. For our soup, instead of buying an entire grouper fish, she would only buy the head, which was an unusual thing to do. She explained to me that not only was this cheaper, but we would receive far more nutrition, because the bone added flavor and calcium. It turned out to be tastier too: she cooked the head with carrots, celery, and ginger, and it was very delicious indeed.

Throughout my two-week visit, mother and I spent all our time together. She showed me everywhere that was dear to heart. We even celebrated our birthdays together. Every day, she had a wonderful, profoundly happy glow about her; it was such a difference from the deep disappointment I had seen in her first time she had come back to Hong Kong from Canada. I was glad to see her happy, but more importantly, I was relieved to see some of her heavy burden lifted off her.

When my trip with mother came to an end, I was sad to leave, and I knew mother and I would miss each other greatly. Mother didn't seem to want to let me go either. I told her how proud I was of her, and if she ever needed anything to just let me know. She waved my offer away, and hugged me tightly, thanking me for coming and saying she would miss me. But even as I left, I could still see the glow of happiness still on her face. This new citizenship was not just a status or a piece of paper; this was a wonderful accomplishment for mother after she had sacrificed so much in her life.

After I left mother, my friends Fanny, Marjorie, and I all took a trip in a recreation vehicle (RV) together. We started our journey in Vancouver, and drove down to Las Vegas. From there, we went up to Utah to visit my sister.

It had been so long since I had seen her; my heart leapt when she grinned at my arrival. She was no longer in the hospital and had been upgraded to a halfway house. This was the last step needed in her recovery process; once she was discharged from the halfway house, she would be free to live a normal life.

As she and I talked, and she told me all about mother's visits, I had flashbacks of our happy childhood together. This was the same brilliant, quiet, beautiful little bundle of joy I had once held so tightly in my small arms. My baby sister was no different now; underneath her illness, she was still the same intelligent, thoughtful, easygoing girl I had grown up with. She was still, and always would be, my dear baby sister.

My visit was soon over, and I said a loving goodbye to my sister. My friends and I drove the RV back up to Canada, going through Calgary first, and then headed back to Vancouver. From there, I departed back to Hong Kong. Once back home, I prayed every day for my sister to remain steady in her progress.

In the summer of 1980, Agnes had progressed so well that she was getting ready to enter into school again for the upcoming fall semester. Suddenly, however, completely without warning, she experienced another relapse.

Mother flew out once again to see her. When she arrived, she found my sister in stable condition in the hospital. But she would not remain there for long; shortly, mother was informed that Agnes's student visa had expired. If Agnes was not going to continue her studies, she would no longer be allowed to remain in America. Agnes could stay in the hospital until she recovered well enough, and then she would be required to return to Hong Kong.

In yet another instant, mother's life was turned upside down again. This time, however, it was worse; mother would not be returning to Hong Kong with her daughter. She was a Canadian citizen now; she had a job, a home, and a life in Vancouver. If she went back to Hong Kong, she would need to start all over once again. At her age, she simply could not do it again.

Agnes recovered well in the hospital and would not be required to stay in Castle Peak Hospital in Hong Kong, as long as she took her prescribed medication. Mother needed to find her a place to live. Immediately, her dear friend, Tony Wong, notified mother that he and his family were currently living in Sheung Shui, Tai Tau Ning Chuen in Hong Kong, and they would be more than happy to have Agnes stay with them.

Mother was beyond grateful. Tony knew mother's situation in detail, and he made Agnes as comfortable as possible. Agnes showed no problems adjusting. From a continent away, mother paid for all of Agnes's living expenses; no matter what Agnes needed, no matter the cost, mother paid for it. She was thankful for Tony's graciousness, but she wanted to make sure he did not pay a cent for anything.

Agnes lived with Tony Wong and his family for three years, until 1983, when she moved in with our number six auntie, my mother's sister Kit Ching, and her husband Daniel. They were pleased to have Agnes. Just as with Tony Wong and his family, they offered Agnes a comfortable environment where she could continue to live her life securely and happily.

Agnes continued her progress, and no issues arose. One day, however, Agnes began to wander out into the street and walked around aimlessly. Soon, a policeman found her and took her to the police station, where he called my uncle Daniel. This had never happened in the short time Agnes had been living with Daniel and Kit Ching, so Daniel of course had no experience dealing with her illness. He didn't know what to do. So he decided to place her in Castle Peak Hospital, where he believed she would be better cared for.

He called my mother immediately to notify her. My mother panicked. There was a reason mother had not placed Agnes in the hospital to begin with; she knew that they were going to force Agnes to have electric shock therapy. According to those doctors, Agnes was just a patient who needed to be tamed and medicated, not cared for like a human being.

Daniel felt awful, and apologized to my mother. My mother quickly said it was not his fault, and she knew he was acting in Agnes's best interest. My mother immediately called Castle Peak to tell them not to administer the electric shock therapy. Even though they said they hadn't, mother didn't trust them, no matter what they said.

Mother tried to book a flight on the next plane out to Hong Kong. Unfortunately, in those days, airlines did not have daily flights, but rather only once a week. The next flight was not for a couple of days. Mother called Castle Peak every day before she left, reminding them not to touch Agnes. Finally, at the end of the week, mother caught a flight, and went right to the hospital upon landing.

When mother arrived, she found her dear daughter lying helplessly in her bed, her hands and feet each tied together to prevent her from struggling. Her worst fears were confirmed: Agnes had already received electric shock treatment.

There was nothing that mother could do. The damage was done. Agnes had no choice but to stay in Castle Peak to recover from the electric shocks. After staying with her daughter for a few days, mother flew home to Vancouver, helpless to do anything else.

I couldn't bear to see mother so beaten and broken down. So in the summer of 1984, I decided to take action. I made the decision to bring Agnes back to Vancouver to stay with my mother. We would figure out some way to help Agnes get back to Canada.

By this time, nearly all of my mother's friends and family knew the ordeal mother had been going through. One of the members at mother's Mormon Church suggested that if a reporter brought the story of my sister to the public, mother could appeal for Agnes to stay on humanitarian grounds, because she did not have any family to take care of her in Hong Kong. Mother thought there was no harm in trying this. She met with a news reporter and told him her entire tragic story, down to every upsetting detail – why she and Agnes were here, why they were hoping to stay, and why Agnes could not possibly live anywhere else without family by her side.

But when the story was published in the newspaper, everything backfired. Instead of receiving attention and appeals for Agnes to stay, mother was informed that because Agnes's visa was expired, she would have to leave once again.

This time, however, there was no way that was happening. Mother knew this might be her last chance. She vowed that she would do anything it took to keep her daughter here with her. She believed she had the grounds to go to court for this. Mother hired an excellent lawyer, Mr. Art Lee, and talked over her situation with him. He agreed that she did have a case, and he too vowed that he would help mother at all costs to help Agnes stay in Canada with mother.

On the day of the court hearing, there was a single judge who was going to make the final decision. Mr. Lee presented mother's case strongly and truthfully, appealing to the judge's humanity and compassion. The last person to speak to the judge was Agnes herself; she acknowledged her condition and told the judge that all she wanted was to learn to be independent, and that even just a year in Canada might make all the difference for her.

After hearing the entire case, the judge took a while to make his final decision. All these years of travelling, hospitals, treatments, countless flights, fights with doctors and nurses—all of it had come down to a single decision.

The judge finally announced his verdict. While he said he agreed and sympathized with my mother humanly, it was just simply the law that Agnes could not stay in Canada. She would have to return to Hong Kong.

It suddenly felt as if all the air had escaped the room. We were all silent. That was it. It was over.

Almost twenty years after she had first arrived, hoping to rebuild her life anew, my mother had to relent. She couldn't fight anymore. Mother had no choice but to finally let go.

A day later, mother watched for the final time as her youngest daughter—her beautiful, well-behaved baby girl, her ideal student, her brilliant piano player, her heart and soul—walked away from her for the final time in Vancouver International Airport to board a plane to leave thousands of miles away. As she watched Agnes walk away, mother had to turn away. She buried her face in her hands, tears streaming down her fingers. Her heart had shattered into a thousand pieces.

In a letter dated July 10, 1985, mother wrote to me:

"Got your letter; knowing that all of you in peace and moved to a new house, I am very happy for you. Your daughters are passing through their lives; girls change 18 times becomes mature. Poor me, until now I have nothing, not even a wooden house and carry a long lasting burden. My only wish is to wait a letter from Canadian immigration to approve Agnes. I've done my duty as a mother in my whole life with all struggle, worry, and sacrifice to fight the environment until now. I hope I will succeed with God's help.

This November I decided to go back to Canada; I need to calm and slow down because of my health and my age. I went to Australia for 14 days, a gift from my #10 sister who lived with me while we were living at Kimberley Mansion. They took me sightseeing everywhere. But still, from the bitter to sweet, I don't know what is ahead; I feel like none of the roads will take me through, but I still find peace in my difficult time."

141

I broke down in tears reading mother's words. She was drained, nearly broken from the pain of so many years of fighting with no end in sight. No mother should ever have to go through her heartbreaking pain.

Mother's heart was no longer in Canada. The new life she had worked so hard to rebuild after losing everything in her family's court case suddenly seemed pointless. Since mother moved in and out at least three times a year to Hong Kong to check on Agnes, many of her possessions eventually had to be put in storage because she travelled so often, and her Mormon friends gave her the nickname "the astronaut."

Agnes had moved into a halfway house in Hong Kong, where she developed the basic skills she needed to become more independent. Every time mother visited her, she was glad to see Agnes was safe and maintaining her illness for now. But what mother always knew that Agnes would always need much more help than she was getting.

After a few years, Agnes was deemed suitable to live a normal, independent life and was discharged from the halfway house. She could live on her own, but mother didn't want anything else to happen to her. This was it; there could be no more regression, no more setbacks. Mother had worked too hard in her growing age and seen too little results. It had been two decades of a constant struggle between hope and heartache, between tears of joy and tears of despair. Mother simply couldn't take it anymore.

Mother made a final choice that put her long journey to an end. She decided to move from Canada back to Hong Kong permanently to be with Agnes.

When she told her Mormon friends of her decision, they were dejected to see mother go. They knew how long and how hard mother had been fighting; to see her fail to reach her dream of staying here in Canada was heartbreaking, but after seeing the lengths mother had gone to for her daughter, they understood mother's need to leave. Mother always remained grateful for everything they had done for her; that had helped her so much in so many ways in Canada. She knew that she could not have endured the roller coaster of events that had happened without their genuine kindness and willingness to help her. Their community had saved her; she would never forget their kindness.

In 1989, my mother sent me a present inside my birthday card. Mother enclosed a photo of my siblings and I when we were young. She had them laminated into a card form, and told me that she loved us all equally. She sent it to comfort me after she could not come and visit me because Agnes needed her attention. She told me in the card that every one of her children was precious to her. That photo, with each of her children in the four square photos side by side, represented the equal love for each one of her children. Agnes simply needed more attention; that didn't mean her heart did not linger to all of her children. She almost cried when on the phone she asked me to tell my brothers how much she loved each one of us equally.

When mother returned to Hong Kong, she was satisfied to be back with Agnes. But she needed a place to stay; Hong Kong's standard of living was very expensive, and mother did not have that kind of money to rent a decent apartment. She moved around from one place to the next, to either friends' or relatives' apartments. Then, in early 1992, the Hong Kong government provided a 350-square foot apartment at Room 622 at Oi Chi House, Yau Oi Estate, Tuen Mun for my sister. The apartment was under Agnes's name, and it was enough for two to five people according to Hong Kong's standards. With the government's permission, mother could stay with Agnes and take care of her.

When mother opened the door to their new apartment for the first time, she could hardly believe her eyes. It looked like a war zone: everything was messy, and the floors and walls were all cement. It was shameful that the Hong Kong government would provide this kind of housing to their tenants. Fortunately, mother's friends from her Mormon church in Tuen Mun came to install laminated floor tiles all through the apartment, porcelain tiles in the kitchen, rewired the electricity, and painted the entire apartment. Then they gave mother basic furniture, including a half manual washing machine, without charging any labor fees. Mother was so grateful for their generosity; she did not want to pay much money for this apartment because she was hoping that very soon she and Agnes would return to Canada. That was why I visited them twice a year and would buy them whatever they needed.

So mother and Agnes settled at Oi Chi House, where they would live for the next decade, together at last. During the day, Agnes worked at the government disability facility four days per week with a small salary.

Mother's residential journey was over. But her emotional journey would forever remain unfinished. My mother would never tell me the full truth about how she was feeling; she always told me she was fine when I asked. But I knew that she never lost hope that she would get to return to Canada for good to give her daughter all the proper care truly needed. This was mother's perpetual dream. It was like a delicate feather floating away on the wind, further and further out of sight.

But still, mother still clung to the last small seed of hope deep inside her that one day, she and Agnes would be able to one day return. Despite all her travels around the world throughout her life, Canada remained her castle in the sky.

I would never know the pain that mother had felt throughout her life. It was something, I wondered, if only a few people on earth that God had allowed to experience. Even as mother recounted all these stories to me as we sat together in those hot, humid afternoons, I still could not imagine how much mother had endured. Mother had always said that God gives the biggest challenges to those who can handle them the most. But she was still a human being; she did not deserve all the pain she had been through. The one thing that always stood out to me in mother's entire life was her incredible and superhuman sacrifice and honor. Nearly every other person in our family had given up part of their dignity when things got tough; greed and envy had clouded their vision. But my mother had always remained truthful and honorable. The promise I had made to myself was that I would take care of mother as best as I could. I felt as if it were up to me to reverse the years of pain and loss mother had gone through. I could never reverse what our family had done to her, nor could I ever pay her back financially for all she had lost. I didn't know how else to help lift this burden she had been carrying for so long.

My mother is living proof that unconditional love is the power and force behind everything. Any normal person would not have been able to handle what she did without assistance. I always told her that I was going to make her a saint on earth; after everything she had been through in her life, only someone who was superhuman could endure everything she had. My mother had learned much from all the obstacles she had been through in her life; they had given her every good quality, strength, and virtue she had. The most important of these was sacrifice and unconditional love.

CHAPTER 8

The rest of 2004 passed without incident. Throughout the year, we had done everything in our power to make mother improve as much as possible. We helped her stay physically active by exercising three times per day and going out to the playground and park to watch the children play. We helped her stay intellectually active by playing Mahjong daily and watching intriguing television programs that would keep her brain stimulated. We challenged her brain by helping her learn new skills, like playing new games, drawing, and writing consistently. We maintained her diet of fish, green vegetables, and other healthy food. We followed our regular, daily routine to a tee, to stimulate her memory and help keep her memory stimulated and make her feel balanced and in control. Finally, we kept her spirits up and her energy high by laughing, playing, and enjoying time with friends and family.

It was clear that we had reached a plateau in mother's health. Although walking across the room remained the pinnacle of mother's progress, she remained steady in her health; she had no further convulsions throughout the rest of the year, and I prayed that we had seen the last of them. Her improvement showed that stroke victims can recover with the proper treatment and care. It also demonstrated that patients with dementia may exhibit a gradual decline that cannot be solved, but can be curbed and aided by constant activity. All I wanted to do was provide my mother with the care that she deserved.

One Saturday at the start of 2005, Mr. Nelson Chan, during one of his faithful weekly house calls to deliver the Holy Eucharist to mother, pulled me aside and mentioned that he knew a particular doctor, Dr. Mok Chun Keung, who belonged to the same Catholic parish as us. After spending so much time with us and getting to know mother quite well, Mr. Chan believed that Dr. Mok would be an excellent addition to our team of caretakers.

His generosity couldn't have come at a better time. On January 9, mother had not felt well and vomited, so we cooked her mint soup to make her feel better. On January 15, at 7:10pm, she had had a convulsion for three minutes; afterward, she did not eat but only drank the beef soup. The following day, she didn't have an appetite, so we gave her some rice congee, red dates, and ginger soup to settle her stomach. She did not begin eating normal food with rice again until January 21. None of these ailments was a major sign of danger for Linda and I, but a trip to see a new doctor might give us some new answers. I thanked Mr. Chan for his thoughtfulness, and assured him we would pay Dr. Mok a visit.

I figured since Dr. Mok was a busy man, and we were just a few of his many patients, we would have to wait quite a while to hear from him. Within the second week of January, however, we had a scheduled visit, and on January 18, we went to see him for a routine checkup.

I wasn't sure what to expect. I was dreading that we would encounter another familiar scenario—long lines, impersonal and inexperienced staff, and vague answers. But Dr. Mok was nothing like the rude young doctors we had in the government hospital. From the moment we shook hands, I could tell he was kind, professional, and very knowledgeable. After looking over mother's medical history, he told us that nothing had changed much; mother's convulsions still could not be helped, and we had to simply endure them for as long as they lasted. After I told him everything we had been doing for mother, he praised me, and said that we should keep up the good work. He was patient with us, and spent a lot of time explaining things to us, instead of rushing through our visit. He did not offer us any new advice, but I appreciated his professionalism, and I knew that we could trust him in the future.

So although we had no new steps to take, my mind was put at ease for a bit. Linda and I continued our daily rituals with mother and approached our work one day at a time. Mother remained fine at the start of the year, aside from a few normal signs of minor disruption.

On January 6, things suddenly changed. As we were eating dinner, Linda and I were having our normal conversation as usual. Mother, however, apparently was not pleased with whatever we were saying. Suddenly, she angrily picked up her spoon and chopsticks and threw them forcefully on the ground, just like a child would. She sat silent and still in her chair, glaring at us.

Linda and I looked at each other, confused; mother had just thrown a temper tantrum, probably for the first time ever in her life. This was something we had never seen before. It had come quickly, without warning, just like her convulsions.

Soon, just as suddenly, her sleeping patterns changed drastically. A month later, on February 5, she refused to sleep at all. Linda and I did everything we could, but mother simply would not go to sleep. She even refused to speak to us, and turned over on her side so her back was facing us. After remaining awake for a full day and a half, she finally went to sleep the night of February 6. Again on February 18, mother only slept for two hours, and three days later, when Mr. Nelson Chan came to deliver the Holy Eucharist to mother at his regularly scheduled time, mother was fast asleep.

These severe changes caught Linda and I by complete surprise. They had come on all at once, and very suddenly. But I didn't need Dr. Mok to tell us what was happening. I knew what it was.

In dementia patients, a common sign of a deteriorating mental state is a drastic change in mood and personality. Often, advanced stages of dementia can also begin to shut off the brain's need for natural things, like sleep. These were the first major warning signs that mother's mind was now beginning the descent that we had worked so hard to prevent.

Linda and I had not wanted to think about this; we had believed that what we had done over the past two years had helped mother in such a way that we had at least prevented her from becoming worse, and would allow her to remain at her peak.

Every day, Linda and I talked out of earshot from mother in hushed tones, trying to figure out ways to combat these new changes. There wasn't much else we could do at this point; we were already doing everything the doctors had asked in exercise, diet, and mind-enhancing activities, and mother had already gone above and beyond our expectations. All at once, I felt as helpless as I had on the day of mother's accident. I didn't know what else to do.

My only outlet was our frequent visits from family and friends. I was hoping their continued presence in our home might alter mother's personality back to the way she was. We were in no shortage of visitors; people still called and came to see mother on a regular basis. On January 17, mother had visits from her nephews Paul and Moses. On February 11, my cousin Thomas Wong, who lives in Singapore, came to visit. On February 12, we celebrated my sister's birthday, and my daughter Iris called my mother on February 20, a day before she returned to New York. On March 10, Mrs. Ho and her daughter Victoria came to visit, after calling mother three times that week.

My brother Paul came to visit once again for a day on March 24, left for a business trip, and came back again on April 1, stopping by before he headed back up to Canada. He was a jeweler, and traveled extensively around Southeast Asia. That day, mother was more ecstatic to see him than anyone else so far. They talked and laughed together for an entire afternoon before Paul had to leave.

Day after day, these people and their phone calls flowed through our home, like a steady, familiar river running through a stormy sea. I observed mother's behavior carefully throughout each visit. On most days, mother's visitors had their desired effects, lifting mother's irritable temperament and allowing her true personality to shine through. She talked and laughed with them as her normal self, fully engaged in the conversation. There were a few times when I could see she was tired and not as welcoming to her guests—but she is only human, of course. The more people she saw, the more her personality seemed to return. The days happily tired her out, and she began sleeping normally again. I was hoping this return to her normal self was permanent.

On April 4, I decided to celebrate the Ching Ming Festival. The Ching Ming Festival is dedicated to looking back to the past and remembering ancestors. All religions in China celebrate the holiday; those of us who practice Catholicism simply go to the cemetery and show our deceased ancestors respect with flowers and prayers. Those who practice Buddhism and believe in reincarnation, have celebrations dedicated to ensuring their ancestors in the other world are happy. People offer them food as an offering and some burn both incense and paper money; burning something, they believed, sends its spirit to the spirit world, where the dead can use it.

I remembered during the festival when I was younger, mother would always remember the three people most important to her who had passed on: her wonderful husband, her lovely mother, and her kind sister. In recent years, on the day of the festival, mother would comically yell up to my father in heaven, "Joseph! You are up there resting peacefully, and I am still down here suffering!" Even under the somber mood of the day, mother always found her way to bring in the light.

On the day of the festival, Agnes and I set out to visit the Cheung Sha Wan Catholic Cemetery in Kowloon. The cemetery itself is over one hundred years old, and is owned by the Hong Kong Catholic Dioceses. It is located high up on a large hill, surrounded by steep steps and winding roads paved for cars and hearses. There are two kinds of plots, temporary and permanent; if the plot was temporary, the body would be dug up after eight years and moved to be buried elsewhere. It was my mother's wish to be buried permanently with my father in the same plot as his in this cemetery when the time came.

Every time I visited the graveyard, I always made sure that each relative's site was well-kept, as the smallest little gesture I could do for them. Agnes and I first visited my father's site, and saw that weeds had grown up through the cracks of the cement lane next to the rows of gravestones, so we pulled them all up. I then used a soft, damp cloth to clean his headstone. I was especially careful in cleaning around his photo, which was placed a little bit below the cross. I placed the lovely bunch of flowers I had brought onto the grave. Agnes and I gave him three bows, which in Chinese culture is a revered sign of respect for the deceased.

We then went to pay our respects to my first grandmother on my father's side, Chow Mo Ching, whose grave was about twenty yards behind my father's. She was a wonderful woman, and very much like my mother in that she had endured a lot of suffering in her life, but always remained diligent and kind. Although she was not my father's actual mother, she was always still a part of our family. I never quite understood this relationship when I was a child, but as I grew older, things became clearer. Back during the time of my parents' births, Chinese tradition allowed men to marry more than one woman in order to bear children, preferably sons. For this reason, both sides of my family are very large and very complicated.

My grandfather Wong Hung Pak was the head of the Eighteen Village in Siu Kiu, China. He had come alone to Hong Kong from Siu Kiu, China when he was fifteen years old, and became an office boy in a shipping company in Hong Kong. From there he worked very hard; the owner of the shipping company noticed his intelligence and diligence and gave him free tuition to study night school. Throughout the years, he was promoted to be a buyer of this big company. It was after he was promoted that he went back to China to marry Chow Mo Ching, to whom he had been introduced by a respected friend.

Chow Mo Ching had always been very short, reaching only about four feet two inches in her lifetime, and, under Chinese tradition, had bounded feet. In the Chinese tradition, bounded feet on females were a symbol of beauty, but were a cruel and painful ritual for young girls. The mother would first soak her child's feet in herbal tonic and rub them with a special ointment to shed any dead skin. The child's four smallest toes would then be bent. Bandages soaked in warm water and herbs would be wrapped tightly around the bent toes. The bandages would be taken off and replaced with a tighter bandage every three days to make the feet grow smaller. After two years, the feet would shrink to become approximately three to four inches in length. To retain this size, the bonding process would continue for at least a decade.

This was extraordinarily painful for the young girls. The toenails would often curl and cut into the flesh, creating an infection. The bent toes created stumped feet that were agonizing to walk on. An early death was not uncommon as a result of this procedure. My grandmother told me her story of how painful it was for her:

"Born into an old-fashioned family in Canton, I was inflicted with the pain of foot binding when I was 5 years old. I was an active child who liked to jump about, but from then on my free and optimistic nature vanished. It was in the first lunar month of my fifth year that my ears were pierced and fitted with gold earrings. I was told that a girl had to suffer twice, through ear piercing and foot binding.

Binding started in the second lunar month; mother consulted references in order to select an auspicious day for it. I wept and hid in a neighbor's home, but mother found me, scolded me, and dragged me home. She shut the bedroom door, boiled water, and from a box withdrew binding, shoes, knife, needle and thread. I begged for a one-day postponement, but mother refused; "Today is a lucky day," she said, "I bound today, your feet will never hurt; if bound tomorrow they will." She washed and placed alum on my feet and cut the toenails. She then bent my toes toward the plantar with a binding cloth ten feet long and two inches wide, doing the right foot and then the left. She finished binding and ordered me to walk, but when I did the pain proved unbearable.

The night, mother would not let me remove my shoes. My feet felt on fire and I could not sleep. Mother struck me for crying. On the following days, I tried to hide but was forced to walk on my feet. Mother hit me on my hands and feet for resisting. Beatings and cures were my lot for covertly loosening the wrappings. The feet were washed and rebound after three or four days, with alum added. After several months, all toes but the big one was pressed against the inner surface. Whenever I ate fish or freshly killed meat, my feet would smell, and the pus would drip. Mother criticized me for placing pressure when I walked on the heel, saying that my feet would never assume a pretty shape. Mother would remove the bindings and wipe the blood and pus which dripped from my feet. She told me that only with the removal of the flesh could my feet become slender. If I mistakenly punctured a score, the blood gushed like a stream. My somewhat fleshy big toes were bound with small pieces of cloth and forced upwards, to assume a new moon shape.

Every two weeks, I changed to new shoes. Each new pair was one-to-two-tenths of an inch smaller than the previous one. The shoes were

149

unyielding, and it took pressure to get into them. After changing more than ten pairs of shoes, my feet were reduced to a little over four inches. I had been in binding for a month when my younger sister started; when no one was around, we would weep together. In the summer, my feet smelled offensively because of pus and blood; in the winter, my feet felt because of poor circulation, and they hurt. Four of the toes were curled in, like so many dead caterpillars, no outsider would ever have believed that they belonged to a human being. It took two years to achieve the three-inch model. My toenails pressed against the flesh like thin paper. The heavily creased plantar could not be scratched when it itched or soothed when it ached. My shanks were thin; my feet became humped, and ugly; how I envied the natural-footed!"

Over the course of their marriage, she and my grandfather only had one daughter. Unfortunately, my grandfather needed a son in order to pass on his family estate. So my grandfather married his first concubine, named Yeung Wai Fan. Unfortunately, her first birth was also a daughter. Then, my grandfather was still not pleased; so in the same year, he married his third wife, the second concubine, my father's mother, Chiu Bo Wo, who was under five feet with blue eyes and a fair complexion. My grandfather adored her; he provided a gift of money to her parents because he wanted to be with her so badly. (In those days, the family of the bride-to-be liked to receive a gift from the potential groom, in the form of money, expensive seafood, or other gifts that demonstrated how much the man liked the woman.) They married in Hong Kong, and lived at their residence at Prince's Terrace. Before their first year of marriage was over, Chiu Bo Wo successfully gave my grandfather what he wanted: a son, whom they named Ambrose. She went on to produced three more sons for my grandfather, which made him very happy. Between the three women, my grandfather had sixteen children altogether.

All of these marriages and children were confusing to me— especially since they all lived under the same roof. One day, I overheard my grandfather talking to his third wife, my real grandmother. He was saying that her first son (my grandfather's third child) Chi Yan's birthday was last month, and he reminded her that his second concubine's son (his fourth child) Hon Yee's birthday would be the following month. I stopped my grandfather; I asked if his memory was okay. It did not make sense to me. My mother had told me that carrying a baby took nine months. It could not take two months. My grandfather patted my head, smiled, and said, "You are young. Your calculations need to become more advanced. When you grow older, you will understand." I didn't realize that Hon Yee was the son of the first concubine, and Chi Yan was the son of the second concubine. I made everyone in the room laugh.

Even though Chow Mo Ching was not my paternal grandmother, I still called her my grandmother and loved her very much. I used to love visiting her when she lived with her only daughter, Wong Tak Kwan, at Diamond Hill in Kowloon. Every time we went to visit her, it was impossible to find our way. In those days, Diamond Hill was merely a village, with buildings that were only about one or two stories high. There were almost no roads for cars to drive on; instead, there were only small lanes running everywhere in random directions. Even if you had the full address, you still could not find the location! We had to remember to go through this lane or that corner and turn left, and finally we would arrive at their two-story home. I always remembered that she had a small garden in the back and lovely flowers and tree next to their gate in front that her son-in-law had planted for her.

Chow Mo Ching had always been so kind to us, and I missed her a great deal now. Agnes and I gave her three bows and left her grave.

Finally, we visited Auntie Lily's grave. She was across a valley from my father's grave, in a large area where all the nuns from her convent were buried. Auntie Lily was the first one to be buried there. I cleaned up Lily's grave a bit, pulled out all the weeds, and placed the beautiful flowers I had brought in their place. Auntie Lily was one of the few members of my family on my mother's side buried in this cemetery. The rest of my mother's family was buried on a hill on their own land in Tai Po Market.

My mother's family dates all the way back to the very founding of the city of Tai Po Market. Tai Po Market is located in an area called the New Territories, which comprises three hundred and sixty-five square miles of Hong Kong, including its two hundred and thirty-five off-shore islands. All of Hong Kong, including the New Territories, is spread out over separate, distinct areas that gradually came together under British governmental rule in the mid-nineteenth century. Hong Kong Island was acquired by Britain from China under the Convention of Chuanbi in 1841. The tip of the Kowloon Peninsula, and nearby Stone Cutter's Island, were not ceded to Britain until 1860, under the First Convention. The New Territories were one of the last pieces of land to be acquired by the British, leased under the Second Convention of Beijing in 1898 for a period of ninety-nine years. In 1997, all British power over Hong Kong was transferred back to China.

Tai Po Market has a long tradition and connection with the Hakkanese people, one of China's oldest traditional cultural sub-groups. They had established themselves as a hard-working and frugal people, the origins of which dated back centuries. In ancient times, the land on the outskirts of Beijing where the Hakkanese lived was not fertile. The cold climate and long winters in that area could not produce enough crops for food to eat. Because of the food shortage, as a group, they decided to move south. The bond between them as a people remained strong; each time they came to a new area to stay, the local people, observing their hard work ethic and closeness, saw them as a threat, fearing that they would eventually take over the businesses of the town, and would then force them out. Finally, they were able to settle in Kwong Tung in Far Yuen and Mui Yuen areas, and established the Haka territory, which still exists today.

Despite the comfort of a secure territory, the Hakkanese constantly wanted to improve the quality of life for their people, and to do this, they were willing to travel outside the comfort of their newly established

151

territory. They eventually expanded to England, adventuring to Europe, South America, the Caribbean, and Mauritius, moving into all corners of the world. In these places they started businesses, primarily in laundry, restaurant, and grocery, all of which expanded greatly and made the Hakkanese people not only very affluent, but global noticed for their hard work ethic. It is this work ethic that has carried over through generations; while their dialect shares forty percent of the same qualities of the Mandarin and remains vastly different from the more common Cantonese that people in Hong Kong speak, the diligent work ethic they have needs no translation.

My mother's family originates in this hard-working Hakkanese tradition. In the nineteenth century, my grandmother Chu's father, Wong Kwong Fook, and his friend, Ip Chi Fun, had formed a brotherhood between their two families. They had been inseparable since they found out the many similarities between them: both had been born on the same date and year, and both of them upheld the conscientiousness of Hakkanese tradition. Though they were not blood relations, Wong Kwong Fook and Ip Chi Fun referred to each other as brothers.

The bond between their two families strengthened as they grew up and had children of their own. Wong Kwong Fook's second daughter was my grandmother, Wong Lai Ching, born on October 2, 1887. She had been raised and educated in the north of China, Nanjing, the second ancient capital of China. My grandmother grew up a devout Christian; her father was a kind and compassionate minister, and my grandmother attended a very old-fashioned Pentecostal church in Tai Po Market. Sundays were devoted completely to God. After going to church in the morning, my grandmother would spend the day meditating or doing any activity that she believed would please God, avoiding spending any money to entertain herself or others. Her appearance followed the strictness of the church; my grandmother grew her hair out in long locks, which she wore in a very tight bun atop her head.

My grandmother grew to be about five feet one inch. Round, black metal glasses always framed her kind eyes, and on her face rested a perpetual smile that showed everyone the kindness in her heart. The rest of her appearance was spotless; throughout her life, she took great care of herself. She had brushed her teeth twice a day for her entire life, and once a month, she would use the white ash from burnt wood to clean her teeth, a practice that helped teeth stay white and clean. For this reason, she never had a single cavity. However, her father did not believe in following unnecessary traditions; he did not want to torture his daughter with the tradition of bonding feet for young Chinese women, so she grew up with large feet. He also allowed her to ride a donkey to school instead of walking, as most children did.

When my grandmother grew to be a young woman, she attracted the attention of a man named Chu Tak Hing, who had been married to Ip Chi Fun's first daughter, who unfortunately had passed away. Chu Tak Hing was my grandfather. He had been born on January 10, 1884 in Far Yuen, Kwong

152

Tung, China, a Hakkanese province. As a male, my grandfather had to adhere to stricter Chinese traditions than my grandmother, especially in the Ching Dynasty in which he was raised. During this time of rule, men were required to wear a hairstyle called a queue to represent the complete control of the imperial ruler. The hairstyle consisted of having the hair on the front of the head shaved off above the temples every ten days and the rest of the hair braided into a long ponytail. It was compulsory on all males, and the penalty for not having it was execution. After the revolution, Sun Yat Sen reformed a Republican Constitution called "The Republic of China" in 1912, replacing the Ching Dynasty and ending over 2,000 years of imperial rule in China. It also was the end of my grandfather's long hair, as most Chinese men abandoned their queue after the Ching Dynasty fell. My grandfather's was a little less than two feet long when he cut it off, and he hung it on the ceiling of his bedroom as a reminder of the oppression of imperial rule. When I was younger, each time when I stepped in to his room, I was scared to look at that piece of hair dangling over. The rest of the room was like looking back at the old days as well. Even though the servants always polished everything sparkling clean, and painters powdered the ground floor's walls and ceiling in my grandfather's home, his room still had the same old fashion, still hanging the same square mosquito's net, and the same old bed.

My grandfather displayed his Hakkanese roots as he matured, and grew into an extremely hard-working and dedicated man. He married once, but unfortunately his wife passed away. Then he met and fell in love with my grandmother. At that time, most of the society did not tolerate free love. But with my grandparents, their families were so close together that they had this free love. They soon married and began their lives together.

Tai Po Market was the ideal place for my grandparents to build their life together. The population mostly was Hakkanese, and they referred to each other as "our own people." When there were job openings, they always picked Hakkanese instead of others. Mostly they were farmers to work for rich people like my grandpa. Quite a few people went overseas to work and left behind their wives & children. That was how they gain their fortune in South East Asia, as far as Africa, Europe. If they needed any helpers, they always find their own people.

This kindness was something that both of my grandparents displayed, my grandmother in particular. My grandmother was a licensed mid-wife by the Hong Kong government. She was well-read in Chinese herbal practices, but was also comfortable using Western medicine. She had a unique, natural instinct for taking care of women who wanted to have a certain gender for their babies. Prior to pregnancy, she would help women devise methods for eating healthy foods and arranging furniture to secure the preferred gender. She had a good success rate, if the women followed her guidelines.

Throughout my grandfather's marriages and his wives' pregnancies, my own grandmother helped deliver every child safely and healthily. This was an amazing act of selflessness for her. It would be natural for any

153

woman to have harsh feelings towards her husband's concubines. If they were asked to assist with the delivery of the concubines' children, many wives would take the opportunity to deliberately harm the children to get revenge on their husbands. But my grandmother did no such thing. She did not hold any bitterness towards her husband, and she took pity on the concubines and offered her services. To deliver her husband's wives' children in her own home took away part of her dignity. But she still remained generous and self-sacrificing. She only wanted to ensure the children were delivered in good health. My grandmother always said, "If I couldn't forgive people, I would go crazy." It was this quality of forgiveness that she passed on to my mother and was how she was able to forgive people later in life.

As my grandparents grew older, they used the money they saved to buy all the real estate that Yam Kwan and Cheung Kiu would eventually seize from them in the court case. My grandfather had received ten cents per foot on the outskirts of Tai Po Market, and after he bought several blocks on Yan Hing Street where he lived and developed much of the real estate, he eventually owned many pieces of land in Tai Po Market. Both he and my grandmother had worked long enough, and were frugal enough, to have saved the money they earned every year to support having two more people in their home.

But although my grandparents were wealthy, such good fortune did not spoil them or cause them to show off. I remember that grandfather once asked a servant to re-patch a pair of his pants instead of buying new ones, unconcerned about what he would look like with the patch. My grandmother never wasted any food, and made sure to store even the leftover rice overnight in a cabinet with a screen door to keep it fresh for the next day. She would then ask the servants to add freshly cooked rice on top of the leftover rice, so nothing would go to waste. When she had an early retirement, she used her time to take care of the poor people who lived out of boats. These people were often ill, but with no money, they could not afford a traditional doctor. My grandmother took care of these people with the best care that any other doctor could offer, and when it came time to pay, she accepted whatever food they had raised on their farms or caught from the sea in place of money at a later date.

My grandparents never let greed or wealth overcome them; they remained humble throughout their lives. This was the respected lineage that went through mother's entire family. As Agnes and I said a silent prayer to Auntie Lily and gave her three bows, I thanked God for being part of such a strong heritage. My mother's family may have had a lot of pain and suffering, but the deep strength of their sacrifice, faith, and brotherhood was the true legacy that would always live on.

CHAPTER 9

After the Ching Ming festival passed, on April 9, I attended the second of two seminars at Hong Kong University that mother's occupational therapist Mr. Lau had mentioned to me called "How to Improve and Maintain the Brain's Cells," which was open only to occupations-experienced employees. I had attended the first class back on March 18 for half a day. This was sponsored by Yan Oi Tong, a non-profit organization specializing in offering services to senior citizens, as well as giving an education to their caretakers, at a low cost. They had several excellent programs, and I was grateful that Mr. Lau had recommended this class to me, so I could bring the ideas back home. The seminars taught me quite a bit about all the things I could do to keep mother's stroke and dementia stable and under control in order to prevent mother's health from declining further. It also confirmed that a lot of the things I was already doing were beneficial to mother.

The most important thing was to strictly follow a daily routine. This could stimulate mother's memory and help her feel more balanced and in control. Mother would often repeat the same thing over and over, as an act of preserving the information in her mind. She also had difficulty to learn new information; if we told her what day and time it was, she would not recall it immediately or for a short period of time. This was where the benefit of routine came in; having something set at a specific time every single day could help mother become less confused and retain important information.

Another thing I learned was the importance of communicating to mother her both her successes and her limits. Many right-brain stroke patients, like people with dementia, remain in denial of their illness. This means that they could place themselves into possibly dangerous situations in which they overestimate their ability to do something. With everything I had observed mother trying to do with her dementia over the last few years (including bending over to pick up that little spot that had gotten her in the hospital in the first place), I knew emphasizing mother's successes was essential. To increase mother's awareness of her limits, I could also give mother simple directions and reminders for tasks she could complete on her own.

Another suggestion emphasized was to challenge mother's brain in any and all ways possible. This included anything from allowing the person to play brain-stimulating games, watching quality or educational television programs, practicing artistic skills like writing, drawing, or playing music, and allowing mother to talk freely about whatever was on her mind. The more the brain was stimulated in the right ways, the greater the chance of improvement.

It was also key to maintain multi-sensory stimulation. This meant stimulating her senses by creating an exciting, but not confusing or distressing environment for her. Things like decorating her room fancifully and placing fresh flowers on her table seem small, but these would still make a big difference for mother.

All of these things together contribute to making sure mother had a joyful, energized, and inspired lifestyle that included plenty of laughing, playing, and enjoying time with family and friends. Not only does such a lifestyle lift a person's spirits, it also actually helps the brain function.

Using this new knowledge, Linda and I continued to monitor mother carefully. Her personality and sleeping habits had returned to normal; however, she was still having frequent convulsions. In early April, we took her to see Dr. Mok at Tuen Mun Hospital by special request, following up on a convulsion she had on March 27. This particular convulsion affected mostly her face: we had seen and felt her face cramping as she had the convulsion, and once it passed, she couldn't open her eyes for the rest of the day.

When we saw Dr. Mok, he told us we had done everything right and that there was really nothing else we could do. So we returned home and continued our routine, day after day, and I continued to pray for mother to remain comfortable and out of pain. But still, her body would not cooperate with us. On April 26, her heartbeat declined to 48, and to 46 the following day. On May 7 at 7:55am, she had a convulsion that had her whole body shaking for two minutes and her heartbeat up to 75. It seemed like for every step forward we took, the convulsions were forcing us two steps back.

As the flowers outside began blooming and the sun began to shine more brightly, I knew it was time for my husband Larry to go back to our home in Massachusetts to escape Hong Kong's hot summer that would begin soon. He must have remembered how much fun we had last year at this time visiting Macau, because he proposed the idea of taking another vacation with me before he headed home.

Against my better judgment, I said yes. I was still concerned with mother's convulsions, and I wanted to be near her at all times. But Linda persuaded me to go; like last year, she said that I needed the time away for myself to clear my head. Dr. Mok had told us there was nothing more we could do right now; it was important to take any chance for a vacation I could get. After a bit of persuasion, I finally agreed.

I let Larry choose the place this time, since last year I had spent the entire trip delving back into mother's past. He decided he wanted to travel to South East Asia, Singapore, Malaysia, and Indonesia. We had already visited Sabah, a big island that belongs to Malaysia, next to Brunei, earlier in the year, visiting both countries four days in a hurry, so I could get back to Hong Kong. We had a lovely time together, just the two of us.

But still, this was nothing like our vacation last year in Macau. All I thought about was whether mother was okay. I called Linda every day during while Larry and I were all over Southeast Asia. She assured me that our household remained quiet in my absence. Linda told me, every time I called, that mother was back to her old self again. She was keeping to her diet, and she was even back to sleeping on a regular basis. Hearing her words calmed my fears a bit; no news was good news, I supposed.

But still, even by the end of our trip, after all the lovely sights Larry and I saw, the only thing that remained on my mind was mother. I was technically scheduled to go back home to Massachusetts with Larry after our vacation. I would bring Larry home and stay with him for two to three weeks. So on May 19, after our vacation, and after I had made sure that everything in our household was functioning perfectly down to the last detail, and after Larry and I had bid our tearful goodbyes to mother, Larry and I headed home to Massachusetts.

When we arrived back in Worcester after our lengthy flight, my home felt strange to me. Like walking back through mother's memory book, I felt as though I was walking up a path that wasn't mine. My house looked oddly out of place to me; I had not seen it in so long, I had almost forgotten what it looked like. Larry and I went in, put our things down, and I collapsed in a heap on my own bed. I inhaled; the cover smelled odd (probably because I had not washed it in quite a long time). It would take me a while to readjust to my new—yet old—surroundings.

I was jet lagged, and my body still remained on Hong Kong time. I woke up during the night, and slept too long in the morning. When I finally woke up, my mind had to adjust accordingly; the light that shone into my room was not the smoggy light of Hong Kong, but the clear light of Worcester. It took me a moment as I lay there to gather my bearings. Here I was, back in the States – and yet the first thing that entered my mind was how mother was doing.

I got up and called Hong Kong immediately. Linda answered the phone, and just hearing her lovely voice again, full of hope and stability, calmed my nerves and put me at ease. I was lucky and blessed to have Linda, who was so diligent and responsible while I was back in America. She told me everything that mother had done in the few days we had been out of contact (they seemed like an eternity to me). She was doing okay – nothing had changed for the worse or better. Still, I worried.

I called frequently – almost too frequently, according to Linda; she would laugh at my worrisome ways, and assure me that everything was okay, and she would let me know if anything was out of place. In June, I got a call from her that mother's heartbeat was abnormally low, between the 40s and 50s; her blood pressure was also higher than normal. On June 7, mother had another convulsion for two minutes, and on June 12, she got a fever for which Linda had to give her a pill to lower her body temperature. But the fever lasted for ten days. On June 24, mom was so tired that she rested and napped the whole afternoon. At the start of July, mom's heartbeat was still low, but on the 11th, it jumped up to 80. On July 15, she got another fever, and her heartbeat lowered to the 60s. By the end of July, her heartbeat went randomly between the 50s to the 70s.

It was hard for Linda and I to trace all these patterns; we worried if she didn't sleep enough, and we worried if she slept too long, too. We were the caretakers, and we had to be alert every single minute.

I headed back to Hong Kong on July 11. It was as if I never left. Mother and Linda were both ecstatic to see me, and the three of us fell right back into our routine without missing a beat. It was almost as if I had never gone home to America at all.

Being closer to mother allowed some of my concern to disappear; in its place, a good-natured, upbeat vibe, just like we had back in 2004, began to spring up on us like a bright sun ray peeking through the clouds. On August 2, Thomas came to visit mom around 4pm, and showed pictures of his family, to which mother was very pleased. On August 5, we had a doctor's appointment with Dr. Mok at Tuen Mun Hospital in the early afternoon. When we went, I opened an umbrella once the van stopped in front of the daily clinic; Linda pushed the wheelchair where mother sat, and the three of us rushed into the air-conditioned hall downstairs to line up in front of the lifts. Going out to see the doctors in the summer looked like we were going to fight a war! We would laugh about it for days afterwards.

I even decided that I would also try to have some fun for myself at Yan Oi Tong, a non-profit organization, by joining some fun classes and meeting new classmates so that I had a few friends to hang out with. I didn't know what had come over our household, but I was glad the energy and happiness were back.

Mother's birthday was also coming up, and I knew this was yet another golden opportunity to keep this energy. For the past two years, I had made sure that mother's birthday was a special event for mother. This year was no different; now, all I wanted to do was to make sure all of her loved ones were gathered in the same place. I did not need to plan any mind-challenging games or activities, or use our mealtime as another opportunity for practicing mother's motor skills. All I wanted was for mother to enjoy the company of those she loved.

So on Sunday, August 28, mother's eighty-eighth birthday, I gathered the gang of six of us—mother, myself, my sister, Linda, Ah King, and Ah Fan—to celebrate at the Gold Coast restaurant. We had a lovely time, and looking at the smile on mother's face, this was exactly what she needed. After all the hard work I had put her through over the past two years, it was time to take a break and simply celebrate mother.

After mother blew out the candles, and we cut the birthday cake, we all took a stroll outside in the beautiful weather, taking many photos along the gold coast shoreline. The restaurant was on the Gold Coast beach, one of the most beautiful beaches in the New Territories. It was part of a hotel, and on weekends, like this one, many craft stores were lined up for the natives or tourists. The shoreline was filled with people buying handmade crafts, taking photos, or just taking a leisurely stroll.

As we walked along the coastline, with mother in her wheelchair, I noticed her holding onto my sister's hand as Agnes walked beside her. My sister would sometimes let go of mother's hand to run ahead, but she would come back to walk beside mother again.

I walked along mother's other side and watched her face as she looked at Agnes. There was nothing but pure pleasure and contentment on her face.

I knew that mother had enjoyed her birthday immensely. But I also knew that there was one thing that made her enjoy it the most: the presence of my sister.

Nearly every day, mother would ask Linda and I where Agnes was; even if we gave her a precise answer, mother was still never satisfied. She wanted to know how Agnes lived without help, whether or not she was taking her medicine and following up with her doctor. I kept explaining to mother that she was being taken care of; I had Ah Fan go to clean her apartment once a week, bringing her soups and food, and I even had Agnes come to our apartment at least two to three times per week. I didn't mind her coming to visit usually; the only problem was her demand to eat exactly at 11am when she visited. Ah Fan had usually just arrived home from the market at that time and was only just beginning to prepare the meal. Because she did not have her food placed in front of her at 11am sharp, Agnes would get angry and leave. I knew it was her illness that caused her to act this way, but that didn't make it any easier to deal with her. My concern was my mother's business, and her business was my sister's business, and taking care of both was not easy to do.

More recently, Agnes had only been dropping in once or twice a week, like a wild bird out of its cage. These were the days when mother would ask more and more about her youngest daughter. It was like a broken rainbow: a beautiful picture that mother had in her mind but somehow could never have all of its colors complete. When mother got anxious about Agnes, I tried to steer our conversation away from the present and focus on the happier past and the possibility of good things to come. But mother always carried that constant burden of worry and anxiety—the knowledge that her youngest daughter, whom she had strived so hard for, would never be fully safe and secure with her. This would forever be her unfinished dream.

With each birthday, mother was counting down when she and Agnes would be able to reunite and move to Canada together permanently. Today was no different. When we got home from the Gold Coast restaurant, she told me quietly, "I am eighty-eight years old, and I am still thinking of how your sister could not immigrate to Canada with me. I have travelled back and forth to both places for so many years; when will the day finally come?" I did not have an answer for her. I never would.

Early in September, I called to check up on my husband Larry at our home in Massachusetts. Not long after I had left home on July 11, Larry started to have heart problems back in Massachusetts; the problems became so severe that he had to be admitted to the hospital on August 20. He made a very quick recovery, however, and was soon back to normal.

It was bad enough that my mother was suffering; I couldn't bear the thought of my husband in pain too. How could I possibly choose which one to be with at this time? I felt like an elastic band, stretched out between opposite ends of the world, between Larry and my mother. I felt like I would snap soon if anything happened to either one of them. Luckily, Larry recovered quickly, and I stayed in Hong Kong for the time being.

159

On September 6, however, when I called home, Larry's voice was not right; he was having breathing problems again. So I immediately flew home on September 11, his birthday. During my stay in Hong Kong, he had been in and out of urgent care and the doctor's office many times, and yet no one had found out what was wrong with him. Finally, on the late night of September 17, a young doctor named Dr. Allen discovered he had too much water in his lungs, a condition called pleuropericarditis. This was a serious situation, and Larry was immediately transported to St. Vincent's Hospital, where he was admitted to Room 3605 North. Six days later, on September 23, the doctor pumped the fluid—over 140 cc—from his lungs through an insertion under his armpit. Larry had almost drowned from a condition he didn't know he had; God had blessed him and allowed him to live.

But things did not go easier for him after the operation; only three days after he was discharged, on the morning of October 1, his pulse was very low, below 45. I checked on him every half hour. That afternoon, around 3pm, I could hardly believe my counting: his pulse was down to 36. I immediately called 911. When the medic tech arrived, he couldn't even feel his pulse, so he rushed Larry to the hospital again. He remained in critical danger in ICU because he stopped breathing for a few minutes. But the doctors were finally able to revive him in the hospital.

Larry told me later that he had an after-death experience after he returned to consciousness. He told me that he was up at the ceiling, looking down; he saw a bunch of people surrounding him. By the time he woke up, it was already two days later. He was still having trouble breathing, so he remained on a ventilator until October 4, when they removed it and moved him to Room 2534 South. The next day, Dr. Pacifico installed a pacemaker in Larry's chest for good; additionally, Larry needed to take long-term medicine to keep his heart rate and his breathing normal. Dr. Gary Blanchard was a house doctor, and we were under his care until Larry was discharged. I became very busy taking care of Larry at home, even though he had a nurse visit daily. It was by God's blessing that I had been home with Larry when his pulse had dropped; now I had to devote all my attention to helping him recover.

While I was back in America, I called frequently to Hong Kong, like I had always done to check on mother. Linda told me that mother was doing fine, and had kept up her fair share of visitors. On September 22, Paul came in the afternoon, and he came again on October 2. Stephen also came that day and played saxophone for mother. She was very pleased and enjoyed the music. The following night, and the next night, mother couldn't sleep after her sons left, perhaps from feeling too excited or overwhelmed. Finally, on October 5, she slept for three hours after breakfast. I kept this information in the back of my mind.

Now I knew a bit what mother had felt like with Agnes. It is more difficult than anyone can imagine, to feel like you are in five different places at once. To care for someone at home is one thing; to do it halfway around the world is another thing entirely.

When I spoke with Linda on the phone again in the middle of October, she said that the pattern we had noticed before mother began her convulsions was beginning to occur again. On October 6, her heartbeat was very low, and went between 42 and 50; we just gave her rice congee to eat because it was easy to swallow. From October 10 to the 15, mother didn't take naps at all, and on the 16, she developed a fever again, and we gave her pills again to lower her temperature. The following day, she went right back to not napping from the 17 to the 21. This was the pattern she had developed before her convulsion, so we knew another one was coming. Sure enough, she had one on October 2, at 7:25am, that shook her whole body for two minutes. During the first part of October, her heartbeat was low, but it gradually increased around mid-month to the end. She began the month with a heartbeat of 42, and by October 24, it was up to 92.

After having these irregular heartbeats, and she was admitted to the Tuen Mun Hospital on November 4 during a regular follow-up appointment with Dr. Mok. I didn't know how serious it was until I called Dr. Mok from America, and he said the hospital had begun administering an IV into her. I refused to let them do so. What kind of service could a cold, unfamiliar hospital with unfriendly nurses and doctors give her? I told Dr. Mok through the phone that I did not want my mother to suffer in the hospital without any familiar faces with her. So Dr. Mok agreed to my request and let mother return home.

Mother was discharged on the 8th at 1pm. She was glad to lie down on her bed, to search around the familiar areas, and Linda was at her side when she woke up. Mother did not have an appetite that evening; she immediately vomited up a bowl of soup that Linda fed her. I didn't know what they had done to her in the hospital, but later, Linda told me that mother had a few small black holes on her arms; I expected it was the injection holes. Mother's skin was very tender and fresh, like a newborn baby's skin; mother had not been treated with the delicate care she needed; I wanted her home now, with her loving family. The next day, the 9th, mother ate a bit more food; I think that after a good sleep at night in her own bed, she would feel much better in her own home. Still, Mother woke up many times during the nights, and hardly slept during the daytime.

Still, despite her irregular health, mother still had her steady stream of visitors come to see her almost every day. They seemed to be the only ones who could heal her emotionally. Mr. Nelson Chan delivered the Holy Eucharist to mother on November 13 for the last time in mother's life. On November 21, Iris brought her boyfriend Danny to visit her grandmother. It really gave mother a wonderful emotional boost, a lovely happy moment for her to cherish. Three days later, on the 24th, they came back again at noon, bringing with them a heart-shaped cake for mother. She finished one piece on her own, and yet, even with her appetite, she finished her dinner too. It was a special treat from her granddaughter Iris. Mother seemed to return to normal the next day—I think seeing her granddaughter made her healthier, at least for a short while.

161

After Linda called me and told me that Iris had stopped by and mother was more energetic than she had seen in some time, my heart felt a little better. I was happy, knowing that Iris had lifted mother's spirits.

But all of that changed on November 26. In the middle of breakfast, mother stopped chewing and stared straight at Linda, not blinking. Linda was scared and did not know what to do; this was something we had not encountered before. It was not another convulsion; mother was not moving or shaking at all. After a moment, mother was fine again, but Linda was concerned, and wondered if this was mother's way to tell us something was wrong.

Sure enough, later that evening, mother had another stroke. This was no usual stroke like she had had before after her accident. A stroke of this kind is when your body goes absolutely rigid; a person loses all control of their motor and mental abilities, and may wet themselves, experience confusion, bodily weakness, hand tremors, and neck and shoulder pains.

Mother's body and mind endured all of this in the span of a few minutes. She shook like she had when she had her convulsions; she lost all control of her body. It passed after a few moments.

When Linda called me in America, she had already taken mother to the doctor. I drew in my breath when she told me what happened.

"How bad is it?" I asked.

Linda paused. Then she said, "The doctors said that this stroke was so severe that it eliminated all of her language skills."

I froze. "What does that mean?"

"Well," Linda said, "she can no longer speak."

Devastated, I thanked Linda for calling me and told her I would be on the next flight out to Hong Kong I could get.

As I hung up the phone, I kicked into high gear. I begin to plan my trip as quickly as possible. I was free to leave Larry in good hands at home, since he was improving well and had nurses come to check on him daily and was going to rehab at the Jewish Health Center.

On December 3, I called Hong Kong and told them I would be coming soon. The next day, I called again, and Linda told me that mother seemed alert, smiling with a good appetite. She had sat on her chair long enough to watch TV, and she slept well during her afternoon nap, as well as at night. Linda guessed that it was because mother seemed excited to hear that I would be coming soon. They were counting the days.

I was counting the days as well. However, I was having trouble booking my ticket. During the fall season, most of the tickets sold out. On December 5, I finally got a ticket with United Airlines and arrived by myself in Hong Kong the following evening.

Linda greeted me warmly; she told me mother had been eagerly awaiting my arrival the whole day, and she remained awake until she heard my voice. When I arrived home, I expected mother to look joyful. Mother looked at me with a smile, but to me, it looked grim and bitter. I still gave her a big hug

162

Linda and I went through her vital signs she had recorded in the logbook. Her heartbeat had grown lower and lower each day; most of the time her heart rate was under 50 beats, and both of her legs were swollen. She was tired all the time, and she slept a lot. I knew that we would have a lot to do to reenergize mother as best we could.

The next morning, as I sat next to her bed, mother looked at me and, very simply, said my name: "Wong Wai Yu." I looked at her. I was shocked. The stroke had eliminated her language skills; this was not supposed to happen. But I had heard her clear as day. I looked in her eyes. Mother looked back at me. She never spoke a word from there on.

This was the shot of energy I needed. It was a miracle that mother had said my name. I needed to do everything in power to continue taking care of her as best I could.

Since I returned home, mother began eating and sleeping better, and her heartbeats returned to nearly normal, from 55 to 70. Since she was speechless, I spent most of the time talking to her while she was awake. She had spent the last year telling me stories; now it was my turn to talk to her. Sometimes with her expression, I could feel she worried about Agnes. On one afternoon, she looked at me with that worried look, and I looked at her eyes, holding her both hands, and I assured her with my golden promise that I would take care of Agnes. She blinked her eyes in response; I knew she understood.

It was on December 19, when mother went to see Dr. Mok for her follow-up appointment, that the inevitable happened. Dr. Mok wanted to check on how mother was doing periodically after she had been discharged from Tuen Mun Hospital, and at this particular appointment, he discovered she had not gotten any worse.

Then he told us, very simply, what our situation was. Mother had declined to the final stages of dementia. From here on out, she would not be progressing any further.

I had known it was coming. All the signs over the past year had been leading up to this. But I couldn't face it.

When I got home, in desperation, I sat down and immediately wrote a letter to Fr. Chiu of Our Lady of Joy Abbey in Lantou Island, who had been praying daily for my mother in his chapel. I asked him to deliver the message to God, to remove my mother's pain as soon as possible. That was my final request.

I signed the letter and put it on the table. In my pile of papers, I noticed an old letter I had taken out and forgotten to put away. It was addressed to me from mother, dated July 27, 1986. It read:

> "How are you? Thinking of you all the time. We are fine. I believe Agnes will go back to Canada in August. The lawyer told me with all reports from the doctors, as well as housing quarter documents already received. He is waiting for official commissioner; this is where they send the permit.

Knowing that you are busy earning money, working full time job, doing house work from inside to outside without help, I know you can manage. God knows how much you can do. Humans are continually fighting in this world, sometimes like war; even our grandparents did the same. If we just depend on ourselves it is not enough; we need to ask our Holy Spirit to lead us to conquer every step of the way. We need to be improved step by step. If you sit on a soft cushion, it has a comfortable feeling, and you will fall asleep. Once you struggle, you start to use your brain to stand up until you settle in peace.

Changing is hard and painful. It happened for me to suffer so much, words can't even describe. It might soon end; I need to care for Agnes continuously. If one day she can be independent or marry, that is one of my hopes too. I am not only following His doctrines, obey His commandments, hoping in my worry, still believe in Him, and receive His blessing. In my past, each day I try to live as normal as possible, to learn how to be happy in my misfortune. All things have an opposite; if there is war, peace will follow; if there is disaster, joy will come.

I know you are a strong daughter; wishing you gain more knowledge, you are chosen to sharpen your mind and skill to gain wisdom. You need to be kind, polite, and joy, and continue to receive God's blessing.

Hope you are happy all the time.

Love you very much and please give my regards to Larry."

Her tearful words shot through to my heart like an arrow. I wanted to collapse on my bed and cry for days. No matter how much I focused on carrying out my duties as a daughter with a neutral face, deep inside my heart, I was aching. I had been across two continents caring, praying for, and worrying about mother constantly. Not a day had gone by that year when I wasn't thinking about her. Now things had changed permanently; deep down inside me, I knew that this could not last forever.

As 2005 left us, I wanted in 2006 to see mother's beautiful eyes shine again with the light she had once had. But that deep heartache I had told me that that light was becoming only a distant memory now, and I had to prepare myself for what was to come.

CHAPTER 10

On January 2, 2006, Mr. Yu Pui Keung came to visit mother. He used to live in Hong Kong, and now he had immigrated to Australia. Once he had heard of mother's illness, he came over immediately. Mother recognized him, and was very happy to see him, and they both had a long hug.

On January 5, my grade school buddy Fanny came to visit. Mother remembered her too; they had been friends since mother had immigrated to Canada and had both lived in Vancouver. Since Fanny was a nurse, she knew how to talk to mother with ease, grace, and gentle care. She made mother content, and mother was able to sleep well that night.

Two days later, mother's sister Suk Ching and her family came to visit. When they arrived, mother opened her eyes, and although she recognized her, she merely nodded grimly. It was heartbreaking to see her greet her sister without speaking. During that night, mother did not go to sleep at all, perhaps with too many thoughts in her mind.

On January 12, at 11am, Nelson Chan came for his usual visit. This time was different. He could sense what everyone else could. He said the prayer for her, and blessed her with the Last Sacrament.

Sunday, January 29, 2006 marked the start of our Chinese New Year. But there would be no celebrations this year. In place of the parties and festivities we had had over the past two years was the dark shadow of Dr. Mok's words. The inevitable news had been weighing on my heart like a dark shadow.

Reality was here. I had no choice but to face it.

After the incredible success we had seen in 2004, and the bright spots of 2005, there was no denying now that mother's dementia had taken over much of her mind, and there was no going back. While last year we had seen little signs of her regression, the only major effect she had was her loss of language skills after her stroke. The dementia was something we had kept stable. But there was no denying now that we were in the final descent of the roller coaster ride.

The dementia began its final stages by taking over the most essential parts of her brain she needed to live. She had lost her language skills. Her irregular sleeping patterns she displayed last year became more evident. She would simply lie there in her bed, not moving but not sleeping. Mother had always been very conscientious about disturbing us; if she couldn't sleep, she would only turn from side to side rather than bother us. Now she was neither sleeping nor turning.

The phlegm in mother's lungs had also increased, and she could not cough it out, so she often had trouble breathing. In order not to take any side effect medication, we pressed the side of her lung up and down, for ten to fifteen minutes, several times per day, and the phlegm would eventually come out. Sometimes, we had Mr. Chan, the physical therapist, come to do the job for us.

Her body could no longer create any heat. Her temperature dropped very low, and stayed around 35 degrees Celsius. She wore at least four or five layers of clothes all the time. Her heartbeat became irregular, but it was always to the extreme, either too fast or too slow; if her heartbeat was high for more than three days, we had to call the doctor.

Most clearly, the dementia had now shut off her desire to eat and drink. During our lunchtime now, when Linda fed mother, she shook her head with every mouthful of food. I tried to fool her to open her mouth, and have Linda then put the spoonful of food into her. Mother just coughed it right back out. We would only usually get to eat half a bowl of food per day, which was not enough to sustain her.

These were all signs of what we knew was going to happen. I just wasn't ready for it yet.

To deal with the symptoms we could actually handle—getting her to eat and drink—Linda and I took her to see Dr. Lau, a private doctor, just three blocks away from our home, instead of lining up in Tuen Mun Hospital. He prescribed mother two kinds of medicine: Cloxacillin (Sodium) capsule 500 milligrams and Ampicillin Syrup 125 milliliters. From that day on, mother stayed in her bed to eat or drink without moving to a chair. Since her bed was exactly like the hospital's bed, we cranked it upward, because each time she ate, she had to sit up at a straight angle, so that she could swallow easily without choking.

Suddenly, we were right back where we were almost three years ago: mother sitting in her bed, cranked up to an angle to swallow. Each time I looked at mother's face, I wanted to console her, but I couldn't find any words.

I wanted the days back when I saw mother hold herself up using the railings in the bed for the first time; I wanted the days back when she first ate real food again all by herself. I wanted to see that energy she had when she was recovering, that strength and self-demand she always had, even when she was ill; that energy showed me that she was alive, bright, lively, and had a long but hopeful road of recovery. What did I see now? Where was that light that I once saw at the end of this long and dark tunnel?

It was time for both of us to begin to let go.

Mother was already ready; it became obvious when she began refusing her food. She was sensing something that none of us could see, that it was time to begin to let go. But I could not do it. I didn't want to recognize that this was the end; I couldn't. I had seen mother recover from so much in her life; for the past few years, I had devoted my life to help her recover from her illnesses, and I thought it had taken all my strength. Now I realized that letting go was going to take far more strength than I had ever had. What could I do? How could I wake up with mother every day and look in her face, helping to keep her comfortable with this darkness clouding my heart and mind? It was suddenly as if the North Star, the brightest light in the sky, was quickly growing dimmer.

In all the sadness of my own emotion, I had forgotten how brightly the North Star shined—and how many people it reached. From the very beginning of the year, every day, we began to see a steadier stream of visitors come to see mother. It was as if a mass message had been sent out that I didn't know about. People that mother had not seen in ages came to pay their respects to her, offering their love and gratitude to her.

Moses and his family came to visit mom on February 2. He knew it was the last time he would ever see her alive. His wife Kin Chun prayed loud and clear, saying that God loved her, and asked mother to let go. God would receive her in heaven. He hugged me tightly as he left, looking back only once at mother.

The day after Moses left, my siblings and I went to see mother all together. My brother Paul had arrived from Canada on February 1, and was staying with me; Stephen had come right after Paul and was staying with Agnes. The time had come for the four of us to see her all at once.

We gathered around her, each saying a soft hello. Mother opened her eyes and looked at her two sons in joy. Paul knelt down beside her and held both of her hands in his. Two pairs of eyes met without words.

I knelt down too and touched her hands. Stephen and Agnes did the same. Together, our touch told her how much we loved her and that we would always be right be our side.

She gripped us back softly; in her touch, we felt her love. We stayed that way for a while. We didn't need words.

In between visitors, mother's eating and sleeping patterns got worse. On February 6th, mother slept well, but did not eat at all. The next day, mother did not sleep but ate fine. I didn't know what to expect from one day to the next.

In what would be our last appointment, I went to see Dr. Mok at Tuen Mun Hospital on February 8. In his gentle, kind way, he told me the words I had not wanted to hear: mother was near her end.

Hearing it from him was appreciated. I could never repay him for his wonderful service to mother. As I got up to leave, I shook his hand firmly, and placed my other hand on top of his. I looked him in the eyes.

"Thank you," I said, "for all you have done for mother."

He smiled back at me and placed his other hand on top of mine. I thought back to mother's time at the hospital in 2003 and the incompetence of the workers. It was amazing how far we had come – and how well mother had done with the right medical professionals.

In a final gesture of kindness, Dr. Mok sent a nurse, Ms. Wong May Fong, to visit mother every five days, and to see if our environment was suitable for mother to stay at home, or if she would have to stay in the hospital. In the law of Hong Kong, all sick people who were nearing death were required to actually die in the hospital. My case was different because I was an American citizen, and they respected my principle of staying home and letting mother die peacefully. I knew mother did not want to stay in the hospital, and both of us preferred her to stay at home if we were approaching the end, to be more comfortable and to see all familiar faces anytime she opened her eyes. Ms. Wong was very accommodating and agreed that our home would remain the right place for mother.

Quietly, things began to slow down, like a clock on its last few precious moments. I stopped all physical and occupational therapy except for Mrs. Cheung, whom I still had come to inject vitamins into mother. Mother did not sleep much, and ate a little, only by force. On the 14th, mother insisted that she would not open her mouth, and did not eat at all. She only allowed us to feed her soup. I called Dr. Mok immediately about how to handle this. He was not at the hospital; I called his private cell phone, which doctors usually would not give away to their patients, but he did for us. I left a message about mother's situation, and he returned my call the next day, telling me that he was out at a conference the night before and was sorry to get back to me so late. I told him that I had a request. In order to make my mother comfortable, I remembered that Mr. Ho (mother's goddaughter's husband) had injections of morphine while he was in the hospital before he died. Dr. Mok agreed, and asked me to go to his office to have the prescription filled immediately.

I started giving 2ml of morphine to mother every four hours, but not more than four times a day. We had to wheel her bed up to a 90 degree angle three times per day to feed it to her to allow her to feel a bit relaxed. But each time we cranked the bed up, mother seemed to be having difficulty sitting up straight. I could feel her pain by looking at her expression. Her mouth also remained very dry from the morphine, so every two hours, we sprayed sterilized water in her mouth and put Chap Stick on her lips.

Her declining strength didn't stop her visitors from coming. Every one of the members at mother's Mormon Church knew she was dying. Suddenly it seemed as though everyone mother had ever met in the church was dropping by to say their farewells to her. I did not allow so many people to jam in to the apartment, so I allowed only four people each round to come in. As they entered, I instructed them not to cry in front of mother, in the fear that it would upset her. Mother remembered each and every one of her visitors, since she was very active in the church. February 19 was our peak day for visitors, when a total of twenty-five people from the church came by.

On February 20, Mrs. Ho, her favorite goddaughter and her friend Mrs. Wong came for the last time. On the morning of the 21st, I was surprised to see Tony Wong's sister, Sally, standing in our doorway without notice. Immediately, she began crying when she saw my mother lying there. I hushed her, and pulled her aside. Between her tears, she told me that a long time ago when she had some personal issues, she went to Vancouver without a place to live. Mother had opened her arms and welcomed Sally into her home to stay when she needed it most. That was my mother's generous love.

In between these visits, we made sure mother was still comfortable. I put on mother's favorite music, "Blue Danube," "Ava Maria," and the semi-classical soft music that she liked. I watched her smile as she would drift off to sleep. My brothers and I did our usual checkups of her temperature, high blood pressure, and pulse, five times a day. Everything remained normal; her heartbeat always hung on between 55 to 70 beats per minutes. Her temperature stayed around 36.4 and her blood pressure stayed at 170 over 90. Each time we checked on her, our hearts were beating fast with anxiety. We didn't know what was going to happen next. Now that she had begun using the oxygen, and I could feel her breathing more heavily. I called Dr. Mok to ask if I needed to increase the oxygen. He reminded me we couldn't give her too much because it would dry out her mouth.

Every day, Paul sat on mother's high chair and I knelt next to her bed when I found mother was awake. Stephen brought Agnes with him to come see mother twice a day. I wanted mother to be surrounded by all her beloved children as much as possible. We were aware that if Agnes were not here, mother would worry about her, and she would not leave us peacefully. My brothers and I consistently repeated to mother how we would take care of Agnes. Every time she heard us say that, she closed her eyes, and a peaceful look would settle on her face. It was time for her to stop fighting.

February 22 was a Wednesday. The sun shone through the living room windows with a gentle force. Every dark corner was filled with light; every surface glowed with brilliant, soft beams.

The sun recognized the face sleeping on the bed. The face had changed a bit since 2003; but underneath, the features remained the same. The almond eyes. The smooth and fair complexion, free of wrinkles. The dark, ebony hair. The teeth, pearly white, dazzling, and full.

The sun traveled down her body and enveloped her fully. She was glowing, encompassed in a giant halo, like the angel she was.

Mother opened her eyes. She kept them open. She was not going back to sleep today.

In the other room, I awoke on schedule. I didn't give her the oxygen mask. When I went in to say good morning, I found her wide awake and breathing fine.

After breakfast, as usual, Paul sat on her high chair and I knelt on the ground next to her bed. She looked at Paul and I with love.

Paul and I talked to her all morning. I reminded her of our childhood days. I mentioned again that time when Paul was in his teens and did not say sorry to mother, and he slept overnight outside on the tree and mother worried the whole night until she discovered him there the next morning. Paul remembered this time, and he admitted he was very naughty, but smart like his parents. I reminded her about the time she taught me the rumba dance and how my legs were so skinny they looked like bamboo sticks. I also told mother how much I adored her integrity, her loyalty, her promises and all the sacrifice she gave to the four of us. As a widow with four children, to raise us with high education, to teach us to love, respect, and serve others, we, her children, would be the fortunate ones.

Our words seem to settle her heart. She looked to us like a small weight was beginning to lift from her, slowly but steadily.

Around 3pm, Linda called us to have lunch. We hadn't eaten since breakfast. As I got up, both of my knees were red from kneeling beside mother for so long, but I did not feel anything. All of my emotions, feelings, and thoughts were fixed on mother. I was barely aware of anything else I was doing; I felt like I was sleepwalking, just a shadowy figure going through the motions of walking, eating, and talking to Linda and Paul. While we ate, mother took a nap. We took her vitals; her temperature had dropped from 33 to 32 at 2pm, and at 4:30pm it was down to 29. Her heartbeat stayed at 53.

Around 5pm, Stephen came in with Agnes. Mother was still sleeping. He told me that he had not slept the night before; I wondered why last night, of all nights, he had not been able to sleep. I wondered if the same anxiety and feelings that something was going to happen soon was on Stephen's mind and heart too. He was exhausted and really wanted to take a nap, so he and Agnes only stayed for a half hour, and then they returned home for a bit, so Stephen could sleep.

Mother did not wake up until 8:45pm, which was the time she needed to take the morphine. I talked to Linda and told her that we still needed to give her the morphine. I cranked the bed slowly to sit her upright.

Mother began moaning with pain. I was standing on her left side and Paul was on her right. "I know it hurts, mom...but you need to have your dessert." With every groan that escaped her lips, another small piece of my heart felt like it had shattered.

I used my two hands to hold my mother's head. These were the same two hands she had held when we climbed the stairs to our family's home when I was younger. I thought back to that time. Her hands were strong; mine were weak. My hands were shaking now, but I steadied them for her. I touched my lips to the left side of her face. I wanted to feel her beautiful skin on my mouth one last time. It was the same skin I had touched with these same lips and hands when I was a child, coming to her for hugs and kisses. I didn't notice the wrinkles that surrounded her eyes and cheeks anymore; as I held her head in my hands, I saw for a brief moment the young woman she used to be—the beautiful bright light in her dark eyes, the shine of her lipstick, and the rosy blush on her cheeks.

I began to speak to her. "Mom," I said, "all your life, you have endured many difficulties—you have suffered so much for your children and your family. You raised four children who are all good members of society. You saved all the money you could, enough to provide for your children. I will always love you; I will always carry on your values and virtues in my family and my life." I told her this to give her comfort in her last hours.

I tried to make sure she was in a comfortable position for her to drink the 2ml of morphine. Mother did not respond. She put it in her mouth without swallowing. Paul and I looked at each other, and spoke to mother, saying "Mom, you can do it. With all the difficulties you have conquered, this little teaspoonful of medicine cannot beat you." And it did. She took the last ounce of strength that she had, somewhere deep down inside her, she held the medicine in her mouth. As she swallowed, I heard a single noise escape from her mouth. "Ggg…" Her mouth was right next to my ear, and the noise was loud. I was using my lips to support her cheeks.

I still held her head gently in my hands. I did not let go. I turned around, still holding her, and asked Linda to give her a little bit of water to clean her mouth. I turned back around to look at mother's face. It was still.

The clock struck 9pm. Linda began to cry. "Shush," I said, as tears began to form in my eyes. "Mother is sleeping…don't wake her up." But Linda continued crying.

Paul walked to the middle of mother's bed. He started to cry and told me mother had left us.

I knew he was right.

He cranked the bed while I was still holding my mother's head. I let go of my mother, and she fell gently back onto her bed. I wiped my eyes and tried not to cry. The Chinese had a saying that if you cried at the bedside of a dying loved one, they would not go to heaven as quickly as they could. When the dead watched their loved ones crying, they would linger to stay, and they might miss their train to their eternal home. I kicked Paul gently under the bed to get him to stop crying; Paul wiped his eyes, and replied to me that he got some sand into his eyes, and that was all.

Paul removed the oxygen tube from mother. I closed mother's eyes, but her mouth was still open. I knew it took her a lot of effort to breathe and swallow her last spoonful of medicine. Paul covered her up to her chest and let her two hands rest comfortably outside the blanket. I knelt on the left side of the bed and Paul knelt at the right to pray.

Then we heard the doorbell ring. Stephen and Agnes were back. They had only just missed mother's last moments. We told them what had happened.

It was the first time I had ever seen my sister cry. We all couldn't help it this time. The four of us together knelt next to mother, and we all said different prayers.

I never had the opportunity to tell mother while she was alive, but I know somehow that she knows that I am very sorry for anything I did to offend her in my past. I know that she is still watching down on me from heaven, and let me assure you, my dear mother, that your children have all became useful citizens in the world. Without your love, teaching and sacrifice, we would not be standing here to tell you that you are the most perfect mother we have ever seen. I thank God that He gave you a special heart to have the ability to march on through all the thick thorns, howling wind, rain, and thunder in your life.

As we said our silent prayers, no one wanted to move. But we had to. Stephen was Buddhist, and he told me it was part of his religion not to remove mother for four hours. I could not do that; because I had special permission to keep mother at home, I had promised Dr. Mok when mother died, I would call the ambulance immediately.

I compromised with Stephen; after one and a half hours, I called 999 for the ambulance and police. Within fifteen minutes, the policemen arrived,

171

later followed by the ambulance men. They had taken a little longer to come than they usually do because I told them my mother already died, and they would not need to try to save her life. They put mother in a wheelchair, covered her body with a big wool blanket, and placed her in the ambulance. Paul and I followed in taxis to Tuen Mun Hospital.

In the hospital, both doctors and policemen questioned us for a long time. It was fortunate that Dr. Mok had already given me a letter stating that I had requested mother to die at home, and he supported me all the way. If I did not have Dr. Mok's letter, I would have gone straight to jail and then to court later. I had five copies of it, just in case I had to prove myself over and over again.

I could never repay Dr. Mok for his kindness and understanding. It was because of him that mother was allowed to pass peacefully, with dignity, and surrounded by her loved ones, instead of in a cold hospital surrounded by strangers.

Even with Dr. Mok's letter, mother still had to be transferred to the mortuary because when she died, no authorities had witnessed her death and signed the papers. She would be transferred the following day to the mortuary on Kwai Hei Road, Kwai Chung. It was very far away from our home, and we had to be there at 8am. We didn't arrive home the night mother died until 2am. We didn't sleep at all that night.

The next morning, very early, my brothers and I took taxis, and we arrived on time, even with heavy traffic. When we entered the hall, there were only a few groups of people there. Two policemen, #PC49804 and #PC4021 greeted us and explained the day's procedure to us. He told us that much of what was going to happen today was just a formality to ensure that we had not purposefully hurt mother, because there were no witnesses to her death. He told us gently that he knew that we had not harmed mother, but officially we needed to follow the rules. This was actually a unique mortuary; besides housing the deceased, it was also a courtroom for some to defend themselves to receive justice for their dead loved ones that others believed had died under suspicious or unordinary conditions. I would be one of those people today.

We waited for over three hours, and when our turn came, two of the policemen went in with us; they were the prosecutors, and we were the defenders. It was a short process; the judge believed me. He honored my wishes about mother's body as well; the coroner only examined mother and did not cut up her body to examine how she died. That was a blessing.

We scheduled a memorial service for mother to be held in the coming days. The service would be held on Saturday, March 4, from 1pm-3pm at the Funeral Parlor at 8 Cheong Hang Road, Hung Hom, Kowloon. After we scheduled the service, my brothers and I shopped for a coffin. We knew mother wanted to have one with a westernized style, since the Chinese style coffins were not as beautiful as the western ones. There were several kinds of woods, styles, handlers, linings, and colors to choose from; most of all, their prices were totally different, even if the coffins looked the same. We needed a fair bargain for the coffin; the funeral home was just a temporary

172

place for us to have a memorial service. There were some sub-contact funeral company that managed the memorial service and its protocol.

My mother's wish was to be buried with my father together in the same lot. I had to help her convert back to Catholicism before she died to ensure this would happen. I then had to deliver the official documents in person, including the original green receipt of my father's burial in 1960, to the office of Catholic Cheung Sha Wan Cemetery, with the burial order # CCMA-1551/2006. When they were approved, I had to bring the documents over to the sub-contact funeral company to arrange for my father's bones to be dug up to be put into a small marble coffin. Both of my parents would finally lie in peace next to each other in the lot.

The timing was very tight; there were only five official days for me to run around in all directions to get all of this accomplished. Stephen accompanied me the entire way. The most important paper to have was the semi-death certificate. On March 2nd at 3pm, I got the official documents at Kwai Chung mortuary and the sub-contact funeral company's staff came to collect my mother. I gave them a set of seven pieces of my mother's favorite clothes to put on; this was the Chinese traditional way. Mother was then transferred back to the Funeral Parlor in Hung Hom.

The next day, the day before the official service, we had a wake from 4pm to 11pm. At first, we did not want to do that since we did not have many friends and relatives living in Hong Kong that we knew of; but we obliged, since the funeral parlor provided the space for the wake for us for free, and we did not want my mother to be alone in the room until the next day.

The room in which the wake was held was very small; it held only around twenty to thirty people. We really did not expect anybody to come. To our surprise, however, many people came to honor my mother; friends from her church, extended friends and relatives. They all poured in, and made this silent room into a solemn and respectful environment, filled with memories of mother. The book of registration signed by the visitors was half full. Beautiful flower arrangements were brought in, sent from well-wishers who wanted to pay respects to mother; some were big and fancy, and others were simple with only wreaths. The four of us, myself, my brothers and Agnes, had bought a heart-shape wreath with red roses on it, a final salute to our mother. My daughter Iris and her boyfriend Danny (now her husband) also flew in from Chicago to say goodbye to her grandmother.

These gestures from all of mother's friends, family members, church members, and everyone else who knew her spoke volumes. As Agnes, Paul, Stephen and I stood there watching person after person sign the guest book, leave flowers, speak silent prayers to mother, and tell us all again and again how much mother meant to them, I knew mother was looking down on us all. She had touched so many lives with her courage, kindness, and firm, unwavering unconditional love – and they were all here to tell her how grateful they were to her.

I wiped tears from my eyes as I thought of all the love mother had given in her lifetime. I knew that despite all her challenges, she was, above all else, a saint at heart.

The day of the funeral service turned out to be a sunny Saturday. From the beginning to the end, I did not cry. After the ceremony was finished, we all went to Cheung Sha Wan Cemetery on several buses to take all our relatives and friends to the location. Four of mother's children stayed and traveled with the funeral hearse. The cemetery was built on a steep hill, and there were around eighty steps to arrive to the middle level of the site where my father was buried.

At the grave site, Fr. Suen said more prayers and the last blessing to my dear mother. The yard was already prepared in the space. The staff slowly guided the coffin down to the bottom of the site to rest next to my father. My brother Paul, being the first son, following Chinese tradition, gave a flower to mother first, followed by me, then Stephen and Agnes; then relatives and friends. Finally, the coffin was covered with dirt.

Family members and relatives, friends and guests stood around us, some weeping into tissues, others holding onto each other for support. I looked straight ahead. I let a single teardrop escape from my eyes. It was all I needed. Mother was with my father now – they forever would be together in heaven. My mother was at peace.

A few days after the funeral, I reread a letter from mother dated August 24, 1986 – a month before mother's sixty-ninth birthday. In full, it read:

> "I received your card and your present; thank you very much…Paul came home from Hong Kong, and he told me Agnes is doing well. Their activities are swimming and dancing lessons. They learn to cook, shopping, typing, and piano and crafts. Of course Agnes would like to come back to Canada. I am wishing our Lord to continue to bless her to be independent. I am her mother; I am always thinking of her, and of you.
>
> A mother's love to each of her child is far more than any kind of love. This love is picking out all hardship; her love is never selfish, even in danger. A mother will sacrifice her comfort in exchange for her child's peace. If her child happens to come across difficulties or shame, a mother should give extra care and attention. Love is personal and it is priceless. The Gospel of John, Chapter 18, verse 37 says 'God's teaching becomes our daily lives; it needs diligence every day; each person sooner or later experiences pain, but if we build our foundation on the rock, our house will stand firm and last forever.'
>
> I have had to receive all kinds of mental pressure, but I did try my best to help and correct Agnes's behavior and reality.

After a seventeen-year struggle, your sister wrote to me in English: 'Mom, all goes well, I have made up my mind not to sin or follow the wrong path. I love God and want to serve His will. The Lord protects me and let me not to meet any accident when I cross the road.' Each day I have to have self-control, and try my best to take care of myself, as well as Agnes.

Wishing God bless you all. Do give my love to the grandchildren."

Throughout her life, my mother had fought long and difficult battles. Most of the dreams she had sought had never come true. A terrible war and illness had taken her husband and left her a widow; her family members had stolen her father's property; her daughter could not get the proper medical treatment; and her dementia would eventually overcome her. My mother's entire life was an unfinished dream, a series of setbacks and challenges that were unthinkable. I never fully realized how hard she was carrying her heavy cross. Mother always told me, that no matter how old I am, I still need to learn how to fight. Our lives in this world are like a long battle; no one can escape or avoid the inevitable challenges that will come to them. Hardship is exercise; failure is encouragement. Only difficulties can polish ourselves; we need to be more practical, have unlimited patience, and self-control; God will help us to choose the path if we continue to use our wisdom to go forward to a better land. If we are just fighting for ourselves without faith, our path would be very cold and hard to carry on. Always have faith, mother said, and always, always put others before yourself.

My mother, Wong Chu Yi Ching, would carry out her own words right to the very end. She was an ordinary woman who did extraordinary things. She enriched our lives beyond belief. She was always willing to help those who were less fortunate than she was. She taught her four children how to become good people, and to love God and others. She was a hero to almost everyone who met her. Her strong character, with her warm heart, will always stay with her friends and her family. She was energetic, firm, and strong. This was the unconquerable spirit of an endless fighter. It burned brightly to hide golden treasures: a wealth of stories, a keen, sharp wit, and a pure, unbroken heart. Her kindness, generosity, and endless, unconditional love to her children, family, and friends made her an immaculate, vivid light in the lives of all who knew her.

With my endless gratitude, I love you, mom.

Joseph Wong and Anna Chu married on October 12, 1940 at St. Theresa's Church, with both sides of the family.

My parents beginning the love of a lifetime.

Mother and me in 1942.

Me, my father, and my
brother Paul in 1946.

Mother and my brother
Stephen in 1947.

My parents with
three kids in 1948.

My father and
three kids in 1951.

Our complete family.

Our family at the
airport.

My mother and her four children at her father's grave after his death in 1964.

My mother and family at the airport when my brother Paul went to study in England in 1966. From left to right: my brother Stephen, my sister Wai Ling, grandfather Wong, Paul, mother, myself, and my husband Dudley.

A widow with her four grown up children in 1999. It was a coincidence that we all visited mother at the same time that day.

My father in 1928. My father in 1930 in Nam Hoi, China.

My father in 1934.

My father in 1935.

My father dating my mother in 1936.

My father in 1950.

My father in 1955.

My father in 1954.

My father's Chinese
writing, "a lonely soul
with his shadow," in 1955.

My parents in 1957.

South Morning Post, Friday, June 27, 1969

Revenue Officer Retires

  Mrs. Anna Wong Chu Yee-ching (above), a Woman Revenue Inspector and a model mother, has just retired after 16 years of service with Government.
  Mrs. Wong first joined the Preventive Service as a Revenue Officer, Class II, in 1953. She was promoted to Class 1 in 1957, and Revenue Sub-Inspector in 1958. She was the first woman to be appointed a Revenue Inspector in 1967.
  Mrs. Wong, a mother of four, was elected "Mother of the year" in a contest sponsored by Chung Sing Benevolent Society earlier this year.
  To mark Mrs. Wong's retirement, the Assistant Commissioner of the Preventive Service, Mr. A. L. Tokley, presented her with a gold medallion last week at a brief ceremony held in the Preventive Service Senior Officers' Mess.

Mother's retirement in 1969.

My grandfather, Chu
Tak Hing.

My grandmother,
Wong Lai Ching.

My grandmother and her eldest daughter, Sister
Lily.

My grandmother, Wong Lai Ching, with her
husband's second concubine and her
children, Lai Keun and Yam Hong.

My third grandmother with her two sons and their wives in Fan Lan in 1951.

My grandfather Wong Hung Pak and his second wife, Yeung Wai Fan, and their four daughters, along with me in the middle and my brother Paul sitting on the floor, in our home in Hung Hom in 1955.

My grandfather and his third wife, Chiu Po Wo, seated in the front, with their five sons in 1957. From the right: my father Joseph, Man Chi, Bernard-Kwok Wai, Ambrose-Chi Yan, and Hon Yee.

183

My mother, my grandmother, and my
brother Stephen and his wife in 1969.

My mother and sister leaving Hong Kong for a better
life in Canada in 1969. From left to right: my sister
Agnes, Sai Dim, my brother Stephen, my mother, my
daughter Stella Shaw, me, and Dudley Shaw.

Mother and her best friend Wong
Koon Kau in 1969.

My mother with Brother Poon
and friends in Utah in 1971.

My mother and her two granddaughters, Stella and
Pui Yee, along with Agnes in 1972.

My mother celebrating her birthday in 1979
in Vancouver with her children.

Mother with her younger sister Kin Ching and her family in 1980.

Mother with her twin sisters.

Celebrating mother's 65th birthday in 1982 in Vancouver with her son and daughter-in-law.

Mother visiting her sister Theresa in Australia in 1985.

In 1994, Theresa (far left) came from Australia to visit her number 5 sister Kin Ching and her family in Tai Po Market, along with her other sisters.

My mother and my
daughter, Stella, in 1995.

Mother and Agnes
enjoying lobster at my
home in Worcester,
Massachusetts in 2001.

Four generations in one photo, taken at O'Hare
Airport in Chicago on the way to an international
flight to Hong Kong. My daughter Stella and her
baby daughter Stephanie met us on June 17, 2001.

My daughter Iris and my mother in November 2003.

Mother and her son Stephen when we first moved to Tai Hing Garden in 2003.

Mother playing Mahjong in 2004.

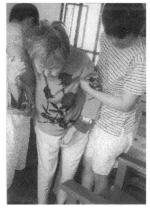

Mother walking with Linda and Ah Fan helping her on June 27, 2004.

My mother celebrating her birthday in 2004.

Me, mother, and my sister celebrating mother's
birthday in 2005 at the Gold Coast Restaurant.

Celebrating my mother's
extraordinary life on March 4, 2006.

The beautiful gravestone of my beloved parents.

The land register of my grandfather's properties
with the signature of Yam Kwan and Cheung Kiu.
There are 263 parcels of land in total, including
mountains and houses in Tai Po Market.

IN THE SUPREME COURT OF HONG KONG
ORIGINAL JURISDICTION
ACTION NO. 162 OF 1963

Chu Tak Hing alias Chu Tak Yam Tong alias
Chu Nam Yuen alias Chu Wai Chi (or Chee)
alias Chu Heung Chi alias Chu Yi Fong   Plaintiff

and

Chu Chan Cheung Kiu   1st Defendant
Chu Yam Kwan   2nd Defendant
Chu Cheong Wai alias Scotch Chu   3rd Defendant
Chu Yam Ko   4th Defendant
Chu Yam Hong   5th Defendant
Chu Yam Ki   6th Defendant
Chu Yam Cheung   7th Defendant
(By Original Action)

and BETWEEN

Chu Yi Shan   1st Plaintiff
Chu Yi Ching alias Anna Chu   2nd Plaintiff
Chu Yau San Tai   3rd Plaintiff
Tsui Chuk Shan   4th Plaintiff
Executors of the said Chu Tak Hing alias
Chu Tak Yam Tong alias Chu Nam Yuen
alias Chu Wai Chi (or Chee) alias Chu
Heung Chi alias Chu Yi Fong, deceased   Plaintiffs

and

Chu Chan Cheung Kiu   1st Defendant
Chu Yam Kwan   2nd Defendant
Chu Cheong Wai alias Scotch Chu   3rd Defendant
Chu Yam Ko   4th Defendant
Chu Yam Hong   5th Defendant
Chu Yam Ki   6th Defendant
Chu Yam Cheung   7th Defendant
Chu Cheung Lun   8th Defendant
Chu Cheung Yan   9th Defendant
Chu Lai Kin   10th Defendant
Chu Lai Tung   11th Defendant
Wong Lai Tsing   12th Defendant
(by Order to carry on proceedings
dated 10th October 1964)

Coram: Scholes, J. in Court.

J U D G M E N T

This case concerns land in the New Territories, and shortly
the facts are that one Chu Tak Hing, who was a clerk in the District Office
Tai Po, retiring in 1940 or 1941, and who lived at No. 1 Yan Hing Street,

The first page of the court case.

192

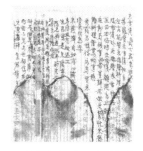

The envelope of the letter my grandfather gave my mother begging her to help protect his second concubine and their three sons.

The letter, soaked in tears and blood.

A Chinese letter written by Chu Tak Hing while he was in the hospital to the judge.

Chu Sut Hon came to Hong Kong at the age of five or six years old. I love him as my own. He started to help me around the age of fourteen already as my assistant. I never trust anyone except him. Sut Hon left Hong Kong during the Japanese War. When he came back, he worked in the post office and yet he came back to help me several times per week to handle my property business.

Yam Wah was my first born son. He got heart disease and never worked. He had a son called Cheung Mong who died young. In 1936, he married Chan Cheung Kiu.

Tsui Sai Ha was brought to serve as a maid, and later became the first concubine to me.

Each of the member's expenses of the family are supplied by myself.

Yam Kwan was born by Sau Ha, and got education from primary school to Hong Kong University, all supported 100% by me.

In 1949 Yau San Dai as the second concubine joined in. Yam Hon was her first son in 1950 and two more sons followed delivered by my wife Wong Lai Ching. Three more girls followed as well. Since San Dai came to my home, she pleased me and gives me children and brings luck.

Therefore, after my death, Wong Lai Ching will legally have my pension.

I am hoping the judge will understand this fact.

The English translation of the letter.

193

業主姓名 NAME OF OWNER	身分 (如非唯一業主人) CAPACITY (IF NOT SOLE OWNER)	註冊摘要編號 MEMORIAL NO.	文件日期 DATE OF INSTRUMENT	註冊日期 DATE OF REGISTRATION	代價 CONSIDERATION
YAU SZ		N89953		08/06/1934	$1,150.00
LEUNG CHUK KWAN		備註 REMARKS: SALE			
YAU SZ		N91038	11/12/1934	11/12/1934	—
		備註 REMARKS: DIVISION OF PROPERTY			
CHU YI CHING		N123135	01/03/1949	01/03/1949	$1,760.00
	M162499 12/10/1968	COURT ORDER RE 1/2 SHARE	CHU CHAN CHEUNG YIU AND OTHERS		—
	M163225 13/04/1969	REGISTRAR'S CERTIFICATE OF COSTS RE 1/2 SHARE	CHU CHAN CHEUNG YIU AND OTHERS		—
	M163539 26/06/1949	AGREEMENT	CHU CHAN CHEUNG YIU		$30,000.00
	M226934 06/05/1988	AGREEMENT FOR SALE AND PURCHASE	PLENTY PROFIT INVESTMENT LTD.		$2,150,000.00 (PT
	8227362 21/06/1988	STATUTORY DECLARATION OF PANG HANG YIU	—	—	—

The deeds to our home in Fan Lan, at 59 Oi Lok Chuen, Fan Lan, New Territories, Hong Kong. My mother purchased this land on March 1, 1949, for $1,760, while my father was still in the hospital. After the court order on December 10, 1968, she was forced to sell it on June 26, 1969 at $30,000. On July 6, 1988, the market price worth was $2,150,000.

土地註冊處 THE LAND REGISTRY
土地業權紀要 LAND REGISTER

業主資料 OWNER PARTICULARS

業主姓名 NAME OF OWNER	身份 (如非一業主) CAPACITY (IF NOT SOLE OWNER)	註冊摘要編號 MEMORIAL NO.	文書日期 DATE OF INSTRUMENT	註冊日期 DATE OF REGISTRATION	代價 CONSIDERATION
JOSEPH WONG OTHERWISE WONG POON LAI		UB308329	17/12/1959	15/01/1960	$26,460.0
		REMARKS: ASSIGNMENT WITH PLANS			
CHU YEE CHING OTHERWISE KNOWN AS ANNA WONG		UB421694	22/03/1962	30/12/1963	
		REMARKS: PROBATE			
CHU YEE CHING OTHERWISE KNOWN AS ANNA WONG		UB666076	17/03/1969	18/03/1969	
		REMARKS: ASSENT			
ELLEN LEE SUNG		UB682214	26/06/1969	08/07/1969	$43,500.0
		REMARKS: ASSIGNMENT			
LAU YEUK LAM		UB7980424	22/12/1999	18/01/2000	$950,000.0
LAU YEUK LAM	JOINT TENANT				

The deeds to our home at Kimberly Mansion, 10th floor, H flat, Kowloon, Hong Kong. My father purchased this land on December 17, 1959 at $26,460. After the court order on December 10, 1968, mother was forced to sell it on June 26, 1969 at $43,500. On December 22, 1999, the market price worth was $950,000.

Laichikok Hospital,
Ward C-1
Kowloon

Dear Miss Ho:

For the welfare of the patients in this hospital, I
am writing this letter to you, telling you some of the problems of
this place, as well as giving you a few suggestions as to their
solution.

As to the treatment and care of patients here, it is
evident that they are in very good hands. I am not going to enlarge
on the subject, as I am an out-sider in the field of medical science.

One of the problems of this place, as any observer can
see it, centers on the matter of discipline. Most of the patients
do not follow the hospital rules. They get up and walk about when they
are supposed to be bed patients. They do many things that they
are not supposed to do - e.g. gambling, swearing, shouting, quarrel-
ing, and even fighting once in a while. Worse of all, as regards its
effect on the more serious patients, they keep on being noisy when it
is time to rest or sleep. According to the "old timers" here, such
conditions have been existed for the past several years.

Now let us come to the solution of this first problem.
There are two approaches to the problem - one positive and the other
negative. Let us consider the negative approach first. This approach
consists mainly of setting up a TIME-TABLE for the patients to follow.
A set of rules, concerning the activities of the patients - what they
could do and what they could not do - should also be made up. The
time-table should be thorough. It should cover every hour of the day.
It should set out precisely the time to get up, the time for meals,
the time to rest, the time for recreation, and lastly the time to retire. The rules also should be in detail and to the point.

A few days ago, a set of several rules, rather in the
form of a notice, was put up in all wards by the authorities here. It
is evident that the notice was put up with the view of improving the
discipline of the patients. However, the purpose has not been realized. For one thing, the notice is far too abbreviated. It is not
thorough enough, and it does not cover enough ground. To spread good
discipline in this Hospital, a precise time-table with the necessary
rules must be set up by the authorities at the earliest possible date.

Now let us come to the second approach to the same problem - the positive approach.

This consists mainly of educating the patients in the simple facts of T.B.; the methods and possibilities of its cure. When
the patients realize that they must rest as much as possible if they
expect to get well, they will try to stop their bad behaviors, and
the enforcement of discipline will become much easier.

There are various ways of educating the patients. For
illiterate patients specially prepared posters, and pictures must be
used. For literate and educated patients, pamphlets and booklets on
the subject should be freely distributed. Besides, movies and lectures on the same subject should be periodically arranged.

As it is, very few patients have any knowledge on the
simple facts of T.B. Their ideas are mostly distorted. Some patients
think that because they can still eat and sleep and move about, they
are not sick at all. They look upon hospitalization here as a holiday. That's why they are fooling around and enjoying themselves most
of the time. On the other extreme some patients think that because they
have T.B., they are doomed. They think they are here to live their
'stolen days' and they just do what they like, disregarding all discipline. With such patients around is there another wonder why discipline has never been successfully enforced?

The second problem is that of sanitation facilities.
To answer the call of nature, around thirty or more patients are using
a single bucket, a foot in diameter, and a foot deep. This is far
from being enough, and far from being hygienic. In the morning, on
an average of ten minutes a person using the bucket, some patients
have to wait for an hour or two before their turns come up. If at all
possible, a number of flush-toilets should be provided for each ward

The first page of a letter my father sent to Lai Chi
Kok Hospital in early 1950 about how poorly the
tuberculosis patients were treated there.

Another thing about toilet facilities is that there are
no such facilities in the upper storey wards. Patients have to climb
up and down a flight of stairs every time they want to urinate or do
a little cleaning. Moreover, the stairs are opened to the elements.
The danger to the delicate patients in rainy days and in cold weather
due to exposure to inclement weather can easily be imagined. Besides,
the climbing of stairs many times a day is too much for weak patients.
I understand that the provision of flush toilets in all wards has been
considered for a long time by the hospital authorities; but for one
reason or other, the project has never been able to materialize. I
therefore suggest that for the time being at least, awning should be
made to cover all the stairs.

The third problem is the lack of X-ray facilities.
That a Government Hospital which caters for hundreds of T.B. cases,
does not possess an X-ray apparatus, is simply amazing. So many
doctors of private practice are having them. As it is, patients who
requires an X-ray are transported by ambulance to Kowloon Hospital a
few miles away, for the purpose. This arrangement, to say the least,
is very inconvenient. I'm going to relate below an actual incident,
personally experienced, to illustrate the inconvenience and danger of
such an arrangement. Such an incident is rather exceptional. Still
it will reveal something that you never could dream of.

About two weeks ago, I was asked to go for an X-ray.
Being a bed-patient I had to be transported all the way on a stretcher.
That morning, there were nine patients (including myself) to go for
X-ray. When I was carried down to the ambulance the other eight walking patients were already seated inside the ambulance on two opposite
benches which lined the two sides of the ambulance. The stretcher on
which I laid was slid under one of the benches. There were not more
than six inches between my face and the bottom of the bench. Then the
doors of the ambulance were slammed shut. Guess what happen? I suddenly realized that I could hardly breathe due to lack of fresh air.
I was seized with fear, and my breathing became even harder. I could
not climb out due to some obstruction in the form of wires stretching
down from the bench above. Besides, the legs of the patients seated
on the bench above me, formed a curtain all along the length of my
stretcher. Even if I shouted for help, which I could hardly do, it
would take some time before the ambulance attendants realized the situation and relieved me from the dilemma.

If I became hysterical, tried to shout or struggle out,
I would probably have passed out in no time. Instead I kept myself perfectly motionless, tried my best to breathe, and at the same time,
prayed hard. "Oh God, give me strength to endure this ordeal. Oh
God, give me strength ....." Then I felt fresh air coming in. The
ambulance had started to move on and air was coming in through a vent-
hole. Probably it was not more than twenty seconds between the time
the doors shut and the time the car started to move. But I felt it
was more like twenty hours. This story did not end here, although
I'm going to stop relating it from this point or else this letter
will be getting too long.

The longer I stay in this Hospital, the more I realize that the condition here, especially regarding discipline and
rest hours, must be improved at the earliest possible date. Criti-
cism is never in my mind. I'm only stating facts. To tell honest-
ly, the first attempt at rule setting by the Hospital authorities
here has failed miserably. 10 p.m. is too late an hour for T.B.
patients to retire. Only an hour of rest in the afternoon is much
too short.

I think I will not write any more right now. I'm
very tired.

Sorry to trouble you.

Yours sincerely,

The second page of the letter.

197

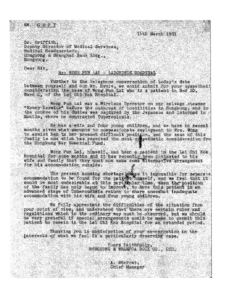

A letter from March 1951 detailing why my father
should be allowed to remain in Lai Chi Kok
Hospital while he is recovering from his
tuberculosis.

A letter from my father in August 1957
describing how often he is on his ship, traveling
back to Hong Kong only every few months.

20 Wuhu Street,
(1st floor)
Hunghom,
Kowloon,
Hongkong,
1st Apr.'58.

Dear Bernard,

It has been quite a long while since I last heard from you. Several months ago I sent you a letter. It probably never reached you. I sent it, together with some other letters, in a small town in the Philippines. As far as I could gathered not one of the letters ever reached their destinations. It was possible that the people in the post office there just took away the stamps and threw away the letters. Such things do happen. Seeing day in and day out so much outright- selfishness and dishonesty, there are times when I seem to lose faith in human nature. But when I come across, once in a while, really good people, my faith is restored.

How are you these days? I understand from Thomas that you were going back to Minnesota. But to play safe I'm sending this letter to your Valyermo address. I'm sure it will be forwarded to you in case you are not there. I haven't heard from Anthony for a long long time. If you will kindly give me his address I'll write to him.

By the way, how did that nominal scholarship for Capt. Yang's son come out? Were you able to arrange it? I have not seen the Capt. for a long time. As I told you before, you were not to go out of your way in the thing. If it is too much trouble, forget it.

I have been continuously working in the same ship for the past two and a half years. Now that my family expenses are so much, I dare not think what will happen if I ever get sick again. My health is quite alright though, thank God. Anna is still working. Our two girls are good enough, but the two boys are exceptionally unruly. For the past year or so, we have been trying to get boarding schools for them, but without success. It is so hard to get schools now-a-days in Hongkong.

A month ago, when my ship called at Formosa, I was able to be with mother for a couple of days. The last time I saw her was three years ago. She has aged a great deal because of a serious illness (high blood pressure) a year ago.

Hope to hear from you soon.

A letter from my father to his brother Bernard in April 1958. My father was working on board a tramp and didn't know when he was going to be able to return home to his wife and children. A tramp is a cargo boat hired to carry things from one place to another, with no regular line or schedule - equivalent to a commercial truck on land.

Mr. W. Derrick Johnston,
Controlled Pressure, Inc.,
1226 Linden Ave.,
Erie, Pennsylvania,
U. S. A.

Dear Sir,

I have recently received your letter dated Oct. 16th, 1958,(Ref: WDJ/H) and the enclosed leaflet describing the Oxy-Hale device. Due to some oversight on the part of my family, your letter was not forwarded to me while I was away from Hongkong. (I am a sea-farer) When I came home a few days ago, the letter was there waiting for me.

I happened to show your leaflet to a friend of mine, and he was very interested in your device; not for personal use, but as a commercial proposition. He is Mr. Edward D. Y. Lau, Managing Director of Chung Ching Medicine Co., a reputable pharmaceutical firm in Hongkong. Besides doing an extensive business, both wholesale and retail, the firm manufactures various pharmaceutical products of its own. The firm is also acting as Agents for a number of foreign pharmaceutical manufacturers.

Mr. Lau will soon write to you regarding his business proposition.

Faithfully Yours

F. L. Wong.

A letter from my father in June 1958 for the power
of attorney, explaining that he is working on the
tramp with no fixed schedule. Most of the ports
had no British consulate. My father stated that he
will arrive in October, hoping he will arrange for
his wife to move into the new apartment, Kimberly
Mansion.

Dear Anthony,

It has been a long while since we last corresponded. I think our feelings are the same regarding this matter of letter-writing. Once in a while, we would think of writing to someone - a relative or a friend. Then we would tell ourselves - well, there is nothing much to write about. Better wait for a little while until we've something particular to tell. Such procrastinations, or rather, excuses, result in our being silent to one another for long periods of time.

Your last letter to me was dated Dec. 19th,'55. I still have it with me. In fact, I've just read it over once again to see what you were trying to tell me.2½ years ago. Since that time, you must have progressed a great deal in your studies. You must have also gained much experience in various spheres. When you write me a reply to this letter, I would like you to tell me how have you been getting along in the past couple of years, and what are your plans for the future - if any!

Meanwhile, let me tell you my side. Since Sept. '55, I've been working in a tramp. As you know, a tramp is a cargo boat running on no regular line or schedule. It is equivalent to a commercial hauling-truck on land. It is out for hire to carry things from one place to another.

After several years of enforced idleness due to ill health, I was more than pleased to come across this job. It pays reasonable well. Better still, my health has even improved. However, there is also a less favourite (I think you spell this word in the States without the u) side of the picture. Our ship goes back to Hongkong every few months on the average, and stays there for a few days each time. It means to say that in one complete year I'll be at home for not more than 15 days. Worse of all, we do not know when we are going Back. It is this waiting, this suspense that saps most of the spirit and joy out of our lives as sea-farers onboard a tramp.

Now, there is something I've been thinking of discussing with you. It is the matter of import and export business between the U.S. and Hongkong. As far as I could gather, it seems that the prospect of this business has been becoming more and more favourable in the past couple of years.

Here are the main reasons. Hongkong products have increased in kinds well as in variety. Many of the products have had their quality "standardised". By being standardised, we mean that the quality of the finished goods must be up to the level of the standard set by a controlling body- the Chinese Manufacturers Union. Hongkong products offer you the best buy in the world for your money, principally due to low labour cost. Owing to Hongkong's participation in various International Trade Fairs in the past few years, her products have become better known throughout the world. Hongkong has recently put up an official agency in the U.S. for the promotion of trade relations between the two places.

Due to the various factors which I've just mentioned, don't you think that we should try to do something on that line. I heard from "twelfth" sister that you were now studying in the evening. If it is so , probably it would be even better. I know of various instances of prosperous I and E. business carried on between brothers or other near relatives, one in Hongkong, and the other in the U.S., in Australia and elsewhere. Between relatives there is the benefit of mutual trust, which is a very important contribute.

Once I know you are interested, we can get started in real earnest. As I'm now away from Hongkong most of the time, I will put you in touch with a very good friend of mine who is really keen in trying a hand on the business. He is such a good fellow that you can trust him as you trust me. Probably the first thing we will do will be to send you some catalogs on Hongkong products, and some printed matters on statistics and market conditions. It will be good also if you can inform us what items will probably command a ready market in your particular location.

So kindly rush me a reply at your earliest convenience.

Your loving brother,

A letter from my father in March 1959 trying to earn
more money for his family while he was in poor health.

Wai Yiu, my daughter, your letter was received, thanks!

It is because of my moving of the house, I cannot reply to your mail, so, please pardon me. On the 18th of this month, I hired a van (for passengers and goods). We had to go from Kwun Chung to Tuen Mun where the route was far away, and even more it made the transport difficult. The reason is that the vehicle cannot get closer to the house. We had to use a cart to take all the items to the house and go to the lift.

The church gave me 3 male members. Including my daughter and I, there were five people working for the whole day. We then put all our belongings and other materials into the house. Now all my belongings are enough. Of course, these include all the logistics. This apartment is a low-rent housing. The monthly rent is $572. I believe that this amount includes electric fee, gas fee, telephone fee and water fee. The amount may be one thousand dollars. The owner of this house is a married woman. She has a husband, a son and a daughter. It is because of her trouble, she has to leave this house and to stay in another place. That is Tuen Mun. If she has to return to this house, we have to find another house. I believe that she will not return to this house, so we can stay here at ease.

In the house, there is furniture, bed and other articles which belong to me. I believe that I can use all these items till my death. The area of the house may have more than one hundred square feet. This room is government housing. It is 24 stories high (top floor) and is cool during the day. At night the heat comes from the roof. We have to sleep on the veranda. When we sleep, we have to cover ourselves with a blanket. There is an iron gate at the main door. I cover the gate with a piece of cloth so that outsiders can see the feet and cannot see the head. The wind can flow freely.

I think I have to move over one hundred times. I am moving upward, do you think so? Wai Ling had seen a doctor on the 25th of this month. The doctor Welfare Department understands our difficulties. They tried to give us the help to look for a double room. However, I have citizenship and enjoy Canadian pension, I cannot stay in public housing. The officer in the Social Welfare Department had checked from the Housing Department. They said there was no such thing before. They said this case has not happened before. Therefore, we have to accept this opportunity. We know that there is someone in the black market. If we do not quarrel with the neighbors and do not throw rubbish in public places, there is no problem for us to stay here. The owner of the house gives thanks to us that we have cleaned the house. We give thanks to her for the allowance of our stay in the house. If the news is broken, the ownership of the owner will be cancelled, but will not be in jail. My sister Kin Ching and her husband came to visit us. They greet you too. Paul has returned to Hong Kong and gave me money and he gave you HK$1,000.00.

Love Mum

A letter to me from my mother on June 30, 1990. Her church official had asked three parishioners to help her move to low cost housing. She had moved so many times and yet she was there only temporarily, with no idea when and where she would settle for the final time.

Yiu, my daughter. There is no washing machine, nor dryer in this apartment) Wai Ling has to go to work by light rail. The fare is only two dollars. It is very convenient. It takes one hour to go to Kowloon by bus. Before 10th of July, I sent out a big photo (by registered mail). I don't know if you have received it or not. I was concerned about it.

Knowing that you have got some hemorrhoids. It is a troublesome matter. Wai Ling has got a piece. I went to a specialist with her for $2,000.00. Now she has recovered completely. Now you have to buy the medicine to see what will happen. You have to clean it with clean water every time after excrement. Then smear with the ointment. It may be helpful. I feel horrible after I think of it. When I was around the age of thirty, I got hemorrhoids too. At that time, it might be clocked. It took a long time to sit, or by using much hidden force. As a result, I saw a specialist. I used the medicine every day. Then the three pieces of hemorrhoid were dried out. I used a pump to get them and put them into a small bottle. Until now the disease has not recurred. It recovered very soon. There are some specialists on hemorrhoids. They are experts. They do a good job.

Talking about the economy, why are you so worried? I am not in debt, and no need to pay the interest. In other words, I feel happy when I have no debt, right? Moreover, we have got shelter. In this world, we have to learn how to manage the pressure from the economy. There is also no need to pay attention to this worldly matter. The challenge from the pressure of the economy will be good for us. (1) Because the economy is difficult, we have to hold a rally, learning to be humble, to help each other and to love each other. (2) To keep our dignity. To become even stronger, going along with circumstance, (3) Learning to be patient. To have more ability and technique. Sometimes personal potential is to be displayed. We have to learn to trust in the Lord to overcome "fear". In a word, we have to be "open and candid", and "to have a clear conscience". We have to treat everybody and God fairly. This is our duty.

Unfortunately, my property was lost, otherwise I will share my residence. After my death you may live with Wai Ling for the rest of your life. Ha! Ha! With regards to American nationality, the relatives and friends of Mrs. Ho have got the nationality certificates. As for the painting of our house, there is no need to work excessively. It is because our body might get hurt. There is no need to worry about worldly matters. We can just finish our daily work. Just as "faith" is written in the card which you sent me, right? You may think that a widow of over 70s and an orphan live in Hong Kong. They have the sickness of moodiness. If I do not have faith to be humble and obedient. How can I get through this difficult time? I hope you have to pray more, to trust in God, asking for guidance from the Holy Spirit, so that you may come close to the Lord. Living in this world, especially in the US, it is not difficult to live without a house. Perhaps I could win the lottery ticket, I will give you a house and you will come to look after me. Ha! Ha! You look very nice from the photo, right? Thanks to the Lord! It is good for me to live in public housing. Although it is on the top floor, it is very hot at night. My daughter and I sleep in the arcade. We feel that it is cool and comfortable. It takes fifteen minutes to walk to buy food. It takes half an hour for a round trip. My hands feel tired. It is because Wai Ling has to go to work in a "shelter workshop". She has to work for six and half hours every day. In the morning, it takes three and half hours. In the afternoon, it takes three hours. It is very hard. If there is a suitable job to work, I will let her try. Now she can earn more than one thousand dollars every day.

Love Mum

A letter to me from my mother on July 28, 1990. She is tired of moving around constantly without a permanent address for her and my sister. This apartment she is in has no washing machine or dryer; she was so sad to lose all her property through the unjust court case. And yet, she still had faith in God, asking to guide her through difficulties.

Yiu, my daughter.

The check US$70.00 you sent was kept in my place. It is because the name of Anna Wong was temporarily cancelled. Only the name of "Chu Yi Ching" can deposit in the bank. Do you understand? If Maggie and Stephen want to send me the money on my birthday, they should use "Chu Yi Ching". How troublesome!

Since 16th April of this year, I have been very busy. In this low cost housing, corrosion happens almost everywhere. The ceiling is leaking. The water in the toilet is not running smoothly. The outgoing water in the kitchen has gone to the toilet. On the other hand, the dirty water from the kitchen sink goes to the toilet. Can you see how ugly it is? Fortunately, the bishop, brothers and sisters are willing to give me help. They solved all the problems. As for furniture and beds, members of the church voluntarily supply all daily needs for us. Otherwise no money left for the future. Thanks to the grace of God! As For the installation of the telephone, gas stove, I have to buy them. In other words, if there was not the help from the sisters, I may even sleep on the cement floor. It looks as if it is plastered by green porcelain. It is easy to clean. The area of the apartment is some-what like the bedroom as in Lee Kung Street. It has a toilet and kitchen.

Since the return to Hong Kong with Wai Ling, this time we can live in the best place within these seven years. We have a washing machine and a small refrigerator. It is considered to be lucky. In other words, a series of moving of houses, this is the tenth times of our moving. We hope that God will grant us special grace to return to Canada. Wai Ling is always willing to give me help. Unfortunately, the government is very poor in Hong Kong. It is very easy to be fooled. Therefore, as a mother, as the saying "bodily unoccupied, but our hearts feel occupied." Moreover, it is not easy that all matters have to be done by me. I am an old woman at the age of 75. It is very difficult. If we (mother and daughter) return to Canada, God will surely arrange all. I dare not to think too much. As for the saying "at home wherever one is". Heavenly Father so loves us and gives us the tests to enable us to be strong and to make progress, right? Pui Ying asks for the telephones of Stephen and Paul. In August, she will go abroad to get a "certificate of self-employment". She will return to Hong Kong by early of September. She asked me to notify Paul and Stephen. The most important thing is to ask Stephen to help her to build a house or to buy a flat. She thinks that he has got lots of cash. The company of Stephen is not a charity and will not earn her money. If you have time, please notify Stephen. In the summer, my rheumatism is not as painful as in winter. My right hand may sometimes feel uncomfortable. In other word, it is not to be a human and it is much harder to hold two jobs simultaneously.

Love, Mum

A letter to me from my mother on July 31, 1992, detailing how much she wishes for my sister to return to Canada. She had moved to another low-cost apartment, with the ceiling leaking, the toilet not running, and the outgoing dirty water from the kitchen sink going to the toilet. Mother had never experienced such a place. Mother still needed to buy a gas stove and install the phone line. once again, her church members were willing to volunteer to help her repair every corner of this dilapidated apartment. Mother was tired of moving, and this is where she and my sister decided to live permanently, at #622 Oi Chi House, Oi Chi Lau, Tuen Mun, New Territories, Hong Kong. This broken apartment was rented by the government because they had applied for housing for a long time.

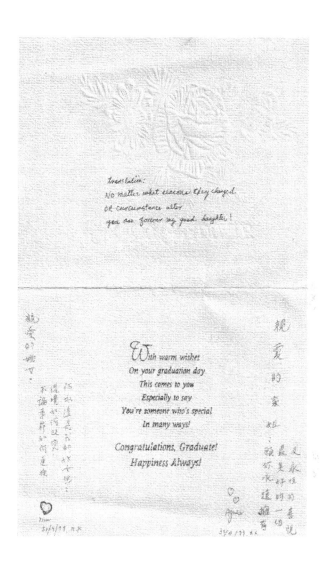

A card mother sent to me in 1999.

206

#10 Fook Ching (Theresa); husband Leung Leung Sun, and their two sons and one daughter, Kam, Ann, and Ming

#11 So Ching: daughter; husband Luk Wing Kai, and their three children

#12 Yam Ko; wife Patsy Chu and their three children

Yau Sun Dai: second concubine of Chu Tak Hing, and their children:

#13 Yam Hong

#14 Yam Ki

#15 Yam Cheung

#16 Lai Kuen

#17 deceased

#18 Lai Yung

#19 deceased

Wong Hung Pak: Joseph's father

Chow Mo Ching: Wong Hung Pak's wife, and their daughter:

#1 Tak Kwan; husband Yip Sing Fong and their four children

Yeung Wai Fan: first concubine of Wong Hung Pak, and their children:

#2 Shui Kwan; husband Cheung Fai, and their seven children (Rosie was the last daughter)

#4 Hon Yee; wife Ko Siu Fan, and their two children

#7 Yui Kwan; husband Pang Siu Tuen and their seven children

#8 deceased

#9 deceased

#11 Kwai Kwong, wife Chan Kit Yok and their three children

#12 Ying Kwan; husband Wong Shui Lun

#13 deceased

#14 Wai Kwan; husband Chan Ying Chiu and their four children

#15 Kwok Sheung, wife Kwok Kam Ngai and their son

#16 Yuen Kwan; husband Yuen Yuk Cheung

Chiu Bo Wo: second concubine of Wong Hung Pak, and their children:

#3 Chi Yan (Ambrose); wife Amy Yuen, and their three children

#5 Pui Lai (Joseph); wife Anna Chu Yi Ching and their four children

#6 Man Chi; wife Ko Bo Fan and their four children

#10 Kwok Wai (Fr. Bernard)

Chu Sut Hon: Chu Tak Hing's nephew that he had raised and educated when Sut Hon had lost his own parents

Chu Yee Shun: minister of Church of Christ in Tai Po Market, one of Chu Tak Hing's trustees

Ip Chi Fun: friend of Wong Kwong Fook, formed a brotherhood

Tsui Chuk Shan: brother of Tsui Sau Ha (first concubine of Chu Tak Hing)

Wong Kwong Fook: father of Chu Tak Hing

Yip May Chun: Anna's cousin (mid-wife)

Chan Bo Chun: Anna's goddaughter husband Lawyer Ho Sun Kuen and their two children, Victoria and William

Nelson Chan: member of the Redeemer Church

Cheung Ching Po (Fanny): best friend of Anna's daughter Seraphina

Ho Chi Ching (Sr. Ho): Lily's best friend, teacher at St. Rose Lima's School

Ho Tin Sung: Anna's godfather

Kwok Wing Sui (Mrs. Man): Anna's best friend

Lan Je (Mrs. Fan): Anna's son Stephen's mother-in-law

David Lau: Anna's occupational therapist

Dr. Mok Chun Keung: Anna's doctor from Tuen Mun Hospital

Cybie Mok: Anna's senior coordinator

Mok Man Kin: helped Anna with his handicap van

Ah Mok: grandfather Chu's nephew

Sr. Verna Poling: Anna's Mormon friend in Vancouver

Elder Poon: Anna's Mormon friend in Utah

Mrs. Tsang: Anna's senior occupational therapist

Wong Koon Kau and his wife Li Sin Woon: Anna's best friend and Seraphina's godparents

Sally Wong: Tony's sister from the Mormon church

Tong Wong: Anna's friend in Hong Kong from the Mormon church

Wong Yee Chun (Rosie): Anna's cousin, and her daughter Karen

Sr. Wu: nun from the Redeemer Church in Tuen Mun

Yu Pui Keung: Anna's Mormon friend

Linda (Chu Shui Lin): Anna's personal assistant from April 28, 2003 – April 2006

Ah Ding: Anna's domestic helper from March 8, 2003 – April 28, 2003

Ah King: Anna's domestic helper from March 20, 2003 – end of June 2003

Ah Fan (Mo Choi Fan): Anna's cook from June 23, 2003 – end of January 2006

Ah Mg (Tsang Lai Wah): Anna's domestic helper 1950-1969

Ah Ye: Anna's domestic helper 1950-1952

Acknowledgements

I would like to acknowledge the extraordinary debt I owe to Nicole Dellasanta who has helped me over the years. I would not be able to get my work done without her continued support and vision as my editor and co-author. I'd also like to express my gratitude to Patricia Siemaszko who gave me suggestions and shared her experience, and I appreciate her constant support for my project. I also wish to express my appreciation to Ann Leung for her gracious help and professional design of the front and back of my book cover.

I'd like to thank the friends and professional advisers who had a great impact on my mother's life during her difficult time:

The Church of Jesus Christ of Latter-day Saints - members in Vancouver, Salt Lake City and Hong Kong

Kwok Wing Shui

Wong Koon Kau

Lawyer Ho Sun Kuen & his wife Chan Bo Chun

Verna Poling in Vancouver

Dr. Mok Chun Keung

Cybie Mok

Mok Man Kin

Nelson Chan

To Nga Pui

Myself, my sister, and my mother in 1986.